Scotsmen in the service of the Czars

*A Highlands clachan or farmtoun ca. 1730 (by kind permission of
Jim Proudfoot, Landmark Press).*

Ian G. Anderson

Scotsmen in the service of the Czars

The Pentland Press Ltd
EDINBURGH

© Ian G. Anderson 1990
First published in 1990 by
The Pentland Press Ltd
Kippielaw, by Haddington
East Lothian, Scotland

Jacket designed by Ann Ross Paterson
ISBN 0946270 74 0
Printed and bound by D. & J. Croal Ltd
Haddington, East Lothian, Scotland

Contents

List of Illustrations

List of Maps

i

Author's Preface

When I was researching and writing this book, the subject matter had long remained largely unexplored territory. I finished writing it by the end of 1982 and delay in publication has permitted numerous competitors in the field to beat me to the finishing post.

Until the late 1970s very little had been published on the Scots in Russia beyond papers in academic periodicals. In 1913 A. Francis Steuart published a book, *Scottish Influences in Russian History* (James Maclehose & Sons, Glasgow). This was a useful, though superficial, work which omitted many characters included in the present work. For instance, there is no mention of Charles Cameron, Catherine the Great's chief architect.

Steuart also was aware of the lack of any previous books on the subject of the Scots in Russia. In the Preface of his book, page v, he says:

> "I am unaware of any book, however, which shows to any degree the part the Scot played in Russia (individually, though hardly as a nation) in helping to 'westernise' the great empire of the Czars, so I have endeavoured shortly to sketch the 'service' given by the Scots who enrolled themselves in the Russian employ."

On page 3 of the same work, he refers to Dr J. Hamel's book, *England and Russia,* translated from the German into English by John Studdy Leigh and published in 1854. He says: "It is very difficult to follow but still remains the best book on the subject." I have perused this book (a copy of which is in the National Library of Scotland, Edinburgh), but found it very boring and of little use in the present context.

Between 1902 and 1907, Thomas A. Fischer wrote three books: *The Scots in Germany* (1902), *The Scots in East and West Prussia* (1903) and *The Scots in Sweden* (1907); but nothing on the Scots in Poland or Russia.

Gordon Donaldson's *The Scots Overseas* (1966) is a general history of Scottish emigration and empire building, but has very little on the Scots in Russia.

Dr J. B. Wilson reported on *Three Scots (Doctors) in the Service of the Czars* in *The Practitioner* of April/May 1973. Professor K. A. Papmehl and Professor A. G. Cross have enlarged our knowledge of two more

Scots doctors in their monographs on Dr M. Guthrie and Dr John Rogerson respectively. Chapter 7 of this book notes the careers of over a score of Scots doctors who lived and worked in Czarist Russia in the century and a half between 1704 and 1854.

Recent publications have made good two serious previous omissions. Both Charles Cameron and Prince Michael Barclay de Tolly had to wait more than a hundred and fifty years after their deaths, in 1812 and 1818 respectively, for full-length biographies; we are indebted to Isobel Rae for her biography of Cameron (1971) and Michael and Diana Josselson for that of Barclay de Tolly (1980).

Slowly sufficient evidence has been accumulated to support the contention of Robert Heron who, in his *History of Scotland* published in 1799, stated:

"If we listen to the fame gained by these Scots in foreign countries, we shall not fail to allow that its *men* were far the most valuable of the exports which Scotland ever sent abroad."

However, delay in publication has given me time in which to make numerous revisions and corrections of the text. In this connection I wish to thank Mr Harvey Pitcher, of Cromer, Norfolk, for valued help in the transliteration of Russian personal and place names; Dr John H. Appleby, of Norwich, for correcting several factual errors in chapter 7; and Dr J. B. Wilson, of Lockerbie, Dumfries, for supplying several illustrations.

I would like to express my deep gratitude to the late Dr N. F. M. Henry, Fellow of St John's College, Cambridge, for his constructive criticism and invaluable help in preparing the manuscript, and for providing information about the altar-piece painted for St John's College by Sir Robert Ker Porter (see page 168); to Mrs A. Rosemary Bigwood, M.A., M. Litt., whose expert help in looking up references in the libraries of Edinburgh has been so helpful in bridging the distance between my study and that great centre of Scottish cultural life; and to Mrs J. Woodman for her careful preparation of the final typescript.

Dates are given in the New Style only, except in chapter 8 where Old and New Style dates are given, e.g. 24 November/6 December. The Julian Calendar (Old Style) ran eleven days behind the Gregorian (New Style) in the eighteenth century and twelve days behind in the nineteenth century. The Gregorian Calendar was adopted at various times by different countries in Europe; in 1752 in Britain, but not in Russia until 1917.

Harare, Zimbabwe, 1988.

Introduction

The Scots were ever a restless folk; coming and going from lowland to highland, from mainland to island back and forth; for many centuries they had no fixed abode and no tenure of territorial possession.

From Northern Ireland they came, and met, clashed with, fought and eventually tolerated, even inter-mingled with the Lowlander, the native Celt, and the equally foreign Dane and Norwegian who, originally a seasonal raider, came to settle in the northern countries and the islands of the Hebrides. Yet the flow was ever both ways — as they came, so they departed, to the islands of the inner and outer Hebrides, to the Orkneys and Shetlands (both acquired from Denmark in 1468), and overseas to the continent of Europe and the shores of the Baltic Sea. This continued even into modern times; a century ago the island of Islay supported, but barely and at a low level of subsistence, a population of 12,000; today the human population has shrunk to a mere 3500, whilst the sheep have multiplied tenfold.

Even in the fifteenth century Scotsmen were busy in the Baltic ports. As early as 1474 there was a Scottish commercial colony at Danzig, and in the two following years as many as twenty-four Scottish vessels entered the port. In the following century twenty to thirty ships were engaged in the Baltic trade from Dundee alone, trading into Prussia and Poland. Lithgow, in his *Travels,* put the number of such pedlars and their families in about 1618 at thirty thousand, which would appear to be a gross exaggeration[1]. At any rate, they were numerous and pushing enough to become as unpopular in Poland as the Jews.*

In 1519 the Scottish Privy Council authorised the King of Denmark to levy soldiers in Scotland for his war against Sweden. The Danish king had Scottish soldiers in his pay again in 1572; and in 1573 there was a Scottish regiment, commanded by Sir Archibald Ruthven of Forteviot,

---

* Thus in Sir John Skene's Law Dictionary we find the following: "Ane pedder is called ane merchand or cremar, quha bears ane pack or crame upon his back, quha are called bearers of the puddill be (by) the Scotsmen in the realme of Polonia, quairof I saw ane great multitude in the town of Cracovia, anno. Dom. 1569."

in the service of the King of Sweden, then at war with the Czar of Muscovy (Ivan IV).

Before 1591 Russia had mercenaries in her ranks and, by the middle of the seventeenth century, Scottish troops were so numerous in all the provinces of Poland that a Scottish Consul, Patrick Gordon of Braco, was sent to Danzig to represent their interests. There had long been a "Conservator of Scottish Privileges" in the Netherlands, the only other Scottish officer of consular rank in the sixteenth century.

By the middle of the seventeenth century the business of hiring mercenaries had become a "buyers' market," there being more mercenaries than could be accommodated. Rates of pay and subsistence had dropped, as the various national paymasters no longer had to compete for supplies of troops. Conditions of employment varied not only from country to country, but from time to time; Sweden, once the favourite goal of the adventurer, later earned a reputation for stinginess.

In 1656 the Swedish standard was much in favour with the Scots when Lord Cranstoun arrived at Pillau with 2500 Scots for the Swedish service. The French army was not so popular. Under the date March 1656, a Scottish annalist records that "at this tyme lykewyse the King of France and the King of Swadin sent over their commissioneris to Scotland for levying of sodgeris. The King of Swadin, by the Lord Cranstoun his commissioner, resavit multitudes; the uther, for France, was not so weill answerit"[2].

When enquiring into the causes of Scottish emigration, it is easy to assume certain facile premises and to summarise them in some such phrase as: "Poverty, Population and Primogeniture."

Yet it is not easy to ascribe to one, or indeed several, reasons the prodigious spread of Scotsmen throughout the world; so that, until the break-up of the British Empire in the years following World War II, there was no corner of the globe that had not felt their pioneering and civilising influence.

This is a big theme; suffice it that this volume is concerned with one small area of Scottish emigration — to the Court of Muscovy in a period roughly limited to the years from 1553 to the end of the eighteenth century.

Although the heyday of Scottish emigration to Russia was the seventeenth century, and the early immigrants were mostly soldiers of fortune, it must not be assumed that all the Scot had to offer was his mercenary sword and his reputation as a tough fighter. Soldiers, indeed, Scotland sent in large numbers, but, as we shall see later, she also contributed her quota of seamen, doctors, engineers, architects, artists, bankers and diplomats to the enrichment of the culture of Russia, as Muscovy was to become.

A remarkable feature of this eastern flow of Scots was the tendency of such immigrants to settle permanently in the land of their adoption. Under Ivan IV and several subsequent Czars, it was often difficult to obtain passports to leave Russia; later when no such restrictions were in force, the Scots tended to settle permanently and die, mostly at an advanced age, in the land they had served so well. Later it became the reproach of the British colonist that he earned a reputation as a bird of passage who, after a lifetime of administering Victoria's far-flung Empire, sighed with relief on reaching pensionable age and retired to Tunbridge Wells or Cheltenham and forgot his long sojourn in foreign parts; or, like Lord Clive, rich with the loot of India, built himself a massive country house which he never lived to occupy, leaving no progeny to inherit his property or to perpetuate his name. The Scot proved himself more adaptable to the life of the inhabitants of his adopted country, settled more permanently, married and founded families, many of which persist to this day.

Indeed, as Robert Heron wrote in his *History of Scotland* in 1799[3]:

"Scotsmen went, in great numbers, in this age, to England, to Flanders, to France, to Italy, as soldiers, as scholars, as merchants — or, in some instances, merely as travellers — to accomplish themselves for the business of life at home, by an acquaintance with the manners and learning of other regions. It we listen to the fame gained by these Scots in foreign countries, we shall not fail to allow that its *men* were far the most valuable of the exports which Scotland ever sent abroad."

INTRODUCTION — BIBLIOGRAPHY

1. Mackinnon, James, Ph.D., D.D., *The Social and Industrial History of Scotland*, Blackie & Son, Glasgow, 1920, p. 85.

2. *Nicholl's Diary of Transactions in Scotland*, p. 175; quoted in *The Diary of General Patrick Gordon*, p. 23 note.

3. Heron, Robert, *History of Scotland* (in six volumes), Edinburgh, 1799, Vol. V, pp. 56-7.

CHAPTER 1

Poverty, Population and Primogeniture in Scotland

> "Scotland by reason of her populousness being constrained to disburden herself did every year send forth swarms, whereof great numbers did haunt Pole (Poland) . . . till now they were compelled to betake themselves to the wars against Russians . . ."
>
> Sir William Alexander, *An Encouragement to Colonise,* 1624 [1].

Poverty there certainly was; populousness is a doubtful quantity in the absence of any accurate census until nearly the end of the eighteenth century; primogeniture was undoubtedly a potent factor towards emigration, estates being entailed on the eldest son and younger brothers having to fend for themselves. Other factors, apart from a general restlessness and "itchy foot," were lack of opportunity for advancement and the inhibiting effects of religious strife. We shall examine these factors in turn.

It is difficult to find a starting place, and a certain amount of space must be allotted to a consideration of the state of Scotland in the sixteenth and seventeenth centuries; of certain events in her history, her economy, her political and religious life; of her relations with her southern neighbours and her overseas trading partners and sometime enemies; all of which have a direct bearing on the fact that Scotland did "send forth swarms" and that, over the period under consideration, the main destination of these emigrants was the Low Countries, the Baltic Ports, Sweden, Poland and Russia.

The very geography of Scotland has a direct bearing on the character and life of its people. Two-thirds of Scotland is mountain and moorland, and a large percentage of the remainder marsh and bog. Only in the remaining one-third south and east of the Highland Line is there any depth of fertile soil, hence its destiny to be fought over by Roman and

Pict, by Scot and Englishman, until the beginning of the eighteenth century. Even in the fertile south-east much of the coveted land was covered with forest and marsh, and communication was interrupted by ranges of hills and incursions of sea-lochs and rivers.

In the sixteenth century, when our story begins, virtually every Scotsman lived by some form of agriculture. Pastoral farming — herding rough-haired cattle, goats and small brown sheep — played a larger part in this activity than primitive tillage of grain crops. In a few more favoured areas on the eastern side, however, there may have been more tillage than herding for many centuries back; yet the principal grains — bear (barley), wheat, rye and oats — were little more than wild grasses, bearing little resemblance to their modern counterparts, and of low productivity. This is reflected in a wry saying of that time:

"Ane to gnaw and ane to saw,

And ane to pay the laird withaw."

Swedes and turnips* were unknown and there was little to augment the meagre grazing of the stunted cattle and small sheep. The potato was not introduced until the 1740s and was not in general use even in 1782: "The great age of the potato as a peasant crop in Scotland, as in Ireland and Norway, was evidently the first half of the nineteenth century rather than the last half of the eighteenth"[2].

A good description of the Scotsman's fare is given by Bishop Leslie, writing in the 1590s:

> "The Scots, to begin at the beginning, whether in peace or war, passed their time in careful eating, and their lives in dainty and delicate dishes, or in tasting fine wines or the sweeter drinks, as is the common custom and habit overall; but their care and effort was wholly at this time to sustain their bodies comfortably and well, of such food as they might have of the ground, and to slake their thirst with herbs or, if beer were lacking, with such drink as fountains and springs gave them they used gladly and with good will. Some used bread of rye, some of wheat, some of pease and beans, but not a few of oats, as this or that ground gave in greater abundance. They had greatest delight in ox flesh, and in cow flesh even, and chiefly when the blood was let out some time they most used them, because then they were more sappy and

---

* The turnip was introduced by John Dalrymple, second Earl of Stair, between 1720 and 1730; it was not much appreciated at first.

better then for the nourishment of the body. Oxen, kine, sheep or goat, if they were sometimes wanting, not only capons, plovers and other kind of fare used they, but fish, of which they had an abundance, and of whelks they had no small use, they satisfied their hunger sweetly.

"Not at daylight, neither at noon but in the evening only they prepared the table, and that very simple and scanty, when all their life they hated nothing more than gluttony, assuring themselves that such sobriety in meat and drink, and such manner of fare and cheer was more profitable otherwise to restore to health the sick and weak, or who were not sick and weak to make fresh and strong. Which through long experience and usage they had learned, when among them there were very few sicknesses, but of age all departed this life; most of them continued (fit for) battle."[3]

And for hard liquor (he mentions whisky only once, under the name *aqua vitae*) he offers a kind of mead: "Both to Argyle, in the Highland Isles, and likewise to the outermost Isles of Ireland, it (Glasgow) sends both wine and ale and suchlike of drink as their nations have pleasure of, to wit, made of ale, of honey, aniseed and some such spices (this drink the common people call Brogat)."[*]

Hector Boece, writing about 1527, would have us believe that his countrymen had grown into a nation of epicures, whose gross self-indulgence had ruined their ancient virtue: "For where our elders had sobriety, we have inebriety and drunkenness; where they had plenty with sufficiency, we have immoderate courses with superfluity; as if he was the most noble and honest that could devour and swill down most."[4]

Other writers, native and foreign, from Andrew of Wyntoun (14th century), through Froissart, Ayala, John of Fourdoun, Hardyng, John Major, Aeneas Silvius (the future Pope Pius II), down to Johnson and Boswell, have left us their impressions of life in Scotland, which vary from the greatest asceticism to the grossest self-indulgence.

It is probable that most of the foreign visitors who have left their impressions based their observations on town life and

---

* Brogwort or Bragwort. 'Bragget: A drink made of honey and ale fermented together; latterly of sugar and spice and ale.' — *Oxford Universal Dictionary*.

penetrated only a little way into the rural areas. There were scarcely any roads outside the burghs, and rutted cart tracks and cattle paths led from one farm settlement to another. Even the villages were not as an Englishman would visualise them; the usual nucleus of village life, as it developed in the south, clustered around the lord's house, the church and the market-place, was not apparent in Scotland. The size of the farmtoun or clachan was determined by the area of arable land, and its distance from the next by the area of moorland, rock or bog which separated it. Mountains and long sea-lochs separated pockets of land into isolated holdings, so that travel by boat was often quicker and less arduous than an ill-defined goat-track up granite mountains or traversing the marshy bottom of the valley.

Dates of planting, reaping, driving cattle to the hills, and all other fixtures of the rural calendar, had been determined long ago by common consent; to alter any of these things caused wrangling and discontent among a group of tenant farmers who, though often separated by considerable distances, were mutually interdependent; therefore much better leave the old customs as they stood.*

In the mid-sixteenth century agriculture in Scotland was primitive in the extreme; and indeed not much improved in the following century and a half. Readers of A.L. Rowse's popular and authoritative book, The England of Elizabeth, especially chapter III, The Land, cannot but envy his southern neighbour the happy, industrious and enlightened use of the land which, starting at some uncertain point of time, maybe a century earlier, blossomed into maturity in Elizabeth's reign. This development has been so copiously examined and described that it requires no more than a passing mention here. One feature however worth stressing, in contrast to the primitive condition of farming in Scotland, is the zeal with which improved methods of husbandry were taken up in England as a conscious aim and with the national welfare at heart. In this the English farmer had the inestimable benefit of a flood of practical assistance in the form of technical books which, starting with Fitzherbert's *Book of Husbandry* (five

---

* To this day the inhabitants of the remote Scottish island of Foula (population 45) celebrate Christmas Day on January 5th. The independent-minded islanders refused to conform more than 200 years ago when Britain switched from the Julian to the Gregorian calendar, claiming that the alteration would affect their farming.

editions before 1600)[5], through Thomas Tusser's popular, rhymed *Five Hundred Points of Good Husbandry*[6] (of which thirteen editions were called for before 1600), Heresbach's *Four Books of Husbandry*[7] (five editions before 1600) to specialist works such as Reginald Scott's *Perfect Platform for a Hop Garden* (1574)[8], Thomas Hill's *The Profitable Art of Gardening* and *The Perfect Ordering of Bees*[9]; books on the planting and grafting of fruit trees, on the management of cattle, and many others. Every aspect of cultivation was explored from the drainage of marshes to the recovery of soils previously considered unsuitable for use; from the use of wood-ash, lime, marl, manure and other organic fertilisers to the introduction of exotic crops from the Continent and from the "Indies," such as the potato and tomato.

Not that the Scottish farmer was illiterate — far from it. A country which, in the preceeding century, could produce such a harvest of literary genius as James I, Robert Henryson, William Dunbar, John Major, Hector Boece, Bishop Leslie, and a score of others, from a population of little over a quarter of a million, could stand comparison with the best of the continent of Europe. "During the fifteenth century Scotland produced a succession of men of literary genius which no country except Italy surpassed or even equalled."[10]

But we must not make the mistake of presuming that the culture of a few towns necessarily reached into rural areas, or that the farmer had access to such books as were available to the burghs.

There were few rich in Scotland and many a "bonnet laird" considered himself passably well-to-do on his few acres of land sublet into small farms. The laird's house was often little better, although larger, than his tenants', and farm buildings with their homely smells and litter abutted on the "great hoose." The walls were bare and the lighting dim; the inclement weather reduced the apertures of window and chimney to a minimum; glass was almost unknown even in Edinburgh. No carpets or fabric (save, perhaps, reeds or grasses) covered the floors, which were usually tamped-down earth or stone. Stark penury rendered the necessity of a rigid thrift, a tradition which is said, particularly by the sassenachs, to persist to this day. But with this poverty and thrift, shared alike by laird, tenant and peasant, went a tradition of hospitality, and indeed conviviality on the rare occasions when the harsh necessity of scratching a living from the unyielding soil permitted it.

The backwardness of Scotland's agriculture was a legacy of the feudal system of tenure, combined with ignorance of modern developments in husbandry. The peasants held their farms on annually terminable leases which gave them no security of tenure and no encouragement to develop their lands.* The laird lacked the capital to effect any material improvements. Though a surprisingly large proportion of even the poorer classes could read and write, there were few books other than psalters and sermons available to them, and text-books of husbandry were almost unknown.

Money was scarce and rarely percolated down to the peasantry. Rents and multures were often paid in kind: in corn, oats, barley, and poultry, or by service in the "infield." The cattle were small and stunted, roaming the outfield and grazing on whatever they could find to eat. There were no root crops to augment their meagre fare.

The habitations of the peasantry were primitive in the extreme. G. M. Trevelyan described them thus.[11]

"The houses of the peasantry were in keeping with the starved aspect of the landscape and the want of any proper system of agricultural improvement. Rightly to imagine the home of a Scots farmer in Queen Anne's reign (i.e. a century and a half later), we must forget the fine stone farms of a later date, and think of something more like the cabins of Western Ireland. It consisted almost always of one storey and often of one room. The style and material of building and the degree of poverty varied in different regions, but walls of turf or of unmortared stone, stopped with grass or straw, were very common; chimneys and glass windows were rare; the floor was the bare ground; in many places the cattle lived at one end of the room, the people at the other, with no partition between. The family often sat on stones or heaps of

---

* A three-years' "tack" was about the longest lease a tenant could obtain. John Major, writing about 1510, recognised the retarding effect of the short-term lease. "If the landlords would let their lands in perpetuity, they might have double and treble of the profit that now comes to them — and for this reason: the country folk would then cultivate their land better beyond all comparison, would grow richer, and would build fair dwellings." Quoted by Hume Brown, *ibid.,* p. 45. However, longer leases were not to become general until the eighteenth century.

turf round a fire of peat, whence the smoke made partial escape through a hole in the thatch overhead. Since they worked on an ill-drained soil, only half reclaimed from marsh and rushes, and came back to a damp home in wet clothes for which they too seldom had any change, it followed that rheumatism and ague plagued and shortened their lives."

Though relations of laird and tenant were generally good and close, meeting almost daily in their round of toil, and speaking the same broad Scots which education was yet to smooth out from the gentry, there was nevertheless a large mass of landless men, or "sorners," said to number between a fifth and a sixth of the population, who terrorised the countryside, robbing cottagers of their few supplies and rustling the ill-protected cattle which ranged outside the protection of the farmlands. Laws restricting beggars to their native parishes were passed in 1535, 1551 and 1555, but not renewed thereafter, as they were difficult to enforce and licences were too easily counterfeited.

In the sixteenth century there was no industry and little commerce. The Dutch drew more herrings from Scotland's offshore than did the Scots. Farms were small, inefficient and productive of very little of commercial value; in fact, subsistence agriculture of which one sees so much in the so-called Third World today. It follows therefore that these small farm estates were capable of supporting the population only barely and at a very low level of subsistence.

Even the wool, on which much of Scotland's slender wealth depended, was of a poor, harsh quality, probably mixed with goat hair; although warm and popular among the peasantry, it was not in much demand in the export trade. It could certainly not compete with English wool which, starting with numerous advantages, was becoming very sophisticated in Elizabeth's reign and diversifying into broadcloths, kerseys, jerseys, fustians, bays and various mixtures of wool and cotton and wool and linen, some of the latter innovations being brought in by immigrants from the Low Countries. By 1572 there were 4000 aliens employed in weaving in Norwich alone. Colchester, Lavenham and Canterbury in the eastern counties and Wiltshire and Devon in the west, were also centres of the wool trade; many a county fortune was founded on wool, such as that of the Grevilles of Chipping Campden. The days of northern domination of the wool trade were in the future, but the foundations were laid in the sixteenth century.

During the reign of Edward III (1327-77), Flanders joined England in a commercial alliance to offset the Franco-Scottish League. During the fifteenth century the chief seat, or staple, of Scottish trade in the Low Countries was moved several times, Bruges, then at the zenith of its pre-eminence, becoming the chief centre of Scottish trade. Later the staple moved to Antwerp, and to Middelburg and Veere on the island of Walcheren. Leith, Dundee and Aberdeen were the main ports of this trade.

The trade with Bruges was comprehensive, not in wool only. Bruges at the time served as a depot for whatever Scotland had to export, and for the import of whatever could not be produced at home. Scotland sent wool in small quantities and some cloth as well as hides, skins, furs, salmon and trout. From Bruges they bought in return whatever they could afford to buy: drugs and spices, finer cloths and embroidery, gold and silver work (for which the church created the demand), sometimes wheat and provisions, and especially wines. Bruges was then the chief northern market for the wines of France, Spain and Portugal, brought by sea, as well as those of the Rhineland and Italy, brought overland. In the fifteenth century Scots ships did not venture on the longer voyages to Bordeaux or la Rochelle, as they did later.

With the decline of Bruges towards the end of the fifteenth century, and the rising prosperity of towns in Holland and Zeeland, the centre again passed to Middelburg. From Middelburg it passed to Campvere (Veere) in the beginning of the sixteenth century, which position it retained practically to the end of the eighteenth century. The duty of looking after the interests of Scots traders at the staple and maintaining their privileges was entrusted to a Conservator whose jurisdiction included the duty of trying disputes between them.

Even as late as 1689, when William III and Mary II together ascended the throne of England and Scotland, agricultural methods in Scotland were still medieval, even in the rich lands of the Lothians. For want of drainage, much of the best land lay waterlogged and unused, while the plough went up the barren hillside from which the soil had been eroded into the bog below. The primeval forests had disappeared, but as yet no modern plantations, hedges or walls broke the monotony of the windswept landscape, where the miserable sheep and cattle shivered in the blast. Improvements were impossible so long as the land was let on short leases, offering no security of tenure. Both laird and tenant lacked capital for development, and the nobles were interested in their estates chiefly as hunting grounds. In the last decade of the seventeenth century, a succession of bad harvests tested the bare productivity of Scottish husbandry and found it wanting. These were the "Ill Years," or the "Dear Years," to which we will refer later.

POPULATION

What is this "populousness" to which Alexander[12] refers?

Let us state immediately that the first census of Scotland's population was carried out in the 1790s and that all estimates prior to this date are only guesses. As Flinn[13] stated: "Before 1755 there is no source from which it is possible to estimate a total of Scottish population and hence to assess secular growth rates. Estimates by earlier historians of a figure of one million or 1.1 million for the beginning of the eighteenth century are based on either their own or other people's guesses."

There was, however, one earlier and unofficial census, made by Alexander Webster in 1755[14], composed from figures collected over the period 1743 to 1755. He gave his estimate as 1,265,000. This provides a useful starting point as his methods inspire a reasonable degree of confidence.

Smout[15], writing of the time of Malcolm Canmore who took the throne of Scotland by killing Macbeth in battle near Lumphanan in Aberdeenshire in 1057, says: "It (Scotland) also sheltered an uncertain number of human beings; it may be guessed about a quarter of a million, but nobody really knows."

William Seton of Pitmidden[16] put the population in 1700 at 800,000; and Sir John Sinclair in his *Analysis*[17] offers a figure of 1,048,000 for 1707; but the basis of these figures is unknown. Andrew Fletcher of Saltoun's estimate[18] that, during the "Ill Years" of the 1690s, there were 200,000 beggars who represented a fifth or a sixth of the total population (which would make the total population 1 to 1.2 millions), is undoubtedly an exaggeration of both figures; he was a fine rhetorician who knew the value of hyperbole, and the speech in which these figures were given was an appeal for an increase in poor relief.

Hints from other sources indicate that Scotland's population varied enormously, not from century to century, but from decade to decade. According to Pedro Ayala, the Spanish Ambassador who spent a year at the court of James IV in 1498, two of the great lords appeared in the field with more than 30,000 men, "all picked soldiers and well armed"; and yet, he adds, they did not array more than half their men. His statement sounds like an exaggeration, and certainly errs on the side of generosity, though he avers that he himself witnessed these arrays. He is however supported to some extent by John Major, who remarks on the docility and fidelity with which the people responded to the call of their lords, whatever the occasion. "They are so kindly affected to their lords," he says, "that 30,000 or 40,000 men will follow them at their own charges."[19]

If, as has been guessed, the population of Scotland did not exceed half a million at the time, of which about one quarter only would be male adults, there can only have been about 125,000 adult males in all Scotland from which to draw these great arrays; it seems inconceivable that one-half of Scotland's entire manhood could be mustered at one time. So either Ayala's and Major's figures are far too high or the population of Scotland must have been far greater than is usually estimated.

It must not be assumed that the population was a steadily increasing figure. "We cannot even be sure that the population of Scotland was, say, less in 1690 than it was in 1755, as is commonly assumed. Nor can we know whether the secular trend in the seventeenth century was upwards or downwards."[20]

Peace, prosperity and good health are needed for a steady positive growth-rate of population. Factors reducing, or even reversing, this rate are war, poverty, pestilence and emigration; all four apocalyptic horsemen afflicted Scotland in the sixteenth century more than in any other century; so it is reasonable to assume that the population in 1600 was probably no greater than in 1500; it may have been appreciably smaller. In the seventeenth century again war, poverty and pestilence were still rampant; and emigration was at a higher rate than ever before.

PLAGUE AND PESTILENCE

In the fourteenth century there were unprecedented outbreaks of bubonic plague — the Black Death — in 1349 and following years. Between 1349 and 1401 there were three subsequent attacks of great severity, general in distribution and so destructive that they may have reduced the population by thirty per cent. Then there was a generation of respite until further outbreaks in the 1430s. In 1450 there was "a great pestilential mortality of men through the whole kingdom;" a more limited outbreak in 1475; widespread but less fatal in 1499 and 1500; and lesser outbreaks in 1514, 1530 and 1539. This is usual with epidemics; in time the organism loses virulence and the population builds up immunity.

The plague situation in the second half of the sixteenth century was more complex. There were certainly some bad outbreaks, such as in 1545 and 1546; in 1568 it was especially severe in Edinburgh; and in 1574 chiefly along the shores of the Firth of Forth. The visitation of 1584 to 1588 was particularly severe, killing, according to contemporary accounts, 1400 in Edinburgh, 1400 in Perth, over 400 in St Andrews and about 300 in Kirkcaldy. In each of these towns the mortality must have amounted to a considerable proportion of the total population. Nevertheless, the area affected seems to have been restricted entirely to the south-eastern quarter of the country and probably to the towns alone. D. C. Calderwood[21] said that the disease "rageth to the utter devastatioun almost of the principall towns, Edinburgh, Sanct Andrews, Sanct Johnstoun (now Perth), etc.;" but there is no mention of it hitting villages. Ayr and Aberdeen had no epidemics between 1546 and 1600.

Later in the 1590s this pattern appeared to change; a pestilence appeared in Dumfries in 1598, spread to Dundee and the countryside of Morayshire, and by 1606 had "spread through manie parts of the countrie and raged in some parts speciallie in the towns of Air, Stirling, Dundie and St Johnstoun."[22]

In 1608 it returned to Dundee and to Perth, dying out in the following year. For a pestilence thus to rage for a decade, to infect the countryside and return several times to the same locality, suggests it may have been a different disease.

From 1609 to 1644, except for a limited outbreak in 1624, Scotland appears to have been free from serious epidemics. From1644 to 1648 the armies of the Covenant and of Montrose, marching and countermarching, carried a pestilence which was further spread by refugees fleeing before the contending armies. This, from the circumstances, would appear to have been typhus, that accompaniment of armies from the plague of Justinian to the Second World War. An epidemic of typhus hit Denmark four years later and was reported to have killed twenty per cent of the population. The mortality in Scotland is not known; but Aberdeen lost 1600, or one-fifth of the population, and Leith 2421, or nearly half. Rentals of Kilcolmkill and Kilblaan parishes in Kintyre in 1651, three years after the epidemic, show that 29 out of 55 holdings were "wholly waste," and 13 "partly waste."

The famine of the "Ill Years" in the 1690s was also accompanied by epidemics, probably of typhus; but the Great Plague of 1665 in London did not reach Scotland.

The effects of pestilence on population rise and fall are better illustrated by a comparison with similar years in England. Halifax, a huge country parish covering many square miles of moorland, every year from 1558 to 1583 showed a surplus of births over deaths; during the first decade at an average rate of nearly 100 a year, during the second decade just over 100 a year, and during the last five years nearly 200 a year. Then came the plague, and in two years, 1586 and 1587, there were 566 more deaths than births. This pulled back the rate of increase sharply; but over the thirty years' record there was an average growth rate of thirteen per cent.

The parish of Ormskirk in Lancashire had epidemics in 1558, 1559, 1563, 1565 and from 1588 to 1597; over the whole period of Elizabeth's reign there was actually a decline in population of 49 on an estimated population of about 2250.

As can be expected, urban parishes suffered most. In St Oswald's, Durham, between 1560 and 1606 there were 78 more deaths than births, although only one year — 1587 — is recorded as a plague year. In St Mary-le-Bow, which the plague visited in 1587, 1596 and 1597, there were 128 more deaths than births from 1572 to 1603.[23]

As one would expect, urban density of population spread the plague faster than in rural areas, and the death rate was higher in the towns than in the country districts. This depopulation of the towns was made up by migration from the countryside whose population declined, not directly by reason of deaths from the plague, but from the attraction of more occupation and better pay that the towns offered. Fluctuations caused by pestilence could be measured in decades rather than generations, one generation's fertility replacing the losses of even a decade of plague. As A. L. Rowse put it.[24]

"It (the plague) made fine opportunities for those who were not carried off and who came in from the country."

In Scotland, as in England, the countryside was the cradle, and the towns the grave, of the people.

WARS WITH ENGLAND

It is unnecessary to recount the chronic internecine strife which England and Scotland intermittently indulged in from the time of Edward I. The facts are well known to every Scottish school-child and need not concern us here, although they have a distinct bearing on

SCOTLAND SHOWING HIGHLAND LINE AND BATTLES MENTIONED IN BOOK

Scotland's poverty and relations with England. Apart from wars between the two countries, internal wars on a tribal basis were endemic for centuries and long delayed the acquisition of that internal cohesion so necessary to maturity of nationhood.

Only the Hundred Years' War (1337-1453) gave Scotland some respite from the devastating forays of the English armies, though the decisive victory of the Scots at Bannockburn (1314) may have helped to persuade the English to exercise their martial prowess elsewhere. The lessons the English foot-soldier learned at Bannockburn were used to good effect against the French at Crécy (1346).

The War of Independence in the reign of Edward I (1272-1302) seriously set back the prosperity of Scotland. Andrew of Wyntoun,[25] writing in the early days of the fourteenth century, lamented the interruption of the golden age of Alexander III (1249-86).

Relevant to our theme, however, is the renewed warfare between the two countries after half a century of peace between the death of James II at the retaking of Roxburgh Castle in 1460 and the tragic campaign of Flodden (1513), at which James IV was killed. After Flodden there was another truce; then came the lamentable defeat of the Scots at Solway Moss in 1542, and the "rough wooing" of the 1540s. The violence of the 'wooing' is epitomised by the barbaric actions of the Earl of Hertford, who was instructed by Henry VIII to put "man, woman and child to fire and sword without exception where any resistance shall be made against you." True to his instructions, Hertford in 1544 plundered and burned Edinburgh, Leith and Holyrood, with Newbattle Abbey, Haddington, Burntisland and Dunbar, taking 10,000 cattle and 12,000 sheep. In 1545 he came again and sacked seven abbeys, including Dryburgh and Melrose, sixteen castles, five market towns and no less than 243 "villages" (clachans or farmtouns). The campaign ended in a further defeat for Scottish arms at Pinkie in 1547.

Although devastation on this scale was probably exceptional, bitter wars and much damage to life and property continued over a long period and had many effects on Scottish economy and society. One lasting effect was to fuse the Lowlanders into a single people, and to foster a new national pride and stubbornness.

One of the main causes of Scotland's military weakness in the sixteenth century stemmed from its lack of a strong monarchy. Great and warlike lords it had a-plenty, but the cohesion which comes from fealty to a supreme head, the warrior king, was lacking. "The English," wrote Froissart, "will never love or honour their king unless he be victorious and a lover of arms and war against their neighbours . . ." England's warlike kings were not matched in Scotland after the death of James II. It was bad luck that, following the death of Robert Bruce in 1329, Scotland was deprived of two kings, David II and James I, who were kept prisoner in England for a total of nearly thirty years. Two others, Robert II and Robert III,* reigned for thirty-five years with desperate incompetence. James I emerged from captivity in 1424 as a strong and reforming monarch, only to be assassinated in 1437. For the next two hundred years every Scottish monarch came to the throne as a child: James II succeeded at the age of six years, James III at eight years, James IV at 15 years, James V at one year, Mary Queen of Scots at one week, and James VI at one year. Between 1406 and 1587 there were nearly two hundred years of minority rule and regency, with great lords contending amongst themselves for control of the crown and securing privileges to build themselves up as petty kings. Barons and magnates thus became the centres of agglutination of power which should have accrued to the crown. In all fairness, the actions of these lords probably prevented Scots society from falling into anarchy; and in the absence of a strong monarch, each lord had to mind his own interests and defend them, lest a strong neighbour take his fief from him. Nevertheless it had disastrous consequences for that internal cohesion which alone could have defended Scotland from English aggression, and which brought Scotland, in the sixteenth century, to its lowest military ebb, as evidenced by Flodden, Solway Moss and Pinkie. For centuries of intermittent warfare, in which Scotland, more often than not, was the victim of harsh oppression, murder, loot, rapine and the burning of homesteads, were not easily forgotten or forgiven; and Flodden, still unavenged at the time of the Union of Crowns, instilled its melancholy into many a Scottish ballad.

RENAISSANCE AND REFORMATION

In Scotland, as in other countries of northern and western Europe, the Renaissance led to the Reformation. The Reformation in Scotland differed from that in England in one important respect: in England it was imposed by the Sovereign and the nobles against the opposition, or indifference, of the people. In Scotland it was largely due to

---

* Robert III alone had a peaceful end; but even he, before his death, saw one of his sons cruelly murdered and the other made a prisoner in England.

widespread discontent amongst the middle classes, the lairds and tenants, and was opposed by the nobles who had largely usurped the powers of monarchy.

From all accounts there was a grave decline in religious life and morality in the fifteenth, and first half of the sixteenth centuries in Scotland. This opinion is supported by numerous Acts of Parliament, in records of Church Councils, and in the writings of reforming churchmen such as John Major, Ninian Winzet, Quentin Kennedy and others; as well as those who, like Lyndsay and Knox, became champions of Church reform in Scotland. According to these reports, the secular clergy were largely ignorant and immoral, and the monastic orders in no better case. Apart from the religious and moral issues (too large a field to be entered into here), there were grave reasons for dissatisfaction on economic grounds. The sloth, corruption and inefficiency of the Church were increasingly being resented by a larger proportion of the population, whose poverty was strained to support an edifice which gave little or nothing in return for the sacrifices made by the people.

The Church was in possession of a large proportion of the land and wealth of the country, and no longer rendered services to the community in return for its wealth and privileges. The monasteries which had been flourishing centres of trade and industry, such as those of the Tweed valley in which much of the manufacture of wool was previously carried on, had long ceased to function usefully and were sunk in sloth. The people, resenting the numerous ecclesiastical dues which even the poor had to pay, looked upon the monks as drones and leeches, whose possessions they itched to acquire for the benefit of the poor, as the *Beggars' Summonds*[26] shows.

The nobility envied the higher churchmen their vast possessions and used any pretext to seize them. In this Scotland suffered a disadvantage compared with England: in the latter the dissolution of the monasteries in Henry VIII's reign yielded a vast sum of money which was available, in his daughter Elizabeth's reign, for the development of agriculture, trade, industry, foreign exploration, harbour works and public amenities; not the least, for arms and ships for the defence of the realm. In Scotland the Crown benefited little from the spoliation of the Old Church, whilst the nobles, unrestrained by any strong monarchy, seized land, buildings, plate and specie to their own enrichment. The Reformed Church in particular suffered from this dispersion of wealth, succeeding to no funds or estates with which to carry out its enlightened schemes for the benefit of the people.

These two movements — Renaissance and Reformation — had profound effects on the social life of Scotland. Travellers who had come under the influence of the new intellectual and religious ferments on the Continent not only returned as adherents of Luther and Calvin and zealots for the reformation of the Faith, but also introduced into Scotland immigrants, chiefly from the Netherlands and Huguenot refugees from France, with their new crafts and trades to vivify and diversify Scotland's industry.

Another disadvantage suffered by Scotland was that in Tudor times it lacked the public-spirited gentry who were emerging from the yeomanry in England. It lacked a merchant class; and after 1603 it lacked a court at Edinburgh which would have attracted the sort of men from whose ranks would have emerged officers and administrators so essential to good order and government. Its middle class consisted of lawyers and clergy, twin pillars of conservatism, whilst that of England was progressive and reformative.

In England population, trade and wealth had steadily increased. New industries, new markets in a richer, more sophisticated society, had created, however unequally, a new comfort and a new culture. In Scotland there was no such growth; there was little trade, little industry and no increase in population. The population of London had quadrupled in a century, whilst that of Edinburgh had barely increased at all.

The Reformation, thanks to humanitarians like George Buchanan and Andrew Melville, strove to render education more effective and practical, to develop both the intelligence and character of the individual, to enable him to render the best possible service as a workman and citizen. The Reformed Church aimed to set up a school in every parish and to bring the new education within the grasp of all. It also nourished the spirit of political liberty as a step towards national progress. It substituted for the cloistered and contemplative life of the Old Church the concept of the active life as a true service of God; in this respect it gave a powerful impulse, ultimately if not immediately, to the economic development of the country.

The Reformation in Scotland was remarkably bloodless, and no Catholic was burnt on account of his religion. Beyond fines for non-attendance at church, only occasionally and irregularly levied, Catholic recusants were not persecuted. So corrupt was the Old Church that it required only a small shove to topple it; and its demise was accompanied by less upheaval and strife than in England.

In the realm of foreign relations the Reformation saw the overthrow not only of the Roman Church but also of the Franco-Scottish League, leading to the substitution of an Anglo-Scottish Alliance.

In the years preceding the Acts of Supremacy and Uniformity in 1559, which legalised the Reformation, the Protestant party in Scotland had the advantage of figuring as patriots. Under the leadership of John Knox, who was as much a political leader as an ecclesiastical reformer, Protestantism as a popular movement took over from Catholicism with the support and goodwill of the people, supported by the lairds and smaller landed gentry (who, in England, would have been called yeomen) against the churchmen of the Old Church. As Trevelyan put it:[27]

"If the year 1559 is to count as the first of modern England, it is still more decidedly the birth year of modern Scotland. The precise coincidence in time of the final breach with Rome to north and south of the Border, though largely accidental, was of great consequence. The double event secured the unbroken permanence of the Reformation in both countries, and drew English and Scottish patriotism, which had hitherto thriven on mutual hostility, into an alliance of mutual defence."

The two countries were brought together by the fact that the Reformation in Scotland, on the secular side, led to its rejection of French, and in England of Spanish, domination. The Anglo-Scottish alliance was further strengthened by their mutual hostility to both France and Spain, which, on the other hand, remained mutually antagonistic. By the time Mary Queen of Scots became the hope and symbol of Catholic counter-reformation, Protestantism in Scotland had become the champion of national independence; and Catholicism was branded as an instrument of French aggression. "The Congregation of the Lord" was army, church and political assembly in one; undivided in its opposition to Mary of Guise and her French troops, and later to Mary Queen of Scots who, for all her feminine attractions, was regarded as the puppet of France and Rome, and not as a child of Scotland.

The struggle between Mary and Knox continued for five or six years, while parish after parish formed their lay councils and chose their own ministers. The Kirk Sessions lent their support to the General Assembly which became, in fact if not in name, the Scottish Parliament.

Darnley's murder of Mary's secretary, Rizzio, made him an unacceptable husband for Mary in the eyes of "her" people; his subsequent murder by Bothwell and her over-hasty marriage to her husband's murderer prejudiced her acceptability by a largely male following who, whilst by no means squeamish about assassination for political ends, objected to murder as a domestic weapon to be wielded by females. The subsequent murder of Bothwell ended the game of "tit-for-tat," but did nothing to restore Mary's tarnished reputation in the eyes of her Scots supporters or of her English enemies. Mary's subsequent flight to England signalled her surrender to Knox and the General Assembly; it is possible that she might have fared better had she physically surrendered herself in Scotland rather than thrown herself on the mercy of Elizabeth, whose throne she endangered.

The Catholic rising in the North of England, in support of Mary and the Mass, led by the Percies, Nevilles and Dacres, failed to excite any response among the Catholic families north of the border, and was dispersed in a single skirmish. Scotland, by now firmly in the arms of the Protestant church, was unmoved by the excitations of English Catholics.

Elizabeth, eventually and reluctantly driven to the execution of Mary in 1587, faced the inevitability of Spanish attack, and could not afford to have a religious civil war raging in her back yard. The Great Armada, threatening the Queen's and her people's lives and liberties, was faced by the resolution of the whole country, all religious differences forgotten. There is nothing like a common external enemy to weld together the resources and resolution of a people; in this respect, the Spanish invasion performed a valuable service to the cause of Anglo-Scottish relations, and assisted the preliminary steps towards the Union of the Crowns in 1603.

James VI's accession to the throne of England and the coming together of the two countries at last under a single monarch did not necessarily imply a common participation by the subjects of either country in all the rights and privileges of the other. Whilst the crowns were vested in the person of one king, the two kingdoms remained substantially distinct, as before, under their respective governments and economic, legal and ecclesiastical institutions.

It was obviously advantageous to both countries to be delivered from the constant threat of war. The Union delivered England from the menace of Scots hostility and enabled it to maintain its national interests against Spain, and later against Holland and France. Freed of the necessity of maintaining armed forces for availability against Scotland, England was liberated to expand her continental and colonial interests.

It was equally advantageous to Scotland to be free of the threat of war; but after the first euphoria had died down, certain disadvantages became apparent. Edinburgh did not seem to bear the same stamp as a royal and capital city with the departure of king and court to England, to say nothing of the loss of patronage and trade that the presence of the court and its numerous appendages afforded. Scotland found itself involved in the effects of English foreign policy over which it had no control; and its trade was affected by England's hostility to France and Holland, long Scotland's trading partners. Furthermore, Scotland was denied the privilege of free trade across the border, which she was prepared reciprocally to bestow on England; the latter, as the stronger partner, tended to regulate matters as they concerned her own prosperity. A further disadvantage was the English Navigation Acts against the Dutch, which had the effect of debarring Scots ships from any share in the English carrying trade.

Between the Union of the Crowns in 1603 and the Union of Parliaments in 1707, relations between England and Scotland were thoroughly unhappy.

The first Church of Scotland after the Reformation was Protestant but not Presbyterian or Puritan; that came later with Cromwell in the second half of the seventeenth century.

In 1572 the Concordat of Leith made the Scottish Church explicitly Episcopalian by filling the old sees with Protestant bishops, the Crown nominating the bishops but the General Assembly holding them under its discipline. The next six decades saw conflict and compromise between Presbyterians and Episcopalians, until Charles I precipitated a crisis by his blundering conduct of affairs. He wanted to turn the clock back to 1540, restore church lands and property to the Old Church, and virtually abolish the Reformation.

In 1638 representatives of the Scots people gathered in Edinburgh to sign a national protest, the National Covenant, and pledged themselves to defend their new Protestant religion to the death. The document was neither anti-royalist nor anti-Episcopalian; it affirmed the people's loyalty to the Crown and did not attack the institutions of church government by bishops. The King played into their hands by treating all signatories as rebels and preparing an army to move into Scotland. The Presbyterian influence, now in the ascendancy, got him to agree to call a General Assembly which, to his horror, abolished the bishops.

The Scots were driven into revolt by Charles I's Act of Revocation and Archbishop Laud's Liturgy. Puritan opposition in England enlisted the Scots rebels as allies and, emboldened by this alliance, forced Charles to call a parliament and prevented him from dissolving it. A personal visit of Charles to Scotland in 1641 failed to disrupt this alliance. The English Parliament in 1643 renewed the alliance and brought a Scottish army into England for the second time. Charles tried to raise a rival party and a rival army and nearly succeeded. Montrose offered to lay all England, as well as Scotland at Charles' feet, but his career was ended by his defeat at Philiphaugh in 1645 and the surrender of the King in the following year to the Scottish Army at Newark. The Scottish Covenanters in 1646 sought to impose their terms on the King's Parliament in England. Failing in this, they returned to Scotland, selling their king (or so the Royalists maintained) for £400,000 to the revolutionary English party, who later cut off his head. Scottish raiding parties had tried to rescue Charles but were destroyed by Cromwell at Preston, Dunbar and Worcester. Thoroughly beaten by the Roundheads, with the Hamiltons executed and Argyll driven back into obscurity in Inverary, the Committee of Estates rounded up and the General Assembly dissolved, Scotland was reduced to a sullen obedience for the remainder of Cromwell's lifetime.

Scotland was still Protestant and not Puritan, though the difference became less marked as the seventeenth century wore on. In the sixteenth century both countries had rejected the supremacy of Rome; to that extent they were similar — but apart from that there were marked differences.

While Scotland, in its hatred of bishops, attempted to impose Presbyterism on England, England moved towards an Anglicanism which, whilst retaining a "moderate episcopacy," largely ignored, or curtailed the powers of, the bishops: a typically English compromise. The frustrated Scottish Commissioners fell back on their own Covenant and fastened on Scotland a dour Calvinism — rigid, conservative, authoritarian and unprogressive — which, in the persons of its Synod, superintendents and elders, was little different, except in name, from the episcopacy which the Kirk was committed to abolish. In effect, the differences between Presbyterianism and Puritanism became less and less noticeable.

A harsh Old Testament discipline settled on the Church and made itself felt on the life of Scots who had joyously or thoughtlessly sinned heretofore. Everything was becoming sinful: ostentation in attire and furniture, over-indulgence in food and drink and dancing. Christmas was abolished in 1638. Weddings and burials were shorn of their customary festivities and condemned as "fruitful seminaries of all lasciviousnesse and debaushtrie." Children were punished for playing on Sundays, and no one could visit a tavern, dance, hear "profane" music, wash, brew ale or even carry water, sweep out the house or cast out ashes on a Sunday. Scotland was becoming more and more a glum and cheerless place to live in. Scotsmen were daily made conscious of their guilt, even if this realisation was not always reflected in their conduct. Repression bred hypocrisy among the high-spirited, and a doomful depression settled upon the humble who, huddled in their wet clothes and comfortless cabins, had little joy of their poverty and their baleful religion. Perhaps some or many, in the long, unlit winter nights, pondered long and despairingly on their lot, and wondered if, somewhere, overseas perhaps, there was not a field of opportunity for the adventurous and the hope of some reward, material and spiritual, for the labours of the poor.

During the seventeenth century Scotland made repeated efforts to get the English Parliament to liberalise its treatment of its poorer and weaker partner. Two commissions sat in Charles II's reign, in 1666 and 1670, but, as usual, nothing came of them. In 1681 an Act was passed forbidding the importation of numerous manufactured goods which it was considered could be made in Scotland; and exempting from duty all the raw materials necessary for their manufacture, as well as the finished products. These measures should have given some impetus to Scottish industry; but the persecuting policies of the English Government continuing and provoking a series of popular uprisings in industrial areas in Scotland, suppressed as usual with English severity and martial law over a large part of the country, almost entirely negated any possible advantage that might have accrued to Scottish industry.

The accession of William III and Mary II in 1689 put an end to the internal strife by finally establishing the Presbyterian Church to the eclipse of the Episcopalian; but it did nothing in itself to improve Scottish industry and commerce. The country was rapidly approaching its nadir of despair. Andrew Fletcher of Saltoun described the country as "sunk in so low a condition as to be despised by all our neighbours and made incapable to repel an injury if any such should be offered." He described the condition of seaports falling to ruin, of a decaying agriculture, of industry languishing for want of capital. The value of land dropped; tenants were unable to pay their rents even in produce (it was long since they had been able to pay in money); numbers of countrymen drifted into the burghs where they burdened the burghers with an ever-increasing load of poor relief, or ravaged the countryside as beggars. "Our trade with France," he said, "was very advantageous by reason of the great privileges we enjoyed in that kingdom. Our commerce with Spain had been very considerable, and began during the wars between England and that nation. We drove a great trade in the Baltic with our fish, before the Dutch had wholly possessed themselves of that advantageous traffic. Upon the Union of the Crowns not only all this went to decay, but our money was spent in England and not among ourselves; the furniture of our houses and the best of our clothes and equipages were bought in London; and though particular persons of the Scots nation had many great and profitable places at court, to the high displeasure of the English, yet that was no advantage to our country, which was totally neglected, like a farm managed by servants, and not under the eye of a master."[28]

William Seton of Pitmidden, however, did not absolve the Scots of their share of the blame, by their lack of enterprise in establishing home industries; by their lack of expertise in agriculture; by too many landlords selling their estates and lusting after the fleshpots of London.* It is only fair to point out that centuries of internal dissension, weak monarchy, bad government and poor leadership, were not entirely the fault of the English.

THE "ILL YEARS"

Scotland reached the bottom of the abyss in the 1690s, known as the "Ill Years," or the "Dear Years," during which everything conspired against her. A series of droughts, harvest failures and floods of almost apocalyptic proportions, resulting in famine on a scale never before experienced and persisting for many years on end, accompanied by at least two epidemics, one described as "the plague" but more probably typhus, the other smallpox, reduced the diminished remnant of the population to skin and bone and even, it is said, to cannibalism.

In desperation large numbers fled to Ireland, from where the migratory flow had for centuries been in the reverse direction. One of the most desperate schemes to relieve the misery of his fellow Scots

* '. . . Sir Alexander Brodie of Brodie, goggling at all the wicked fancies and earthly delights of London, reminds us of a bedouin of the desert blinking in the bazaar of Cairo or Damascus.'[29]

was devised by William Paterson, founder of the Bank of England, who had made his fortune in the West Indies trade. In 1695 Paterson started a "Company trading to Africa and the Indies,"[30] also known as the Company of Scotland, to establish a free-trade colony at Darien in the Isthmus of Panama, which should provide a field for Scottish enterprise and cultivate the raw materials for a great manufacturing future in the home country.

The scheme was doomed from the start. It was bitterly opposed by the English Parliament as contrary to that country's interests. It embarrassed William III, as the land which the colonists proposed to occupy belonged to Spain, and his approval of the scheme might have provoked war with that country. It was originally intended to raise £300,000 each in England and Scotland, but English subscribers withdrew their support and exerted pressure on their Dutch counterparts to withold their contributions. Nevertheless, in spite of her poverty, Scotland succeeded in raising £400,000, about half the total capital of Scotland, from her own resources; and in May 1698 a flotilla of assorted vessels set sail with quantities of supplies, fifteen hundred optimistic settlers and the prayers and hopes of the nation, to establish New Edinburgh in central America.

Nothing went right. The Spanish naturally resented this intrusion into their territory; no one seems to have checked the ownership, or even the exact location, of the land to be occupied. The heat, humidity and tropical conditions, as well as the fevers (malaria, yellow fever) which, two centuries later almost caused the abandonment of the cutting of the Panama Canal, took their toll of the settlers. In June 1699 the survivors embarked on four vessels, intending to return home. One vessel was abandoned at sea. The *St Andrew* reached Jamaica, having lost her captain and a hundred men; the *Caledonia* and the *Unicorn* reached New York, having lost three hundred persons.

Meanwhile the organisers at home, having no news of these disasters, were busy organising a second relay of fifteen hundred emigrants. One advance party set off from Leith in two ships with three hundred men who reached Darien two months after it had been abandoned. One of the ships caught fire in harbour and was destroyed. The despairing colonists embarked on the other ship and left the scene of desolation long before the news of this second misfortune could reach Scotland. The remaining portion of the second expedition left Britain on September 24th, 1699, in four ships containing thirteen hundred people. They were to experience even worse trials.

After an attack by Spaniards the colonists abandoned the Isthmus. They embarked on seven remaining vessels but only two reached Scotland. Many died on the way home and one account says: ". . . of the entire colony not more than thirty, saved from pestilence, shipwreck and famine, ever saw their native land again." But many more survived and found new homes in America. Amongst these was a Presbyterian minister, Archibald Stobo, who, after seeing his wife and several children drowned before his eyes, settled in Charleston. He had one surviving daughter, Jean, who married James Bulloch in 1729; their direct descendant, Martha Bulloch, married Theodore Roosevelt; their son became President Theodore Roosevelt, and so a survivor of the ill-fated Darien Scheme became the ancestor, matrilineally, of a future President of the United States.[31]

The news of the total failure of the scheme, coming as the climax of the years of famine and pestilence at home, was the last straw for Scotland. In her despair Scotland lashed out against the English merchants for their pusillanimity, against the English Parliament for its hostility, against the English Crown for its opposition. Torrents of violent and passionate speeches and protests ventilated their pent-up hostility on the English, rather than admit their own inexperience and lack of foresight.*

To give William III his due, his opposition was based on his fears of Spanish reprisals. He was, however, an ardent advocate of justice for Scotland and realised the necessity for Scottish participation in foreign policy and colonisation. On the eve of his death in 1702 he exhorted the English Parliament to cultivate Scottish co-operation in the interests of both countries.

However, as usual, it was the greed and self-interest of the City of London which proved the most obdurate stumbling-block. For the price of Union — political, economic and cultural union — of the two countries was free trade for Scotland.

The battle raged on in the early years of Queen Anne's reign, with Scotland threatening to secede from the regal Union of 1603, and English obstinacy and greed refusing to make any concessions which might affect the prosperity of the English merchants. In the end it was over Spain that the issue was forced to a conclusion: the War of the

---

* It is to Paterson's credit that he sailed with the settlers and remained in Darien until the final evacuation in 1699, when he returned to England broken in health and pocket. He was awarded $18,000 in 1715 as indemnity for his losses at Darien, and died in 1719.

Spanish Succession had broken out in Europe and the English Government could ill afford to have a rebellious and hostile Scotland threatening its northern border. The parliamentary battle continued through 1705 and 1706; Scotland must give up her Parliament and England must grant free trade to Scotland. Both sacrifices were odious to both countries; but in the end both countries gave ground, and the United Kingdom of Great Britain came into being on January 16th, 1707 (O.S.)

Although immediate prosperity for Scotland did not arrive overnight, the subsequent history of the United Kingdom bears witness to the opinion that Scotland's loss of independence was the best thing that had happened to that country; for of what value is national independence without order, good government, internal cohesion and an economic base to sustain it, as many Third World countries are finding out for themselves today?

From 1707 onwards the British people, Scots and English, proceeded to pool their respective talents in their common cause which, starting to bear fruit in the middle of the eighteenth century, saw the dawning of a golden era in the history of Scotland.

CHAPTER 1 — BIBLIOGRAPHY

1. Sir William Alexander, *An Encouragement to Colonise,* 1624, quoted by A. L. Rowse, *The Elizabethans and America,* p. 179. Professor Rowse is in turn quoting from E. F. Slater, *Sir William Alexander and American Civilisation,* (Prince Society), Boston, Mass., 1865, pp. 205-6.

2. Flinn, Michael, ed., *Scottish Population History,* Cambridge University Press, 1977, p. 246.

3. Hume Brown, P., *Scotland before 1700 from Contemporary Documents,* David Douglas, Edinburgh, 1893, pp. 160-1 (Spelling modernised by author).

4. Hume Brown, *ibid.,* Preface, p. xiv.

5. Quoted from Rowse, A. L., *The England of Elizabeth,* Reprint Society, 1953, pp.121 ff.

6. Quoted from Rowse, *ibid.,* pp. 115-123.

7. Quoted from Rowse, *ibid.,* p. 124.

8. Quoted from Rowse, *ibid.,* p. 125.

9. Quoted from Rowse, *ibid.,* p. 126.

10. Mackinnon, James, *The Social and Industrial History of Scotland,* Blackie & Son, Glasgow, 1920, Preface, p. xv.

11. Trevelyan, G. M., *English Social History,* Longmans, Green & Co., London, 1946, p. 430.

12. *An Encouragement to Colonise* . . . See above, n. 1.

13. Flinn, M., *ibid.,* p. 4.

14. Flinn, M., *ibid.,* p. 4.

15. Smout, T. C., *A History of the Scottish People 1560-1830,* Collins, London, 1969, p. 20.

16. Flinn, M., *ibid.,* p. 241.

17. Flinn, M., *ibid.,* p. 241.

18. Hume Brown, P., *ibid.,* preface, p. xiii; and Flinn, M., *ibid.,* p. 170.

19. Mackinnon, J., *ibid.,* p. 82.

20. Flinn, M., *ibid.,* p. 4.

21. Calderwood, D. C., *Historie of the Kirk of Scotland,* Wodrow Society, 1843, Vol. IV, p. 377; quoted in Smout, p. 163.

22. Calderwood, *ibid.,* Vol. iv, p. 591. Quoted in Smout, p. 164.

23. Rowse, A. L., *ibid.,* p. 249-254.

24. Rowse, A. L., *ibid.,* p. 254 footnote.

25. Mackinnon, J., *ibid.,* p. 83.

26. Mackinnon, J. *ibid.,* p. 119.

27. Trevelyan, G. M., *History of England,* Longmans, Green & Co., London, 1926, p. 330.

28. Mackinnon, J., *ibid.*, p. 131-2.

29. Trevor-Roper, H. R. Essay on "Scotland and the Puritan Revolution" in *Historical Essays 1600-1750, presented to David Ogg.*, H. E. Bell and R. H. Ollard, edd., A. and C. Black, London, 1963, p. 81.

30. Insh, G. P., *The Company of Scotland, trading to Africa and the Indies,* Charles Schreibner's Sons, London and New York, 1932, cf. also the same author's pamphlet entitled *The Darien Scheme,* Historical Association, London, 1947.

31. Millar, A. H., "The Scottish Ancestors of President (Theodore) Roosevelt," *Scottish Historical Review,* Vol. 1, 1904, p. 416.

CHAPTER 2

Early Migrations: Scotsmen in the Baltic: the Russia Company

PRIMOGENITURE

The institution of primogeniture owed its origins to the introduction of feudalism by the Normans. Under the earlier Gaelic law the right of the eldest son to succeed his father was unknown: the clan required for its survival a strong leader who would defend the clan and whom it could respect; it was not much concerned with the question of who emerged first from his mother's womb.

As feudalism spread in Scotland and the strength of the clan began to reside as much in its territorial possessions as in the number of men it could muster to the lord's service, primogeniture gradually became the rule; but as late as 1513 the Macdonalds of Moidart deposed and murdered what they considered an unworthy eldest son of their late chief and replaced him with the latter's brother[1]. By the mid-sixteenth century primogeniture had been generally accepted and was mostly occasioned by sheer economic necessity. Farms were small, of low productivity and rarely prosperous enough to support more than one family, that of the eldest son, so that his brothers had to seek employment elsewhere.

Typical of this situation was the family of Patrick Gordon, the subject of a later chapter. Patrick Gordon was one of seven children, five boys and two girls. The estate of Auchleuchries came into the Gordon family through his mother, née Mary Ogilvy. In a legal deed dated Moscow, 11th January, 1682, General Gordon left to his eldest son, John, "the touns and lands of Auchleuchries, Easter and Wester, with the pendicles* thereof called Muirtak, the Milne of Auchleuchries, multuris, sequells, sucken, and knaveships of the samine (same), in the barronie of Ardenred, parochies of Cruden, shireffdome of Aberdeine, and Kingdom of Scotland . . ."

All this sounds an impressive property, but probably amounted to very little. Its five or six small farms yielded in those days an annual income of 360 pounds Scots, or thirty pounds sterling; but it was so overwhelmed with mortgages that probably half of this scanty rent went in payment of interest. Years of successful service in the Russian army enabled the thrifty general to pay off all but one inconsiderable bond; but within thirty years of his death, his grandson was a landless man, and another family of Gordons dwelt in Auchleuchries.

So, while Patrick was still a young man, the family estate went to his eldest brother, James, and Patrick had to seek his fortune elsewhere.

Opportunities for such younger sons were rarely sought in England, where Scottish immigrants were not welcome. In the early sixteenth century there had been a certain amount of colonisation of the Orkney Islands, and even of the remoter Shetlands (both acquired from Denmark in 1468) where conditions were even more rugged and bleak than in the northern counties of Sutherland and Caithness, Aberdeen and Moray, from which the majority of the colonists derived.

From the beginning of the sixteenth century the main outlet for Scottish vitality was service in continental armies. From the 1560s onwards it had been a common occurrence for the Scottish government to grant licences to individuals for the raising of bands of men for service in Denmark, Sweden and the Low Countries. After 1600 the traffic increased and the Thirty Years' War (1618-1648) was the heyday of the soldier-adventurer.

Christian IV of Denmark, and Gustavus Adolphus of Sweden, kings of countries already accustomed to employing Scots, led the Protestant armies of the north into Germany against the House of Hapsburg.

Pendicles: Something dependent on something else; an appurtenance, appendage, dependency; a small piece of property, esp. when sublet—1530. *Multures*: a toll in kind paid to the miller for grinding corn; the right to exact this. *Sequells*: in feudal law the offspring, retinue, chattels and appurtenances of a villein; descendants, posterity; successors in inheritance—1572. *Sucken* (=soken) resort of tenants or others to a particular mill to have their corn ground; the right of the miller to such custom. *Knaveships*: a small due, in meal, payable to the miller's servant on each lot of corn ground at a thirlage mill. (*Thirlage*: a state of obligation in which tenants of certain lands are bound to restrict their custom to a particular mill.)
(All definitions from the *Oxford Universal Dictionary*.)

Donald MacKay, first Lord Reay, raised 3600 men for Christian IV and served under Gustavus Adolphus, along with members of other Scottish noble and landed families. Gustavus Adolphus was said to have had 10,000 Scots at his command, maybe many more.There exists a list of 54 Scots who served as colonels under him, and 20 in even higher ranks. When France, under Cardinal Richelieu, entered the war in 1630, backing Sweden in order to curb the ambitions of Wallenstein, who was expanding his own territories at the expense of Catholic and Protestant interests alike, there was more enrolment of Scotsmen. A brother of the Earl of Argyll raised 4500 men for this service; and John Hepburn, who had commanded a brigade under Gustavus Adolphus, transferred to the French service and died a Marshal of France in 1636.[2]

The Thirty Years' War was primarily a religious war waged by the Protestant powers against the Emperor Ferdinand II, a crowned Jesuit, the first pupil of a Jesuit college to mount the imperial throne, whose intelligence, narrowed, embittered and directed by Jesuit teaching, was directed to a single purpose: to destroy Protestantism and uproot all its adherents from his dominions.

The Peace of Westphalia (1648), however, left unsolved the question of the future control of the Baltic trade routes. "The great days of the Hanseatic League had passed, and Lisbon and Antwerp, Amsterdam and London had, with the opening out of the new oceanic routes, long outstripped Lübeck and Rostock, Stralsund and Danzig. The serious competitors for supremacy in the Baltic were no longer the German republics of the League, but the rival kingdoms of Denmark, Sweden and Poland."[3]

Sweden, whilst battling for the Protestant cause and making a decisive contribution to its ultimate victory, was also vitally concerned in securing control of the eastern Baltic coast. Russia's Baltic provinces were wrested from her by the Swedes, under whose control they remained until the time of Peter the Great.

After 1660 service in the Dutch armies became the main outlet for Scots' energies, recruitment in Sweden and Poland declining. It was said that Sweden was the worst paymaster and provider of mercenaries in Europe, with Poland not far behind. The middle of the seventeenth century saw the zenith of Dutch mercantilism; and Holland's suddenly increased prosperity allowed it to pay its army better than most other employers of mercenaries.

THE RUSSIA, OR MUSCOVY, COMPANY

Although the Russia Company was organised, financed and manned entirely from the City of London, a brief account of it must here be inserted in order, later, to draw together two strands of a cord which eventually bound together English and Scots interests in Russia.

Whereas the Scots adventured into Russia as mercenary soldiers, the interest of the English was purely commercial. The wool trade, which had been the main source of England's prosperity for centuries, was in the doldrums. The loss of Calais, where the wool staple had operated for so many generations past, occurred a few months before the accession of Elizabeth I on 17 November, 1558. There still remained Bruges and Antwerp as markets for English wool and cloth; but in the next few years these outlets were to be closed by the clash between English and Dutch interests. Excluded from the Netherlands, the English cloth merchants moved, in 1567, to Hamburg as their port of entry into Europe, only to be driven thence ten years later by the jealousy of the Hansa merchants. The Baltic Sea was dominated by the Netherlands and Denmark at its entrance from the North Sea, and by Sweden at its eastern end; in particular, the Gulf of Finland had fallen to Sweden, which annexed the Baltic states of Esthonia and Livonia after the end of the Thirty Years' War.

In 1553, "The Mysterie and Company of the Merchants Adventurers of England for the Discoverie of Lands, Territories, Isles, Dominions and Seignories unknown and not before that late adventure or enterprise by sea or navigation commonly frequented," was founded in London, largely at the instigation of Sebastian Cabot, son of the discoverer of the North American land and of the Hudson's Bay passage, who was appointed Inspector of the Navy under Edward VI in 1548. This was subsequently known, for short, as the Russia, or Muscovy, Company.

The Company outfitted three ships to look for a new sea route to Cathay and India via the North Cape. The ships, each of about 160 tons, were very solidly built with special care, and cost £6000 each to equip. They were under the command of Sir Hugh Willoughby, the principal captain being Richard Chancellor, and set out from the Thames north-eastwards towards the North Cape.

The Arctic Ocean was at that time a totally unknown sea. All went well until the little flotilla had rounded the North Cape, but off Vardö, near Varanger Fjord, a frightful storm arose and dispersed the ships. The *Buona Esperanza* and the *Buona Confidenza* became locked in ice, and Sir Hugh Willoughby and all members of both crews perished of cold and starvation.

Richard Chancellor, captain of the *Edward Bonaventura*, sailed on into the White Sea and, on August 24th,1553, came to anchor in one of the mouths of the northern Dvina River, near the Monastery of St Nicholas. Chancellor sent word to Moscow that he was ready to wait on the Czar. This decision to visit the Czar's capital, and not only Novgorod (as all other foreign merchants had done), proved of decisive importance. Chancellor laid up his ship and cargo at Kholmogory, about fifty miles up the Dvina, and, when the messenger eventually arrived with a summons to an audience, set off on the long and arduous journey to Moscow.

MAP OF PART OF THE MUSCOVITE EMPIRE, by Matthäus Seutter, 1678-1757.

Although traders of many nationalities—German, Dutch, Persian, Tartar and Arabic—had previously displayed their goods in Moscow, the English wares were apparently more to the Russians' taste, and the English party received a cordial, indeed an enthusiastic reception. Upon receiving assurances of regular supplies of the varied goods shown, the Czar's government readily granted the Russia Company a licence for customs-free trade by sea or land.

By the end of the same year a fleet of fourteen heavily laden ships full of valuable English products landed at the mouth of the Dvina and started organising the export of Russian raw materials: furs, hides, timber, flax, train oil, tallow and more besides.

Edward VI had died during the first voyage to the White Sea, to be succeeded by Mary Tudor. In 1556 Richard Chancellor, accompanied by Richard Gray and George Killingworth, set sail again for the Dvina and arrived safely in Moscow. This time they obtained from Czar Ivan letters-patent formally authorising the Russia Company to establish factories (i.e. a depot and warehouses) at Kholmogory and Vologda.

Chancellor in the *Edward Bonaventura,* with the *Philip and Mary* and the *Buona Esperanza* and the *Buona Confidenza*, which had been found safe and ice-free on the outward voyage, set sail for England. On board the *Bonaventura* was Osip Nepea, Governor of Vologda and Russia's first ambassador to England, accompanied by a suite of sixteen Russians, with letters and presents from Ivan IV to Queen Mary. A tempest scattered the fleet, sent the *Philip and Mary* as far as the coast of Norway, sunk the *Esperanza* and the *Confidenza,* and threw the *Bonaventura* on to the inhospitable coast of Aberdeenshire. Chancellor succeeded in rescuing the Russian Ambassor, but himself perished with his son and nearly all his crew. 'The cargo and the presents of the Czar were plundered by the savage natives of the country.'[4]

The Russian Ambassador and his suite, minus seven who were drowned when they attempted to gain the shore in a small boat, remained in London for about a year. Indeed, it appeared they outstayed their welcome; and towards the end of Nepea's stay in England, members of the Russia Company found him a difficult man to deal with. Hamel[5] says: "In a postscript, dated the 10th of May, 1557, to a letter previously dispatched to the agents at Moscow, they say:'Wee doe not finde the Ambassador nowe at the last so comfortable to reason as wee thought wee shoulde. Hee is very mistrustfull, and thinketh everie man will beguile him; therefore you had neede to take heed how you have to doe with him, or with any such, and to make your bargaines plain, and to set them downe in writing.'"

The English Russia Company were the first Westerners to organise trade with the interior of Russia. It was started with a capital of £6000 and came to have some 200 to 240 members. The Czar looked upon the venture as his personal perquisite, as became the descendant of

Ivan Kalita ("Moneybags"), and business was brisk so long as it was profitable to the Czar personally.

On another mouth of the Dvina River was the Monastery of St. Michael the Archangel; and here, in 1583, with the help and active encouragement of the Czar, the Russia Company founded the port and city of Archangel (Arkhangelsk). Through Archangel the English merchants expected to have the entire monopoly of imports into and exports out of Russia; but the capture of Narva in 1558 opened up a new and shorter route via the Baltic and into the Gulf of Finland. This gave the Dutch their opportunity; but trade remained profitable for the English pioneers up to about 1585, after which it declined in favour of the Dutch.

In the reigns of James I and Charles I the merchants of the Dutch East India Company had greater resources behind them than their English rivals. It was the day of the amazing wealth and power of little Holland, safe at last from Spain and not yet threatened by France. The Dutch became Europe's sea-carriers, largely to the detriment of English shipping.

The early years of Elizabeth's reign saw the rise of a number of overseas trading corporations. They were of two kinds: first, the 'regulated' company, in which each member traded on his own capital, subject to the common rules of the Company; such were the Merchants Adventurers, the Eastland, or Baltic, Company, the Russia, or Muscovy, Company, and the Levant Company. The other type was the joint-stock company, such as the East India Company, the Africa and—two generations later—the Hudson's Bay Company. In this class of company, trade was conducted by the corporation as a whole, and the profits and losses were divided among the shareholders. Exploration went hand-in-hand with trade, and Persia was first reached by the Russia Company by way of the Russian river system. "The Persian expedition of 1568-73 showed how profitable trade could be; although two-thirds of the goods were lost on the journey, the profit made equalled the whole capital."[6]

After the English Civil War, business with Russia almost came to a standstill, as Czar Alexis disapproved of a people who cut off their sovereign's head. There was some revival in the reign of Charles II, but by the end of the century trade had fallen into the hands of a small group. In 1699, however, the entrance fee was reduced from £50 to £5 and certain restrictions on membership were removed. This seems to have given the necessary stimulus to the Russian trade, and by 1762 the English were said to be "entire masters" of the trade with Russia.

Subsequently the Russia Company became known as the British Factory, established in Moscow. In accordance with an edict of Peter I in 1723, the British Factory was obliged to remove to St Petersburg, where it prospered and acquired some of the best locations in the new city, including what became known as the English Quay in the reign of Catherine II.

One of the first Englishmen to be resident in Muscovy for any length of time was Sir Jerome Horsey, an agent or resident director of the Russia Company. He, as will be seen in a later chapter, was kindly disposed to the Scots refugees from the Swedish wars, recommended their employment by Ivan IV, and even contributed towards the building of the first non-Russian church in Moscow.

So began the first incursions of persons of British stock into the barbaric state of Muscovy in the reign of Ivan the Terrible: the English to engage in Trade, especially in woollens and cloth, in exchange for furs, hides, tallow and blubber, etc., much of it destined for the outfitting of Elizabeth's navy; the Scots to escape the poverty and lack of opportunity in their native country, as soldiers and adventurers in a country as wild and backward as their own.

In the course of time these traders and adventurers were to take a large part in the development of Russia, contributing doctors, engineers, architects, scholars and instructors in many arts and trades, to the enrichment of the culture of Russia.

CHAPTER 2 — BIBLIOGRAPHY

1. Smout, T. C., *A History of the Scottish People, 1560-1830*, Collins, London, 1969, p.46.

2. Donaldson, Gordon. *The Scots Overseas*, Albert Hale, London, 1966, pp. 30-1.

3. Fisher, H. A. L., *A History of Europe*, Edward Arnold & Co., London, 1942, one-vol. edition, p. 613.

4. Rambaud, A., *History of Russia*, Sampson Low, Searle and Rivington, London, 1879 (2 vols.), Vol. I, p. 293.

5. Hamel, J., *England and Russia; comprising The Voyages of John Tradescant the Elder, Sir John Willoughby, Richard Chancellor, Nelson, and others, to the White Sea, etc.*, Translated by John Studdy Leigh, Richard Bentley, London, 1854, p. 157.

6. Rowse, A. L., *The England of Elizabeth*. Reprint Society, p. 180.

For the History of the Russia Company: Willan, T. S. *The Early History of the Russia Company, 1553-1603*, University Press, Manchester, 1956. (Edition used: reprinted 1968.)

CHAPTER 3

The Scots Soldier of Fortune

The Scots soldier of fortune has a long history reaching back to the days of the "Auld Alliance" with France; and the history of the Garde Ecossaise is both long and honourable. In pre-Reformation days Scotsmen fought for Spain in the Low Countries, but after the Reformation Scots tended to fight only for Protestant princes; the outbreak of the Thirty Years' War in 1618 provided their greatest opportunity.

The first Scots in Russia arrived as prisoners of war taken in Sweden about 1581. "The Emperor's souldiers and army, farr greater in number, ranged far into the Swethians country, and did much spoill and rapine; brought many captive awaye to remote places in his land, Liefflanders, French, Scotts, Dutchmen and some English."[1]

Horsey says he was instrumental in getting permission for them to build a church in Moscow to which he contributed: "At which tyme, among other nacions, there wear fower score and five pore Scotts souldiers leaft of 700 sent from Stockhollme, and three Englishmen in their company, brought amonge other captives, in most miserable manner, pittious to behold."[2]

The Emperor was dealing very harshly with these captives and Horsey, who was the chief agent of the Russia Company, put in a word for the Scots to be treated differently. " ' They wear (were) a nacion (of) strangers remote, a venturous and warlicke people, readie to serve any Christian prince for maintenance and paye; as they would apear and prove, if it pleases his Majestie to imploie and spare them such maintenance, now owt of hart and cloths and arms, as they may show themselves and valure against his mortell enemy the Cryme Tartor.' Yt seems some use was made of this advice, for shortly the best souldiers and men-at-arms of these strangers were spared and putt apart, and captaines of each nacion appointed to govern the rest; Jeamy Lingett for the Scottish men, a valliant honest man."[3]

This arrangement seems to have worked well and stranded Scots were grateful for it. Later Horsey remarks: "Twelve hundred of them did better service against the Tartor then (than) 12 thousand Russes."

SCOTS IN SWEDEN

The influx of Scots into Sweden began soon after the troubles following on the renunciation by Sweden of the Danish yoke, when Gustavus Vasa firmly established his new dynasty on the Swedish throne early in the sixteenth century.

Denmark, Norway and Sweden never really got on well together, although since 1397, by the Union of Kalmar, they had agreed on a common monarch for the three territories. This arrangement persisted uneasily until the end of the reign of King John (or Hans) in 1513. In 1520 Christian II of Denmark (c. 1513-1532) attacked Sweden, captured Stockholm and carried out a fearful massacre, almost as bad as that of St Bartholomew's Day in France, and for which the Swedes have never really forgiven the Danes. Sweden rebelled under Gustavus Vasa who, with the assistance of Frederick I, Duke of Holstein, and the Hansa port of Lübeck, defeated Christian, who fled to the Netherlands. Sweden became independent in 1523, although there was a further war of ferocious intensity lasting seven years between Erik XIV of Sweden, "more than half a madman", and Christian IV of Denmark. Gustavus Vasa's fourth son succeeded Erik as Charles IX, who died in 1611, and was succeeded by his famous son, Gustavus Adolphus.

In 1573 Sir Andrew Keith of Forssa employed a body of Scottish mercenaries in Sweden "whose conduct scarcely redounded greatly to Scottish fame."[5] In the same year a Scoto-French adventurer , Carolus de Mornay, brought to Sweden 3000 Scots whom he enrolled to serve in the Swedish army in Esthonia against the Russians (Sweden had seized Esthonia in 1561). The chief Scots under de Mornay were Archibald Ruthven of Forteviot, brother of Lord Ruthven, the Lord Treasurer, and Gilbert Balfour of Westray, a noted intriguer, who had been implicated in the murders of Bothwell and Cardinal Beaton. They were involved in a plot to depose John III, who had seized the throne from his brother Erik XIV, and restore Erik. De Mornay and Balfour were caught, imprisoned, tortured and finally executed. Ruthven was spared on the intervention of the King of Scotland.

Sweden, perennially at war with Denmark or the maritime provinces of Russia, was always greedy for soldiers and not too particular how they came into her service. In 1609 Colonel William Stewart of

Egilshay, brother of the Earl of Orkney, appointed his trusty friend John Ury (or Hurie) as lieutenant-colonel. In 1611, in war with Denmark, General Rutherford, Lieutenant Learmonth and Captain Greig (who commanded the artillery) were employed with a regiment of eight or nine companies; and in 1612 one "Samuel Khebron" (Hepburn) commanded a regiment of Scots in Sweden which included Sir Patrick Ruthven who, from his fondness for the bottle, was nicknamed "Rotwein" (red wine), and who, after a long career of war, died as Earl of Forth and Brentford.

James VI of Scotland was highly displeased by levies of Scots being employed in Sweden against his brother-in-law, the King of Denmark, and forbade further levies; recruitment, however, continued, but less openly. In 1612 Captain Andrew Ramsay and his recruiting officers were tried for kidnapping and impressing men for service in Sweden; they were laid under a heavy bail, their ships searched and the captives released. About the same time some few hundred Scots, levied by Ramsay, left Caithness secretly under the command of his brother, Colonel Alexander Ramsay, Captain Hay and Captain George Sinclair, landed on the coast of Norway, intending to march through Sweden, but were fired on by Norwegian border guards and only a few escaped alive. Nevertheless, in 1624, Sir James Spens of Wormiston raised a levy of 1200 Scots for the Swedish service; and in the reign of Charles I six warrants were issued permitting the King of Sweden to levy 12,600 Scots.

As can be imagined, not all Scots were saints and it is probable that the Scots abroad included a number whom the mother country saw leave without regret. William Gordon, 7th Earl of Menteith (1591-1661) denounced these such in the following terms: "Shame on the pack of these mercenary swordsmen! They have made the name of Scot throughout all Europe equivalent to that of a pitiful mercenary, who knows neither honour nor principle but (only) his month's pay; who transfers his allegiance from standard to standard at the pleasure of fortune and to the highest bidder; and to whose insatiable thirst for plunder and warm quarters we owe much of that civil dissension which is now turning our swords against our own bowels."[6]

Sir Thomas Urquhart[7] says: " . . . at one time he (Gustavus Adolphus) had six-and-thirty Scottish colonels about him . . . the half of the names of which colonels are not here inserted, though they were men of notable prowesse, and in martial atchievements of most exquisite dexterity . . . many regiments of English, Scots, Danes, Sweds, Fins,

Liflanders, Laplanders, High-Dutch, and other nations serving in the confederate war of Germany under the command of Scottish colonels."

There were, one way and the other, a good many Scots in Russia in the time of Ivan IV. Dr Collins, the English physician to Czar Alexis, said: "Some old residents in Russia have noticed that out of two hundred English, Scots and Dutch, who have embraced the Russian Faith, hardly one has died a natural death."[8]

Horsey mentions, among the captive Scots, one "Gabriell Elphingsten, a valiant Scots captain," and there must have been at least one Hamilton, as "Swedish Hamiltons" were known later.

Some, however, were not captives, like General Carmichael, who entered the service of Ivan IV, apparently voluntarily. Scottish history is altogether silent about him, though he was uncle to Sir John Carmichael, Warden of the Border, of the Hyndford family. In 1570 he was in command of 5000 troops of the Czar's army during the Polish war, and later became Governor of Pskov.[9]

It is from the time of Ivan IV ("The Terrible") that Russia began to be largely dependent on foreigners. Up till his time most foreigners in Russia were "Latins," i.e. Catholics; but from now on Protestants, or "Germans," predominated. "It is doubly ironic that the point of no return in opening up Russia to western influences occurred under this most ostensibly xenophobic and traditionalist of czars and that the 'West' into whose hands he unconsciously committed Russia was that of the Protestant innovators whom he professed to hate even more than the Catholics."[10]

The term "German" included English, Scots, Holsteiners, Dutch, Danes, etc.. Scottish settlers, like all "heretics," were excluded from residence in the Kitai Gorod (China City) and Byeli Gorod (White City) of Moscow, and only permitted to live in the Nemetskaya Sloboda, the "dumb suburb." (*Nemetz* means dumb, i.e., not speaking Russian, and soon came to refer to all foreigners.)

The Scots married with foreign exiles, usually Livonians and Germans. One Hamilton, almost certainly one of the Swedish prisoners, had, in course of time, two descendants, sisters, who both married Russians: one to Artamon Sergeevich Matveev and the other to Fedor Poleukhtovich Narynsky—names prominent in Russian history.

In the time of Boris Godunov Captain David Gilbert, a Scot, with a Frenchman, Captain Margaret, entered Russian service. After Boris' death Gilbert served in the bodyguard of the first "False Dmitri," which was, significantly, entirely composed of foreigners. It comprised

300 English, French and Scots, divided into three squadrons and commanded by officers of each nation. Gilbert chopped and changed, like the Vicar of Bray, between the first "False Dmitri," then to the Polish Army, then back to the second "False Dmitri." He was lucky to keep his head. He remained in Russia under Czar Michael Romanov and probably died there.

In 1610 Captain Robert Carr, accompanied by Gilbert's son, entered Russian service. He commanded one of the six companies of British cavalry which, on June 24th, 1610, remained for the longest time on the battlefield on the occasion of the defeat of the Czar's (Vasili Shuisky's) army by the Poles at Kluchino, under the Grand Hetman Zolkiewsky. There Carr lost his entire company, but remained unwounded himself. Carr left for England in 1619, but presumably returned to Russia, as the noble house of Kar existed until 1917.

In 1614 foreign soldiers from Protestant countries began to pour into Russia. By 1624 445 foreign officers were noted: 168 Poles, 113 "Germans" (in which, probably, Scots such as Leslie, Keith and Matthison were included, as they are not listed separately), a few English, such as Fox and Sanderson, and 64 Irish.

The heyday of the Scots soldier of fortune was undoubtedly the Thirty Years' War, which was, ostensibly at least, a war of counter-revolution. Between the Reformation (1552) and the onset of the war in 1618, Lutheran Protestantism had made great inroads in Europe, with the result that in the Germanic countries the last strongholds of Catholicism were Austria and Bavaria, with isolated pockets in the Rhein Palatinate. Bohemia had recently become Protestant and Ferdinand II, elected Holy Roman Emperor in 1619, was determined to regain Bohemia from Frederick of Hohenzollern.

The main Catholic forces were the Catholic League under the command of Maximilian of Bavaria, and the army of the Empire under Ferdinand II. Maximilian moved against Frederick in Bohemia, crushing him at the Battle of the White Mountain, outside Prague, in 1620. Bohemia was regained for the Catholic Church.

In the second phase of the war Maximilian moved against the Protestants in the Palatinate which, although a stronghold of Protestantism, was disunited and fragmented, and proved no match for the Bavarian forces of the Catholic League. In 1623 the Emperor transferred the electoral dignity from Frederick to Maximilian, whom he made a Duke and Elector of Bavaria, and made over to him the Upper Palatinate, contiguous to Bavaria.

Continuing disasters to Protestant armies in Europe at last alerted the Protestant powers of northern Europe: England, the Netherlands, Denmark and Sweden, resolved to form a Protestant alliance under the leadership of England, whose king, James I, was father-in-law to the deposed Elector Frederick. But the Dutch, after a twelve years' truce, had recently resumed war with Spain; and Sweden was involved in war with Prussia and Poland.

Denmark's king, Christian IV, was willing to help, provided James would supply him liberally with men, money and arms. James agreed to do this, but falling into argument with his Parliament (which led to civil war a generation later under Charles I), failed to obtain the money and left Christian in the lurch.

Undeterred by this, Christian gamely invaded northern Germany and moved against General Tilly, now commanding the armies of the Catholic League. However, a new force threatened him from the east: this new force was led by Wallenstein and was the first *imperial* force to take the field. A single campaign only was necessary to force Denmark out of the war. By the Peace of Lübeck (1629) Denmark was allowed to keep her pre-war territories on condition of no more assistance to the Protestant League.

By 1629 it seemed that the Catholic triumph was complete. The Emperor issued an Edict of Restitution by which Protestants were to be dispossessed of all church properties in the area now under Catholic control. By a stroke of the pen two archbishoprics, twelve bishoprics and hundreds of monasteries were reappropriated to the Catholic Church. But the Emperor made a fatal mistake in disbanding his army, which was his only means of enforcing the Edict. The German lands were in a state of ruination due to Wallenstein's policy of allowing his troops to live off the land and to appropriate without payment whatever they might require. Moreover, his ambitions in Europe seemed boundless and now threatened Catholic and Protestant interests alike.

Gustavus Adolphus had by now finished his war with Poland, and tried to reunite the now hopelessly disunited Protestants; but the latter, although they had no affection for the Emperor, hesitated to ally themselves with a foreign upstart who, once he had obtained a foothold in Europe, might be difficult to dislodge later.

At this stage unexpected help came from, of all places, France, which, although Catholic, viewed with apprehension the prospects of a strong Germany arising from Wallenstein's ambitions.

Cardinal Richelieu concluded an agreement with Gustavus Adolphus to pay Sweden a large subsidy to prosecute the war. In 1631 Tilly stormed, took and burned Magdeburg, on the Elbe, a Protestant stronghold, which finally forced the Protestants to unite and support Gustavus Adolphus. Emboldened by this, Gustavus advanced eagerly on Tilly and, in September 1631, at Breitenfeld, near Leipzig, astonished the world by completely crushing the imperial army. Next year he moved against Bavaria and defeated Tilly again, who died in this encounter. The Catholic armies which, only two years before, had been masters of Europe, were now in total disarray.

The Emperor Ferdinand succeeded in persuading Wallenstein who, since his dismissal in 1630, had been sulking on his estates, to take the field again. Gustavus Adolphus and Wallenstein, the two greatest military commanders in Europe at the time, met in decisive battle at Lützen, near Leipzig, in November 1632. The Swedes won, but at a terrible cost, and Gustavus Adolphus was killed in battle.

Germany was now in total chaos. Wallenstein, now virtually dictator of Europe, evolved a plan of German pacification on the basis of toleration for Protestants. Since he could never hope to persuade the Emperor to such a plan, he opened negotiations with his Protestant adversaries, thus formally committing treason. In February 1634, at Eger in Bavaria, he was assassinated by two Scots, Walter Lesley and John Gordon.

Meanwhile in Sweden Oxenstiern, the Chancellor, who ruled as regent for Gustavus Adolphus' infant daughter, Christina, continued the war under several capable generals who had trained under Gustavus Adolphus; but, defeated by the Catholic League at Nördlingen in 1634, Sweden was forced to evacuate south Germany. The war could have ended there with the Emperor's attempts at reconciliation; but just then France entered the war, which continued for another fourteen years. This phase of the war is irrelevant to Russia's interests.

Ferdinand II died in 1637, and it was left to his successor, Ferdinand III (1637-1657), to make terms with France and Sweden at the Peace of Westphalia in 1648.

The rise of Sweden to the position of a leading power in northern Europe dates from the heroic time of Gustavus Adolphus (1611-1632). In his early years Gustavus had successfully extended Sweden's territory along the eastern shores of the Baltic. Although he did not live to see the end of the war, his successes in Germany enabled his successor, Christina, to demand as her share of the spoils western Pomerania and lands at the mouths of the Weser and the Elbe.

For the remainder of the 17th century Sweden ranked with the great powers of Europe; but her greatness rested only on her military prowess which, as history so often shows, is no basis for the continuation of power after the departure from the scene of the military genius who brought it about. Denmark to the west, Brandenburg-Prussia and Poland to the south, Russia to the east, had all paid for Sweden's gains with severe losses, and bided their time to be revenged.

It will readily be seen that a war of this dimension and duration called for enormous resources of manpower. We have no accurate figures of the populations of Denmark, Sweden and other countries at the time; even if we had, they would be only approximate, as the boundaries varied rapidly from decade to decade, and as the fortunes of war added and subtracted whole provinces to and from the contending countries.

In the initial phases of the war the main need for Protestant recruits was to Denmark, Sweden and the Low Countries; Russia largely kept out of the war and it was only later that the mercenaries, in search of a job, began to join the Russian service in any numbers. Many veterans of Danish, Swedish or Polish service eventually ended up in Russia.

An excellent portrait of the Scots soldier-adventurer was drawn by Sir Walter Scott, in the character of Dugald Dalgetty, in *The Legend of Montrose*. As Professor Mackie has shown,[11] Scott based the character on two actual models: Sir James Turner, who, besides his *Memoirs,* left a learned book on the art of war, *Pallas Armata;* and Colonel Robert Munro, who was with the Scots regiment levied in 1626 by Sir Donald Mackay, afterwards Lord Reay, "Colonell for His Majesties Service of Denmark," who also wrote an account of his adventures in the Thirty Years' War. Many incidents in both books confirm the opinion that Scott borrowed extensively from both.

Monro served his military apprenticeship in France and obtained a captaincy in Mackay's regiment in 1626. Owing to severe casualties in the Holstein campaign, he was soon promoted to major, and as such took part in the defence of Stralsund which Wallenstein had sworn to take. He was later a lieutenant-colonel and, after the return to Scotland of Lord Reay in August 1626, he commanded the regiment as Colonel.

Serious casualties had depleted regimental strengths, so along with three other Scots regiments, his men were formed into the Green Brigade by Gustavus Adolphus, and put under the command of Sir John Hepburn, from whose name the unit was known as the "Regiment of Khebron," which became the Lothian regiment, later known as the Royal Scots.

Another fictional portrait of a Scots soldier of fortune is to be found in *Loot and Loyalty,* a novel by Jerzy Pietrkiewicz (William Heinemann, London, 1955). However fantastic were his adventures as invented by the author, who makes him the central figure in the promotion of a simple Polish peasant into the Second False Dmitri, Tobias Hume was a real person. Little is know of him except that he was a soldier of fortune, first in the service of the King of Poland, later in that of the Czar of Russia; that he was a poet and musician who played the viol da gamba; that he was an inventor of new military instruments of destruction, but could persuade no government or potentate to finance their construction; that he fell upon lean times and repeatedly petitioned Parliament for employment or subsistence, apparently without success.

He published two books of musical compositions which are today in the British Museum. One is entitled *The FIRST PART of Ayres, French, Pollish, and others . . . some in Tàbliture . . . and Almaines for the Viole de Gambo alone . . . Some Songes to bee sung to the Viole, with the Lute . . . Also an Invention for two to play . . . Composed by Tobias Hume Gentleman;* and was published in London in 1605.

The other relic of his long life in military service is a curious work: *The True Petition of Colonel Hume, As it was presented to the Lords assembled in the high Court of Parliament: Being then one of the poore Brethren of that famous Foundation of the Charter House. London, Printed for John Giles, 1642.* In this he laments the low state to which fortune has reduced him and pleads for employment in Ireland, of the conduct of which he is most critical. ". . . if you please to send me for Ireland, and make me Commander of all those men who are now to goe over for Ireland, I will undertake to get in all Ireland in three or foure Months at the farthest, or else if I doe it not, I will give them leave to take off my head. . . ."

He offers his credentials: "I am an old and experienced Souldier, and have done great service in other forraine Countries as when I was in Russia, I did put thirty thousand to flight, and killed six or seven thousand Polonians by the art of my instruments of warre when I first invented them, and did that great service for the Emperor of Russia. . . ."

We are not told the outcome of this petition which, from its contents, appears to be the last of a series of such petitions; and Captain or Colonel Tobias Hume (the latter title almost certainly self-conferred) fades away as all old soldiers should.

As shown already, Mackay's levies were for the Danish service when Christian IV made his reckless entry into the war. At the same time Sweden, engaged in a desperate struggle for expansion, found it impossible to supply the necessary manpower from her own resources. The two streams met and intermingled when Gustavus Adolphus made his sudden and successful irruption into northern Germany.

The great recruiting officer, Sir Alexander Leslie of Auchintoul,* arrived in 1631 with a letter from Charles I to Czar Michael Romanov. The Patriarch Philaret (Czar Michael's father) sent him to Sweden to "borrow" 5000 infantrymen, and to persuade smiths, wheelwrights, carpenters, gunners, etc., to come to Russia.

By the end of 1631 there were reported to be some 66,000 mercenaries in Muscovy. Captain William Gordon arrived in 1634; Lieutenant Col. Alexander Gordon (mentioned in Sir Thomas Urquhart's *The Jewel*), and the giant Colonel Thomas Carne (or Garne) arrived about the same time.

In March and May 1633, Captain James Forbes received warrants to raise 200 men on each warrant in Scotland for service under Sir Alexander Leslie, now "Generall Colonel of the Forrain Forces of the Emperour of Russia." Although, in England, the war of King and Parliament broke out soon after, this does not seem to have reduced the number of Scots who went to Russia; indeed many of them possibly went to Russia to avoid committing themselves politically in Britain.

The next Czar, Aleksei Mikhailovich (1645-1676), received the news of the execution of Charles I with shocked amazement; and issued a *ukase* forbidding English merchants residence within his empire. "At the request of your sovereign, King Charles," he wrote, "and because of our brotherly love and friendship towards him, you were allowed to trade with us by virtue of letters of commerce; but it has been made known to us that you English have done a great

---

* Three Leslies were generals in three countries at the same time; the other two being Walter, Count Leslie, in Germany; and Alexander Leslie, later Earl of Leven, in Scotland. Sir Alexander Leslie remained in Russia for the rest of his long life. He became a general, Governor of Smolensk, and died in 1661 at the age of 95. Other Leslies in Russia included Alexander Leslie of Kininvie, a Leslie of Wardis, and a George Leslie, who became a Capuchin monk at Archangel.

wickedness by killing your Sovereign, King Charles, for which evil deed you cannot be suffered to remain in the realm of Muscovy."[12]

This did not affect the Scots, whom the Czar welcomed as he appreciated their loyalty. He refused all recognition to Cromwell, and sympathy for the Stuart cause, as we shall see in the eighteenth century, dates from this regicide.

In 1661, Patrick Gordon enrolled as major, Paul Menzies as captain in the foot regiment commanded by Colonel Daniel Crawfurd. Czar Alexis promptly married Menzies off to a Russian wife, and in 1661 and 1662 he became a member of the suite of the Boyar Fedor Mikhailovich Milatovsky, envoy to Persia. In 1672 Menzies acted as the Czar's envoy to Prussia and Vienna to propose a league against the Turks. He proceeded to Rome to petition Pope Clement X to assist Poland against the Sultan of Turkey and accomplished his mission with dignity. He returned to Moscow in 1674 and was advanced in rank. He was tutor to Peter I until 1682 when the Regent, the Princess Sophia, sent him to Smolensk to take part in the war against the Crimean Tatars. He was a direct contemporary of Patrick Gordon, his friend and witness to his will. He died a lieutenant-general in 1694, leaving a wife and children in Russia. Another member of the same family serving in Russia was Lieut.-Col. Thomas Menzies of Balgownie.

Lest it may appear that undue emphasis has been put on the virtue of the Scots adventurer in the time of Peter the Great, one fairly villainous example of the darker side of life as a mercenary is included.

Count Gustaf Otto Douglas was born in 1687, son of Count Gustaf Douglas and grandson of Count Robert Douglas of the Whittinghame family, and the first of his name in Sweden. After sundry "wonderful adventures," he was taken prisoner at Poltava (1709), but in 1717 reappeared as Governor of Finland. During his rule there, 3000 Finnish recruits were taken by force and sent to Astrakhan, from whence only a few over 400 ever returned to their homes. The very name Otto was held in horror among the Finns.[13]

One day, in 1719, at a wedding in Åbo, he, in a fit of temper, murdered a Russian General of Police, and was sent in chains to St Petersburg. "Peter the Great, chancing to meet Douglas wheeling a barrow with other convicts, straightway pardoned him and reinstated him in his high offices."[14]

No sentiment of honour towards the country of his birth influenced his conduct. In 1719 he piloted the Russian fleet into Norrköping, stole the bones of the English St Henry from the Cathedral at Åbo and carried them off to St Petersburg. The more wicked he became, the more honours were heaped upon him. Later Douglas removed to Esthonia where he became Governor of Reval from 1737-1741. Later, on a commission to Livonia, he caused a noble of high rank to be whipped to death. This was more than even Peter could stand. Count Otto was advised to retire to his estates, which he did in 1751, where he was still living in 1763, at that time 76 years of age.

THE RUSSIAN BRUCES

Bruces were so numerous in Russia as almost to comprise a separate clan. The earliest Bruce immigrant to Russia was Colonel William Bruce, who claimed to belong to the old house of Bruce of Airth, and who arrived in Russia in 1650 and died at Pskov in 1680. He had two sons, Major-General James Daniel (Yakov Vilemovich) Bruce (1669-1735), and Robert (Roman Vilemovich) Bruce (1668-1720), who married into Russian families and became thoroughly assimilated.

Both young men prospered exceedingly in Russia. James "passed at Court for a chemist and astrologer of genius, but was held in the City as a Sorcerer." A whole legend has grown up around the light which streamed, on long winter nights, from the windows of his laboratory in the Sukharev Tower. Some, however, were less impressed; Waliczewski wrote of him: "His astronomical discoveries bordered closely on Astrology, and his celebrated *Calendar,* published in 1711, is all moonshine."[15]

James had a great capacity for hard work, which made him a man after Peter's heart. There was not much he did not have a finger in. He was placed at the head of the artillery and was suspected of peculation. His career was subject to sudden vicissitudes; he was at one time disgraced in favour of Prince Ivan Trubetskoi for "lack of expedition," and at another time for "abuse of his office," though he had a reputation for never accepting bribes. He must have been an engaging rogue, for the Czar always ended by forgiving him.

The Peace of Nystadt in 1721, which ended the Swedish wars, gave the Baltic provinces to Russia and left Sweden with no lands south of the Gulf of Finland. James Bruce played a significant part in these negotiations and was rewarded with the title of Count. He it was who induced Peter to correspond with Leibnitz, translated many foreign books into Russian for his master, and directed the Czar's schools of navigation, artillery and military engineering. He also collated the codes of law of other nations for Peter, and was made a Senator in 1718. He later retired to his estate at Glinki, 42 versts from Moscow, where he died without issue in 1735.

His title passed to his nephew, Alexander Romanovich Bruce, son of his brother Robert (Roman), who was born in 1705. He took part in the war with the Turks and became a major-general in 1739. He retired in 1751 on account of ill health and died in the same year. He married twice into the family of Dolgorouki: his first wife was Princess Anastasia Mikhailovna Dolgoroukaya; his second (her cousin?) Princess Yekaterina Alekseevna Dolgoroukaya, the bereaved fiancée of the young Czar Peter III. She was described as "beautiful but arrogant."

James' brother Robert (who russified his name into Roman Vilemovich, i.e. Robert son of William) accompanied Peter the Great on his travels in 1697-98, and took part in the siege of Schlüsselburg. In 1704 he was made lieutenant-general and commandant at St Petersburg where he remained until his death in 1720, largely occupied in building Peter's new capital. He was buried in the Fort of St Peter and St Paul, which he built, beside the Cathedral and opposite the altar. It was through his influence that the first evangelical church, St Anne's, was built in St Petersburg. It was during General Bruce's brief time in St Petersburg that the great exodus from Moscow to St Petersburg took place by order of Peter I. A thousand of the leading families of Moscow received orders to move, which they did, for the most part, with ill grace. With their removal Moscow was never the same, which "once the pleasantest and most agreeable city in all Russia, became quite deserted, none remaining in it but the vulgar, which was a great mortification to all ranks of people being obliged to leave a place of much plenty for one where everything was both scarce and dear."[16]

Peter Henry Bruce was deeply impressed with the expeditious manner in which St Petersburg grew: "It was surprising to see so many great things undertaken and put in execution by one single person, without the assistance and help of anyone; his own great genius and indefatigable application to things presiding over all, and seeing everything with his own eyes . . . so that never monarch was less imposed on than himself."

Peter Henry Bruce, grandson of John Bruce, the "Prussian Bruce," was born in Germany but served for many years in the Russian army. He left some very entertaining *Memoirs* in which are interesting vignettes of life at the Court of Peter the Great. In these memoirs he tells the story of how his grandfather (John) and grand-uncle (James) decided to leave Scotland, in the time of Oliver Cromwell, and pursue their fortunes abroad. They went to Leith where there were ships bound for the Baltic. "As there were some ships in the port of Leith ready to sail for the Baltic, they agreed to go together to that part of the world; but as there happened to be two of these ship-masters of the same name, by an odd mistake the cousins embarked in different vessels, the one bound to Prussia, the other to Russia, by which accident they never again saw each other."

Peter Henry entered Russian service in 1710 at the invitation of General James Bruce, the one who had taken the wrong ship and ended up in Russia, and who was now one of Peter the Great's right-hand men and head of ordnance in Moscow, and was already a knight of four orders: St Andrew, the White Eagle, the Black Eagle, and the Elephant. Peter Henry was sent on an embassy to Constantinople and returned to St Petersburg when the city was in its infancy and accommodation scarce, but soon found a protector of his own kin there (how those Scots stuck together!). "I had the good fortune to be accommodated in Lieutenant-General (Roman Vilemovich) Bruce's house, who was commandant of St Petersburg, brother of the Master-General of the Ordnance (James Daniel, or Yakov Vilemovich, Bruce)." However, the latter, being still in Germany, ordered Peter Henry to occupy his (James') house in Moscow until he arrived back.

Peter Henry, who later had a company of artillery under General Bruce, was not happy in Muscovite service and was anxious to rejoin the Prussian army; he applied for his discharge but "could by no means obtain it, so I was obliged to continue in the Muscovite service, very much against my inclination." In his enforced continuance in the country he saw and heard much of the trial and death of the unfortunate Tsarevich, Peter's son: "various were the reports that were spread concerning his death . . . very few believed he died a natural death, but it was dangerous to speak as they thought." Peter Bruce had military charge of the dead Tsarevich's son, Piotr Alekseevich, afterwards Peter III. He took part in several Caspian and Persian campaigns, and did many tours of duty in Russia, until he could obtain his liberty. He was promised that as soon as the Empress Catherine's coronation was over (in 1725) he would receive his papers, as his relative Count Bruce was now a privy counsellor, Master of the Horse, and carried the crown at Catherine's coronation, his wife following as one of the Empress's train-bearers. Eventually he did get permission to go on leave and even then he "received the pay and forage money due to me from the regiment, but could not get the two years' pay that was due to me as an Engineer, and which amounted to twelve hundred roubles, but was told the money appropriated for the payment of the service was at St Petersburg, and I must go there to receive it, which, if I had done, would have effectually put a stop to my journey. I empowered Major-General Lefort* to receive my pay, and sell my house and furniture in St Petersburg, and to remit me the money in Scotland; but a stop was put to it till my return, and at the expiration of my furlough, everything I had left there was seized so that I had no reason to boast of any advantage I reaped in Russia after thirteen years' service.[17]

After the battle of Poltava (1709), being in Poland on a separate command, he took the opportunity to send to Moscow for his wife and daughters, and on their arrival in Poland he carried them to Danzig whence they took a ship to Scotland. He went into British service and in 1745 was engaged in fortifying Berwick. He retired soon after and died in 1757.

The Counts Bruce were prominent in the reign of Catherine the Great, and Brusovski Street in Moscow was named after them. Count James Alexandrevich Bruce (1742-1790) was Governor of Moscow from 1781 to 1786. Another Count Bruce was a Senator, General-in Chief and Governor of Novgorod and Tver. His wife was Praskovya Aleksandrovna Rumiantseva, a sister of General Rumiansev. She was a favourite and confidante of Catherine's until she supplanted the Empress in the affections of Count Korsakov, which resulted in her exile.

The Scots soldier of fortune had come a long way from the mercenary levy, pressed into service in foreign armies by poverty and lack of opportunity at home. He had passed through various stages of development, from raw recruit to training officer and regimental commander. He had become a trusted adviser and organiser of the armies of the Czars and had carried out many diplomatic missions with competence and dignity. On the way the Russian soldier grew up

---

* Lefort, François Jacob (1653-1699), born at Geneva of Scottish extraction, served in the Swiss Guard in Paris, but entered the Russian service in 1675, and, heading the intrigues which made Peter sole ruler, became his first favourite, backed up his reforms, and in 1694 was made admiral and generalissimo. *(Chambers's Biographical Dictionary,* p. 580). He was almost eighteen years younger than Patrick Gordon and, to a certain extent, a rival for Peter's favour. He gets very few mentions in Gordon's *Diary.*

with him: from raw peasant material to professional soldier. Now they stood shoulder to shoulder as equals, and the Russian army was about to receive its severest test as Napoleon, the supreme dictator of Europe from the Ebro to the Vistula, prepared to launch his attack on the soil of Russia.

CHAPTER 3 — BIBLIOGRAPHY

1. Steuart, A. F., *Scottish Influences in Russian History,* James Maclehose & Sons, Glasgow, 1913 (Quoted from *Travels of Sir Jerome Horsey,* Hakluyt Society, Vol. xx, p. 182), p. 13.

2. Steuart, *idem,* p. 14 (Hakluyt, p. 182).

3. Steuart, *idem,* p.15 (Hakluyt, p. 183); also quoted in Klyuchevsky, V.O., *The Rise of the Romanovs,* Trans. and ed. by Liliana Archibald, assisted by Mark Scholl, Macmillan & Co., London, 1970; footnote to p. 299.

4. Steuart, *idem.,* p. 16 (Hakluyt, p. 183).

5. Steuart, A. F., "Scottish Officers in Sweden," *Scottish Historical Review,* Vol. i, p. 191.

6. Burton, John Hill, *The Scot Abroad,* Vol. ii, pp. 133-4.

7. Quoted in Burton, *ibid.,* p. 151.

8. Collins, Samuel, *The Present State of Russia,* London, 1671; quoted in Steuart, *Scottish Influences in Russian History,* p. 17.

9. Steuart, A. F., *Scottish Influences in Russian History,* p. 19; quoted in Steuart (see n. 1 above), p. 17.

10. Billington, James, H. *The Icon and the Axe,* Weidenfeld and Nicholson, London, 1966, p. 97.

11. Mackie, J. D., "Dugald Dalgetty; and Scottish Soldiers of Fortune," *Scottish Historical Review,* Vol. xii (April 1915). No. 47, pp. 221-37.

12. Bain, R. Nisbet, *The First Romanovs,* London, 1905., p. 98.

13 Donner, Otto, *A Brief Sketch of the Scottish Families in Finland and Sweden,* Helsingfors, 1884.

14. Marryat, Horace, *One year in Sweden,* Vol. ii, p. 463.

15. Quoted in Steuart, *Scottish Influences in Russian History,* p. 93.

16. Bruce, *Memoirs of Peter Henry, a Military Officer in the Services of Prussia, Russia and Great Britain,* printed for the author's widow, 1782, edition of Frank Cass & Co., 1970.

17. Bruce, *ibid.,* p. 114.

For the background of the Thirty Years' War see Schevill, Frederick, *A History of Europe from the Reformation to the Present Day,* G. Bell & Sons, London, 1939.

CHAPTER 4

Soldier - Adventurers in Muscovy

Patrick Gordon was by no means the first Scot to venture into Europe to seek his fortune; but by reason of the fame he acquired, the exalted rank he attained in the service of a succession of Czars, and of the diary he kept for so many years, he remains the exemplar of the Scots soldier-adventurer par excellence.

Prior to Patrick Gordon, the most famous Scot in Russian service was Thomas Dalyell, or Dalzell[2] (either way pronounced Dee-ell), the

General Thomas Dalzell 1599-1685

"Muscovy General," who was born at Binns, Linlithgowshire, in 1599. He served in the expedition to La Rochelle in 1628 and in Ireland. Taken prisoner at Worcester in 1651, he escaped to the Continent and, in 1655, entered the Russian army, for which he fought in several engagements against Tatars and Turks in the Crimea. In 1666 he returned to Scotland and was appointed Commander-in-Chief of the army which defeated the Covenanters at Rullion Green in the Pentlands. Scott, in his *Tales of a Grandfather,* says the Presbyterians said that at the battle of Rullion Green, musket balls were seen hopping like hailstones from General Dalzell's buff coat and hat. They believed that he, like Claverhouse, was under the special protection of the Devil. He was renowned for his cruelty and severity, possibly learned in Russia, and was alluded to as "a Muscovy beast who roasted men." After the execution of Charles I, Dalzell, a devoted royalist, never shaved his beard again (a custom also probably picked up in Russia); his beard grew white and bushy and descended almost to his waist, whilst his head was completely bald, giving him a ferocious appearance, as can be seen from his portrait (see A. & H. Tayler, facing page 36). He is chiefly to be remembered as the man who raised the Scots Greys, which regiment was originally known as "Tom Dalzell's Dragoons."

"Old Tom of Muscovy," as King Charles II used to call him, died in 1685, his command in Scotland being taken over by General Claverhouse, born John Graham of Claverhouse, later Viscount Dundee. In the service of James II, he was a relentless pursuer of Covenanters, of whom he destroyed some two thousand in the Pass of Killiecrankie in 1689. In hunting down the miscreants he "evinced the utmost activity;" no doubt a worthy successor to the bloodthirsty "Muscovy General." It is difficult to appreciate that the epithets, "Bloody Claver'se" and "Bonnie Dundee," refer to the same person; it just depends on which side you stood in the bloody war of Episcopalians and Covenanters.

There were Gordons in Russia before General Patrick Gordon. There are said to be frequent mentions of William Gordon, a seaman engaged in the early trade between England and Russia, in Dr Hamel's "England and Russia," quoted in the preface of Gordon's Diary (p. xxiii); and "the researches of Dr Posselt have discovered, among the military archives of St Petersburg, certain documents regarding a Captain William Gordon in 1631, and a Lieutenant-Colonel Alexander Gordon in 1634. The latter, no doubt, is the person of the same name who appears in Sir Thomas Urquhart's *The Jewel,* among "those Scottish colonels that served under the great duke of Muscovy against the Tartar and Polonian."*

We would also like to hear more of the semi-mythical Scottish giant, "Colonel Thomas Garne, agnamed the Sclavonian and upright Gentile, who, for the height and grossness of his person, being in his stature taller and greater in his compass than any within six kingdoms about him, was elected King of Bucharia" (wherever that might be: Bokhara?).

Another contemporary of Patrick Gordon was George Ogilvy (1648-1710).[3] Although he reached the exalted rank of Field-Marshal, very little is known of him. He was the son of George, Baron Ogilvy Governor of Spielberg in Moravia, who was a son of Patrick Ogilvy of Muirtown and a grandson of James, Lord Ogilvy of Airlie. In his youth he entered the service of Czar Alexis, becoming Gentleman of the Bedchamber and a major-general. After the death of General Lefort in 1699, he became Field-Marshal under Peter the Great.

From the few references available one gets the impression of a fussy, obstinate martinet who took little pains to disguise his contempt for the Russian soldiery, and who imposed on the forces under his command a Teutonic discipline.

His main claim to fame is the capture of Narva (August 9th, 1704), a month after the fall of Dorpat, in one of Peter's innumerable wars with Sweden, which was concluded by the Peace of Ivangorod. This, however, did not last long, as the Russians and Swedes were at it again in 1706.

At Grodno there was considerable danger that the Russian army would be surrounded and obliged to surrender *en masse.* Peter advised a retreat from the salient, but Ogilvy dared not risk pursuit by the considerable force of cavalry which was at Charles XII's disposal. Peter overrode his objections and again ordered him to retire; Ogilvy ignored this until, after several further letters and orders, he was obliged

---

* Sir Thomas Urquhart of Cromarty (1611-1660) was a true Scots eccentric. He wrote several books, including one on the resolution of triangles; he also wrote *The Pedigree,* in which he gave "an exact account of the Urquhart family right back to Adam;" and *The Jewel,* which extolled the great deeds of Scottish history. In addition, he made the first translation into English of Rabelais. Far from being a dry scholar, his sense of humour killed him; he is said to have died abroad in a fit of mirth on hearing the news of the restoration of Charles II.

to obey. Peter relieved him of his command (March 12th, 1706), which was given to Prince Menshikov, who was a very capable soldier.

Whilst there was no doubt of his loyalty and courage, he was a thorn in the sides of Peter and Menshikov; and when he was finally dismissed from Russian service in September 1706, "with politeness and gifts," they must have sighed with relief.

General Patrick Gordon 1635-1699.

With Peter's permission he transferred to the army of Augustus, Elector of Saxony, whose service he considered more refined, and where he retained his rank of Field-Marshal. However,within a week of joining the Saxon army, peace was signed between Saxony and Sweden, and Ogilvy's military career came to an end. Still, he had not done too badly out of it. He bought for 120,000 ducats the feudal estate of Sauershau. He died at Danzig in October, 1710, at the age of 62.

Patrick Gordon was born at Easter Auchleuchries, Aberdeenshire, on March 31st, 1635, second son of John Gordon and his wife, née Mary Ogilvy. His eldest brother, George, born in 1634, would naturally be presumed to succeed to the estate, but predeceased his father, dying in 1665. His father died in 1675, so that the estate, which Patrick had never expected to inherit, passed to him then. This, however, could not have been anticipated when, in 1651, Patrick set forth overseas to seek his fortune, being, as he stated, "the younger son of a younger brother of a younger house."

One can imagine the pain with which his parents bade him goodbye. He was a little over sixteen years of age when, "on the third of June (1651), after a sadd parting with my loveing mother, brothers and sister, I took my jorney to Aberdeen in company of my father and unkle, who, after two days stay, wherein I was furnished with cloths, money and necessaries, returned. My mother came foure days thereafter, of whom I received the benediction and tooke my leave."[4] This laconic statement, devoid of emotion, characterises his diary throughout; facts we shall find a-plenty; minute details of transactions, military and financial, abound; great names and encounters are recorded, but little insight is given into Patrick Gordon as a person, and his diary is almost entirely devoid of any personal feelings or reactions to the great persons he met and the great events in which he participated.

So he set sail on June 12th in a Dutch schooner out of Danzig, skipper Jacob Bartelman. By Skagen and Jutland the ship reached Elsinore where "wee went ashore, and dined in a Scotsman's house very well for twelve pence a man;"* and so on to Danzig where he lodged in a Scotsman's house in Holy Ghost Street, his landlord being John Donaldson. Here also he met Thomas Menzies and his brother Alexander Michael Menzies, the latter a priest in charge of a small church, who persuaded Patrick to join the Jesuit College at nearby Braunsberg where, from a break in his diary of nearly two years, it appears that he remained until "albeit I wanted not for any thing, the Jesuits alwayes bestowing extraordinary paines, and takeing great care in educating youth, yet could not my humor endure such a still and strict way of liveing."[6]

So he left Braunsberg and, after a year or two of wandering, during which time he resolved to seek employment with Duke Jan Radzewill who had "a lyfe company, all or most Scottismen," he came to Posnan (Posen), where he lodged with a Scotsman, James Lindsay,

---

* i.e. pence Scots; not much above one penny by today's values.

and met other fellow-countrymen such as Robert Farquhar, James Ferguson, James White and James Watson. However, in the end, and after a detour via Hamburg and Lübeck, he came to Stettin, where he joined the Swedish army and took part in the siege of Cracow (Sept. 1655) under General Patrick Douglas. This was the youngest of four brothers, the others being William, Archibald and Richard, all of whom served and died in the Swedish service. Patrick Douglas was a General in 1655 and a Lieutenant-Field Marshal the following year.

Early the next year, Gordon was returning late from a reconnoitre, missed his unit and was captured by the Poles. After seventeen weeks in confinement, he obtained his release only by promising to join the Polish army. Whilst in their ranks he augmented his pay by a device strongly suggestive of having been learned from the reivers and caterans of his native land. He would organise his comrades to drive off the cattle of a neighbouring noble, who would then seek his aid to recover the missing herds, Gordon duly receiving a reward for his successful exertions. This, and the blandishments of the local Mayor's pretty daughter, helped him to pass the time pleasantly and profitably during the siege of Warsaw. Shortly after, Gordon was recaptured by the Swedes and taken before his former commanding officer, General Douglas. His explanation, that he had been forced to join the Polish ranks, was readily accepted and once more Gordon entered the Swedish service where he was to remain for three years. But in 1657 he was surprised by some Polish peasants and captured; again he was urged to take service with the Poles but refused; not long after he was set free by exchange.

Reading Gordon's diary of this period one gets the impression that the Thirty Years' War was organised for the employment and profit of Scottish adventurers; and that the Swedes and Poles took little part in the proceedings. It was far more profitable to make forays into the enemy lines, seize a number of prisoners, preferably of officer rank, and hold them to ransom, than to kill the enemy. This was a sport in which Gordon excelled; on one occasion his party of eighteen captured a village in which there were 23 men-at-arms, 35 dragoons and 40 horses, with which they returned in triumph to the Swedish headquarters. The Scots acquired such a reputation as foragers that whenever prisoners were brought in, the credit was usually given to them, whether justified or not. It all sounds great sport and profitable enterprise; military objectives, if there were any, being of secondary importance.

So successful was the business side of the war that, when Gordon eventually asked for his discharge from Douglas' unit, because, as he claimed, he had never received a farthing in pay or maintenance during the whole period of his service, his "emoluments" were sufficient to make him well satisfied with his progress to date.

The game, however, was not entirely devoid of risk. Gordon was wounded in the forehead in 1656, and a year later was prostrated with some fever which kept him out of action for several months. Then he was again wounded, in two places, and taken prisoner, but escaped after a six weeks' confinement. He also got severe frostbite of the feet; the doctor pronounced his case hopeless, but an old woman cured him with her homely remedies.

The next few pages of Gordon's diary abound in names such as Meldrum, Drummond, Fullerton, Scott, Crawfurd, Menzies, Erskine, etc., etc. One such redoubtable character was his namesake, possibly kinsman, Patrick Gordon of the Steel Hand, then a captain in the Polish cavalry. In the ranks of the Emperor Ferdinand II was famous Walter Lesley, who had acquired a great estate in Germany and, with another Scotsman, John Gordon, distinguished himself by killing Wallenstein (Feb. 25, 1634).[6] Lesley's subsequent honours read like a roll of drums or a fanfare of trumpets: Marshal-General of the Imperial Army, Privy Councillor, Count of the Holy Roman Empire, Lord of Pettau and Neustadt, Governor of Versdan, etc. He was made Ambassador to the Pope and to the Grand Seignior at Constantinople. He married a Princess of Dietriechstein and died, overwhelmed with honours but without issue, shortly after his successful embassy to the Grand Seignior, who, on beholding his entry into the seraglio through a window, was heard to say that never in all his life had he seen such a show.

Gordon now entered the Swedish service as an ensign in Colonel Anderson's regiment. "While on duty at Stum, he one day, in company with his friend Captain Forbes, rode after some Poles who were carrying off horses belonging to the garrison. Falling into an ambuscade, they were set upon by about a hundred of the enemy, when Forbes was wounded and taken prisoner. Gordon, floundering through a bog, dashed through three Poles who had marked him for their prey, and, spurring past twenty others, escaped with the loss of his sabre, his cap, and a handful of hair which was torn with it from his head. His clothes were riddled with shot and had three arrows stuck in them, one of which wounded him in the side. On regaining the Swedish lines, his colonel, who, with some of the officers, had quietly beheld the whole affair, rode up to him with a cocked pistol and threatened to shoot him for venturing so far without orders. Gordon made no other answer than that he would not desert his captain; but he was so far affected by this incident and by the loss of his friend that, in despair, he rode back to seek death in another skirmish with the Poles."[7] He escaped once more, and Captain Forbes, after a captivity of six weeks, recovered his liberty.

In Nov. 1658, in a sally by a handful of the garrison against a numerous body of the enemy, Gordon again fell into the hands of the Poles. Proposals to liberate Gordon by exchange were made by the Swedes but refused by the Poles, who wished to see him again in their service. Gordon was offered several posts as ensign, the same rank he had held in the Swedish army, but played hard to get. At length he accepted the post of quartermaster in the Polish army.

In 1660, hearing news of the restoration of Charles II, he resolved to return home and offer his services to King Charles; but his father wrote that Charles had disbanded most of his armies, only a few troops being retained in pay, the charge of these being given to such persons as had suffered for or deserved well of his Majesty. Gordon, who was a Catholic, could not have foreseen that his religion would prove an obstacle to employment in Scotland. By proclamation dated Dec. 16, 1673, King Charles inhibited and discharged "any person or persons who are of Popish profession after the first of March nixt to accept of or exercise any public imployment or office either civill or military within this kingdome."[8]

In 1661, now aged 26, he tried to enter the service of the Roman Emperor as it was the best paid in Europe, but there were no vacancies. So, instead, he joined the Czar's service on a three-year commission, one year as a major and two as a lieutenant-colonel.

On Sept. 6th, 1661, he enrolled as Major, Paul Menzies as Captain, William Hay as Lieutenant and John Hamilton as Ensign, in the foot regiment of Colonel Daniel Crawfurd. He received as a gratuity 25 roubles in money, and as much in sables, four ells of cloth and 18 ells of damask. Other fellow countrymen enrolled in this regiment included Walter Airth, William Guild, George Keith, Andrew Burnet, Andrew Calderwood and Robert Stuart.

In January 1665 he married Katherine, daughter of Colonel Philip Albrecht von Bockhoven, she being 15 and he 30.

There is a long gap from 1667 to 1677 in his diary; he presumably continued to keep his diary, but there are several volumes lost. In 1670 he was sent with a regiment into the Ukraine to assist in subduing the Cossacks of Little Russia. He remained in the province for seven years, devoting his leisure to the study of mechanics, fortification and strategy. In 1676 Czar Alexis died and was succeeded by his son Fedor. In 1677 Gordon was back in the Ukraine, after a brief period in Moscow, taking part against the Turks and Tartars who were besieging Chigirin, the capital of the Zaporozhian Cossacks. His successful defence of the town greatly enhanced his military reputation.

During the second defence of Chigirin, in July 1678, the Turks mustered some 50,000 and the Tartars about the same. They had four great cannons, each of them drawn by 32 yoke of buffaloes; 27 battery pieces of various sizes; 130 field guns, six mortars throwing shells of 120 lbs weight, and nine smaller pieces throwing 30 to 40 lbs. They also brought 100,000 wagons with provisions and 8000 herdsmen. This formidable army was commanded by the Grand Vizier Kara Mustapha. The garrison which had to hold Chigirin numbered rather less than 12,000. Gordon had command of his own dragoons and a regiment of Streltsys; he was also chief engineer.

The siege started on July 8th. On August 8th the Governor was killed by a bursting bomb. Certain colonels and other officers asked Gordon to take command. Eventually the town had to be evacuated after repeated demands for reinforcements had been ignored. Shortly after the Russian troops had left, the main magazine at Chigirin blew up, killing 4000 Turks. Gordon's services in this affair were rewarded by promotion to the rank of Major-General; he was now 43. There is a further gap in his diary from 1679 to 1684, but we know that he was appointed to the chief command in Kiev in 1679; and in 1683 he was made Lieutenant-General.

One of the first entries after the resumption records the death of his son, George Stephen Gordon, on November 1st, 1684.

Czar Fedor died in 1682, leaving two brothers, Ivan and Peter. The former being an imbecile and the latter only ten years of age, the government fell into the hands of their sister, Sophia, who ruled as Princess Regent with the aid of her Prime Minister and favourite, Prince Vasili Vasilievich Golitsyn.

It appears that Gordon fell out of favour with the Kremlin for about three years, between 1683 and 1686; why, it is difficult to see. But by

1687 he is fully in favour again and in command of select regiments of the second division in a war against the Tartars in the Crimea.

He was promoted to full General on September 11th, 1687.

GORDON AND PETER THE GREAT

Patrick Gordon's life is so generally associated with that of Peter the Great that it must be appreciated that he was, in fact, 38 years older than his royal patron; and that his service under Peter occupied the last ten years only of his life.

For seven years since the death of Czar Fedor in 1682, the country had been ruled nominally by Peter's sister Sophia, but in practice by her first Minister Prince Golitsyn. His elder brother Ivan was co-Czar, but by reason of mental infirmity was largely ignored.

In 1689, Peter, now in his seventeenth year, was married to Eudoxia Fedorovna Lopukhina on January 20th. In August of the same year news reached Peter of a conspiracy against his life. A regiment of Streltsys and soldiers of the guard had received orders from the Kremlin to march to Preobrazhenskoe to seize his person. He instantly sprang from his bed, ran to the stables and, flinging himself on a horse, galloped to the nearest wood. Here he remained until his clothes were brought to him, when, accompanied by a few attendants, he renewed his flight and riding in hot haste reached the Troitsky monastery about 40 miles from the capital. There he besought the protection and help of the Abbot.

It was now an open struggle between the young Czar (or co-Czar really) and the Princess Sophia. Peter summoned the Streltsys and other troops in Moscow to join him at the monastery; Sophia forbade their march. Peter renewed his command in a written order, addressed to the foreign officers stating that there was a conspiracy against his life. Gordon consulted Minister Golitsyn, who was alarmed and undertook to consult the elder Czar, Ivan, and the princess. Gordon answered that if he and his brother officers were to disobey the Princess's orders, their heads would be in danger.

Golitsyn promised to let him know by midnight and requested that Gordon's son-in-law, Colonel Strasburg, should remain behind to receive the answer. This seems to have decided Gordon. He went home and immediately prepared to march. When the other officers came to him, he told them that, whatever orders might come from the

Kremlin, he was resolved to set out for the monastery that night. They agreed to follow his example, and the next day saw them all at the gates of the monastery. Peter was at lunch when their arrival was announced. Gordon was admitted at once to Peter's presence and ordered to remain by his side, whilst the other officers remained outside with their regiments.

Four days later Peter entered Moscow in triumph and the trial of the conspirators began. Shaklovitov, the second favourite as Gordon calls him, was tortured and beheaded, along with many others; the Czar's reluctance to shed blood being overcome by the Patriarch. Golitsyn was banished and his estates confiscated. Princess Sophia was sent to a convent where she died after a seclusion of fifteen years. The imbecile Ivan was persuaded to leave the rule of the empire in the hands of his younger and more energetic brother. The revolution was complete; and Gordon, who had done so much to bring it about, enjoyed a fair share of its advantages.

Peter owed his throne to Gordon and never forgot it. As time went by, Peter came to lean more and more on the advice of the older man, whom he treated with the respect due from a nephew to a favourite uncle, a position Gordon had to share with François Joseph Lefort (1653-1699), born at Geneva of Scottish extraction, who was eighteen years' Gordon's junior, but physically more able to sustain the pace set by their six-foot-nine-inch royal master, whose energy was such as to outlast a score of royal favourites. Thereafter there are frequent references to Gordon's growing intimacy with the young Czar and his presence at numerous dinners and entertainments. After most of these dinners, during which "there was an abundance of everything," Gordon was usually far from well, suffering severe headaches, colic, vomiting and diarrhoea. He was, after all, thirty-eight years older than Peter and not a debauchee by habit. As his son-in-law, Alexander Gordon, wrote of him: "General Gordon was a sober man, in a country where drinking is much in fashion; and though he used to to be much in the Czar's company, his Majesty, knowing his inclinations, would never allow him to be urged."[9] After a while Peter took pity on the older man and permitted him to retire when the going looked like becoming rough.

On September 23rd, 1690, Gordon's daughter Mary was married to his old commanding officer, Colonel Daniel Crawfurd, the Czar gracing the nuptials with his presence.

In 1688 James II was deposed and his daughter Mary, with her husband William of Orange, ascended the throne. Gordon was too stalwart a Jacobite and Catholic tamely to accept the "Glorious Revolution". In several of his letters to the Duke of Gordon, to the Earl of Melfort and others, Gordon refers to the "pretended king of England, calling himself William the Third"; and references to "His Majesty" refer to the deposed James II. In a letter to the Earl of Melfort from Moscow (Nov. 15th, 1690) he writes:

"I am glad to heare of the least hopes or appearance of any good in his Majesties affaires, and am sorry that in Irland things have gone so cross. Wee have nothing here but what wee learne from the Hollands Gazette, from which, though partiall, wee may gather that all does not go in our countreyes according to Orange his wishes; so that it may be hoped that by tyme a strong partie may appear, and act vigorously for his Majesties restauration. I wonder how they can endure so long such slavery and oppression by forreigne forces and intollerable taxations. I looke upon that revolution as another conquest by a medley of forreigne nations. I am sorry that I must, in such a tyme, be a looker on, and not capacitated to serve his Majestie with any thing but prayers, wishes, and goodwill."[10]

Since his visit to Britain in 1686, on which occasion he was honoured by a private audience with King James II, who pressed him to leave Russia and return to Britain where his outstanding talents of military organisation could be usefully employed, Gordon had made several efforts to leave the Czar's service; but Czar Peter not only depended heavily on him in his military capacity but had also a sincere affection for him as a person, and would not let him go.

In a letter to the Duke of Gordon, May 22nd, 1691, General Gordon wrote:

". . . wee may collect that Orange is not so well setled but he may be removed. For I cannot imagine but that, when the English see their purses emptied, their trade ruined, and their necks bowing under a forreigne yoke, and small hopes of prevailing against the Most Christian King[of France], a sense of loyalty and generosity, at least of their owne ruine and slavery, may prevaill so as to move the most generous of them to other measures. There is nothing here more highly commended in the Most Christian King, as his generous and most Christian resolution, not to give eare to any peace untill his Sacred Majestie, our Gracious King, be restored."[11]

Now with the Protestant William firmly in possession of the English throne, and hopes of a counter-revolution fading every year, Gordon appears to have become reconciled to lifelong exile in Russia; and his diary reveals no further applications to be relieved of his service to the Czar.

This year (1692) was further saddened by the deaths of two sons-in-law, Colonel Strasburg and Colonel Daniel Crawfurd; the former left a son and two daughters, the latter a posthumous son.

His diary tells us almost nothing of his family life. We learn that he married Katherine, daughter of Colonel Philip Albrecht von Bockhoven, by whom he had three sons and two daughters. His wife died some time before 1682 and he remarried, before 1686, Elizabeth Barnoe Roonaer, a buxom dame of Dutch extraction, by whom he had one further son.

Although there are almost no references to his wife or his domestic life in his diary, it appears that Patrick Gordon was happy enough with his wife, and kept the day of her death as a day of mourning: "Oct. 10th, 1696, the anniversary of the death of my first wife — the dear, the beloved."[12]

He was, however, not so happy in his children; he had three sons and two daughters by his first wife, and one son by his second wife, all of whom survived him. John, the eldest son, entered the Russian army when young, but was dismissed for reasons which do not appear. He inherited Auchleuchries from his father and died before 1712, leaving five sons and two daughters.

One son, George Stephen, died young, in 1684, as already recorded. James, Gordon's other son by his first wife, also saw service in Russia. In 1690 he had a Lieutenant-Colonel's commission from the Czar, was taken prisoner by the Swedes in 1700 and escaped two years later.

His fourth son, Theodore, entered his father's Butyrsky Regiment as an ensign in 1697. He had risen to the rank of colonel by 1709, after which all trace of him is lost.

His elder daughter, Katherine Elizabeth, born in 1665, married Colonel Strasburg, a German serving in the Russian army. He died from wounds caused by an explosion of fireworks, of which Peter the Great was so fond.

His younger daughter, Mary, was married to Captain, later Colonel, Daniel Crawfurd, who died in 1692. She subsequently married Alexander Gordon of Auchintoul in 1700. She left Russia in 1711 and died in Scotland in 1739, having outlived all the children of both her marriages. Her second husband, known in Russia as Alexander Alexandrovich, left the French army where he had gained a captain's commission, was made a major in General Gordon's regiment, was present at the capture of Azov, and rose, in ten or twelve years, to the rank of major-general. He returned to Scotland in 1711, where he acted as Lieutenant-General of the insurgent army in the 1715 rising. He escaped attainder by a mistake in the Act, and in 1727 returned to Scotland where he died in 1752 in his eighty-second year. In his old age he employed himself in writing a "History of Peter the Great".

In 1695 war broke out again with the Turks and Gordon was ordered to march on Azov. He came within sight of the city on March 27th and two days later the army was joined by the Czar and the Commander-in-Chief of the expedition, General Aleksei Simonovich Schein. It was mid-June before the place could be invested. One of the two forts, called Callanshaes, having been stormed by Colonel James Gordon, the other was evacuated the following night.

In mid-July the besieged made a sally on General Gordon's division but were repulsed. The following night a German engineer went over to the Turks and betrayed to them the weak points of the Muscovite lines. The next sally was, in consequence, directed against Lefort's quarters, and was so nearly successful that the division was saved only by the opportune interposition of General Gordon. The Czar scolded and threatened the Streltsys for failing in their duty.

At the beginning of August, Peter was determined to assault the town. It was in vain that Gordon remonstrated; the attack was made and failed, as he had foretold. "Such," he writes, "was the unfortunate result of this ill-timed and rash undertaking, urged on, as I might say, by Rehoboam's councillors. Of the four regiments, fifteen hundred men were killed, besides officers. About nine o'clock, his Majesty sent for me and the other officers. There was nothing to be seen but angry looks and sad countenances."[13]

A further assault, towards the end of August, was equally fruitless; and a few days afterwards, the siege was raised. The Czar, with his generals, returned to Moscow about the end of October.

By March 1696 Gordon was again advancing upon Azov at the

head of 15,000 infantry. He was at Voronezh on the 19th of April.

The second siege of Azov began in June, of which we have an eye-witness account by Gordon's son-in-law, Alexander Gordon of Auchintoul:

"The Czar, considering the great loss of time he had sustained the preceding year, called a council of war to know the opinions of the generals about the safest and most expeditious methods of becoming masters of the place. Most of them delivered their sentiments in the common way, by carrying on attacks, making of great breaches with mines and batteries; which (they said) would infallibly oblige the Governor to capitulate in terms of war, or expect the worse. Then General Gordon, as the oldest general (he was 61), gave his opinion that the safest and most expeditious way to become masters of the town, would be to carry before them a whole rampart of earth along the front of the town which, as they advanced , would hourly increase. By having ten or twelve thousand men night and day at work, said he, we shall carry and roll as much earth before us as will not only be sufficient to fill up the fosse, but we will have more over and above than will exceed the height of the town walls; by which means, in a few weeks, we shall oblige the enemy to surrender, or we shall bury them alive. The Czar preferred this opinion, and told them to do as he proposed. So to work they went with such cheerfulness that, within the space of five weeks, the fosse was actually full, and the earth above the height of the ramparts rolling in over them; which obliged the Governor to put out the white flag. Though this seems to be a very extraordinary and uncommon method of taking towns, yet here it proved very successful and safe, the loss of men during the siege not amounting to above 300 . . . The only officer of distinction the Czar lost during the siege was one, Colonel Stevenson, a Scots gentleman. He was shot in the mouth, being a little too curious, and raising himself too high on top of the loose earth to observe the enemy. He died of hunger, not being able to swallow any kind of nourishment. He was a good officer, and much regretted by the Czar, who caused him to be buried with all the honours of war.

"On June 28th the Governor demanded to capitulate . . . They marched out of the town about 6000 persons, whereof 3600 were armed men."[14]

The Muscovite army returned to Moscow in triumph on October

9th. Rewards were bestowed on the victorious generals; and Gordon received a medal with six ducats, a gold cup, a costly robe of sables, and an estate with ninety serfs.

In 1698 he was instrumental in putting down a serious revolt of the Streltsys, which he did with the utmost severity. One hundred and thirty men were executed, seventy were killed in the engagement or died of wounds; and 845 were sent to detention or prison. On July 6th he was confirmed in the Russian Orthodox Church, taking the name of Leopoldus. The years were beginning to take their toll of him; he was now 63 and had been in almost continuous action in the Czar's service and elsewhere for about 43 years. On September 19th he notes: "I was unwell and kept the house." The diary ends on the last day of this year with these pious aspirations:

"Almighty God be praised for his gracious long suffering towards me in sparing my life so long. Grant, Gracious God, that I may make a good use of the time that thou mayest be pleased yet to grant me for repentance. This year I have felt a sensible decrease of health and strength. Yet thy will be done, Gracious God!"[15]

These were the last words that Gordon was to enter in the journal which he had kept for so many years. His strength was now failing fast, and during the following summer he became so weak that he was unable to leave his bed. He died at 7 o'clock in the morning of November 29th, 1699. The Czar, who had visited him five times during his last illness, and had been with him twice during his last night, stood weeping by his bed as he drew his last breath; and the eyes of him who had left Scotland as a poor unfriended wanderer were closed by the hands of an Emperor.

Peter himself ordered the funeral procession, and took his place in the long line, accompanied by all the pomp of the empire, and followed by representatives of most of the great powers of Europe. The body was carried on the shoulders of twenty-eight colonels, two generals supported the footsteps of his widow, and twenty ladies, the wives of high Muscovite dignitaries, walked in her train. The religious obsequies were performed by the priests of the church he had loved, in the first chapel of stone which the Roman Catholics were suffered to raise in Moscow. It was built chiefly by his bounty; and his tomb was dug before the high altar, in a vault, where this inscription may still be read.:*

---

* At least it was still in place in 1859, the date of the first publication of his diary.

SACRAE TZAREAE MAJESTATIS MILITIAE GENERALIS

PATRICIUS LEOPOLDUS GORDON

NATUS ANNO DOMINI 1635 DIE 31 MARTII

DENATUS ANNO DOMINI 1699 DIE 29 NOVEMBRIS

REQUIESCAT IN PACE.

CHAPTER 4 — BIBLIOGRAPHY

1. The main source is *The Diary of General Patrick Gordon,* first published by the Spalding Club in 1859; the edition used is that published by Frank Cass & Co., London, 1968.

    The palace revolt which secured the throne for Peter the Great is not well dealt with in the Diary. A more detailed description is to be found in Stephen Graham's *Life of Peter the Great,* Ernest Benn, London, 1929.

2. For Thomas Dalzell, see the *Dictionary of National Biography* and A. and H. Tayler, *James Graham of Claverhouse,* Duckworth, London, 1939. (See also the portrait facing p. 36).

3. For Field-Marshal George Ogilvy see Stephen Graham, *Life of Peter the Great,* pp. 144, 155-57 and 162; also A. Francis Steuart, *Scottish Influences on Russian History,* p. 73.

4. *The Diary of General Patrick Gordon,* p. 5.

5. *ibid.,* p. 7.

6. See Chapter 3, p. 42.

7. *The Diary of General Patrick Gordon,* pp. 28-9.

8. p. 34, footnote.

9. Alexander Gordon, *History of Peter the Great,* Vol. I, p. 138; quoted in *The Diary of General Patrick Gordon,* Preface, p. XVI.

10. *The Diary . . .,* p. 171.

11. *ibid.,* p. 173-4.

12. *ibid.,* Preface p XXI, footnote.

13. *ibid.*, p. 184.

14. *ibid.*, pp. 185-6.

15. *ibid.*, p. 193.

CHAPTER 5

Scotland's Contributions to the Russian Navy

Admiral Sir Samuel Greig (1735-1788).
Rear-Admiral John Elphinston (1722-1785).
Admiral Thomas Gordon (1662-1741).
Rear-Admiral John Paul Jones (1747-1792).

From an early age Peter the Great had shown an interest in the sea
and had realised the importance of securing ports and of sea power for
a country which, when he came to the throne in 1689, was almost
entirely landlocked. The Baltic Sea and the Gulf of Finland were in
Swedish hands; the Black Sea ports at the mouths of the Don and the
Dnieper were controlled by Crim Tatars and Turks; moreover, ports in
the Sea of Azov were useless so long as the Turks controlled the
outlet to the Black Sea, the Strait of Kerch; and the only true Black
Sea port, Odessa, near the mouth of the Dniester River, then the
boundary between Russia and Poland-Lithuania, was too vulnerable
to Polish and Turkish attack.

In the first year of Peter's reign the mouth of the Amur River was
ceded to China by the Treaty of Nerchinsk. This left Archangel in the
White Sea as the only outlet for maritime trade; a port which was ice-
bound for more than six months every year.

Peter visited Archangel in 1693 and was not impressed by the
limited facilities of the port and the few Russian vessels trading from
it. He soon realised he must have more ports, but all likely sites were
in enemy hands. Therefore military campaigns were needed to obtain
the land on which ports could be built. Hence the numerous wars
against Sweden, Turkey and the Tatars of the northern Black Sea
shore, which occupied him almost continuously for the whole of his
reign.

Peter had served a practical apprenticeship in ship-building in

Archangel, Holland and London. Immediately after his visit to Archangel he started, with the able assistance of Count (later General-Admiral) Fedor Matveevich Apraksin, ship-building at Archangel. His first completed ships were the *Apostol Pavel* of 24 guns, the *St Pierre et Von* 12 and the *Sainte Prophetie* 44.

Military expeditions against the Turks in the south were undertaken in 1687 and 1689; in his first expedition, in 1695, Peter attacked Azov with 30,000 men.[1] This attempt fared no better than previous attacks.

Peter established shipbuilding yards at Voronezh on the Don and at Briansk on the Desna, a tributary of the Dnieper; and within one year had completed 22 galleys, 24 fireships, some larger craft and about 1500 barges, rafts and small boats. A further assault on Azov in June 1696 was made; and after a month of siege and determined assault, Azov surrendered.

War between Russia and Turkey continued for several years and shipbuilding progressed at a pace. Larger vessels were built at Voronezh under the direction of Dutch, Italian and English engineers. Smaller craft were built at Briansk. 686 vessels were built between 1701 and 1714. The Admiralty Yard at St Petersburg, established in 1705, completed the first Russian battleship, the *Poltava,* in 1712. Other yards were established at Archangel, Vyborg and Åbo, and were soon turning out ships of up to 2000 tons, armed with 50 to 100 guns that fired cannonballs weighing from 6 to 20 pounds. A naval base was established at Taganrog on the Sea of Azov, and in 1698 an elementary naval college was opened.

In the north the first naval action between Sweden and Russia occurred in 1701, when the Swedes sent seven ships to the White Sea to attack Archangel; this engagement was inconclusive, the Swedes losing two six-gun ships due to Russian prisoners, pressed into service as pilots, deliberately running them aground. But in the next two years Russia took the offensive; and by 1704 Peter had eliminated the Swedes from Lake Ladoga and Lake Peipus, and controlled a narrow corridor to the Baltic along both sides of the Neva River, as well as the strategic island which, later, would become the naval base of Kronstadt. The swampy marsh opposite this island was the unpromising site on which Peter proceeded to build St Petersburg.

By 1714 the Russian navy had ten battleships and seven frigates. That year was climaxed by a Russian victory at Gangut, or Hangö Head, as it is more commonly known, where a Russian galley fleet under Admiral Apraksin destroyed a weaker Swedish detachment of some twenty-eight units. Russia lost one galley, 466 men killed and wounded. Sweden lost ten galleys, 116 guns captured, 361 men killed and 941 taken prisoner. The battle would scarcely have been noteworthy for any established navy; but as their first naval success of any importance, Gangut has a prideful place in Russian history.

Considering that Russia had no tradition or experience in shipbuilding, that it had to rely entirely on foreign labour,* that suitable materials were not only not available (at first thousands of ships were built of fir, spruce, larch and other soft woods which had a very limited life), but had to be transported hundreds of miles on non-existent roads, Peter achieved miracles by his personal supervision and energy.

Personnel remained a major problem; although Russians used the inland waterways extensively for trading and fishing, they shuddered at the thought of going to sea. There was no merchant service and seamen were pressed into service from peasants and soldiers, and only increased rates of pay persuaded them; as it was, the majority left as soon as possible, and long servicemen rarely exceeded ten per cent of the manpower.

A number of naval officers were, like Peter himself, self-taught; and many, like Apraksin, Russia's first admiral, who had been a general before he took to the sea, turned naval officer late in life and made considerable reputations for themselves. But for a while Russia had to import experienced seamen and officers and export raw material to be trained overseas. Before Peter, Boris Godunov had sent a party of Russian students into Europe to learn western ways; this was a failure as none of them returned to Russia. Most of the nobles sent by Peter to learn in foreign navies were not genuinely interested in learning. Many devoted their time, and their Emperor's money, to riotous living; and those who returned to Russia were found to have learned very little and were promptly demoted to the rank of common seaman.

General Gordon's son-in-law, Alexander Gordon of Auchintoul, however, had a high regard for the nobles sent abroad. Most of them, he observed, remained in Europe "seven years (until they were perfect)," and upon return were employed "to their capacities, either in the land or sea service; and those who had no inclination for either

---

*Two of his first shipbuilders were British: Richard Brown and Peter Bent, who were recruited in England and sent to Russia about 1704.

were employed in the police. (i.e. the civil service)." Peter himself agreed with Gordon, and boasted that ". . . seamen sprung up from *Russian* blood . . . from foreign countries (were) return(ing) home able Men."[2]

It is paradoxical that Peter, the most autocratic of all the Russian autocrats, was also a great leveller. He had no great respect for the Russian nobility, and encouraged ability before rank in the Russian navy. Pay varied enormously, ranging from 2 roubles 40 kopecs *a year* for a common seaman to 7000 roubles for a general-admiral; a captain's pay being about 400 roubles a year. Pay for foreign officers was determined by contract and was invariably higher than that of Russians of corresponding rank. This made the Russian navy a very expensive service; and short-term contracts made it difficult to develop continuity, or build up a tradition, of service.

The long-term solution of Russia's educational problems would obviously depend on her ability to build up an adequate indigenous school system. Before 1700 seamanship, anywhere in Europe, was mostly a matter of apprenticeship and practical experience in either navy or merchant marine. Officers were drawn from the nobility and usually had some military training background; it is remarkable that, under such circumstances, so many became highly proficient. After 1700 theoretical and scientific training began to assume importance, and could be obtained at such institutions as the British Royal Mathematical School at Christ's Hospital, John Colson's school at Wapping, and Louis XIV's naval schools at Toulon, Brest and Rochefort.[3]

One such school which combined book instruction with practical seamanship was that of Marco Martinović of Perast in Dalmatia (then under the rule of Venice), to which a number of Russian students were sent, and from which two Dalmatian seamen were recruited into the Russian navy. One of these, Matvej Melankovic, in March 1698, was put in charge of Russian youths for naval training.[4] In 1701 the Moscow School of mathematics and navigation was founded on the model of the Christ's Hospital school. Its first director was Henry Farquharson, formerly Liddel Mathematical Tutor at Marischal College, Aberdeen. He was assisted by two Edinburgh teachers, Richard Grice and Steven Gegn, who taught navigation. All three became professors between 1709 and 1715, during which time the school instructed some 1200 students.

From the beginning the students were of diverse social origins, and included clerics' and soldiers' sons, but also those of the gentry, urban classes and administrative ranks. In age they ranged from 16 to 28, most being in their early twenties. With the opening of the St Petersburg Naval Academy in 1715, recruitment among the gentry became more frequent; the Moscow school being intended to produce seamen, and the St Petersburg School officers and administrators. Nevertheless ability still dominated choice of students, and within a few years almost all the vacancies were filled by commoners, while non-nobles occupied many of the administrative positions until the Academy closed in 1752.

However, all this activity did not produce instant admirals; and until the new generation of professional seamen acquired experience in the course of time, the senior ranks were filled with nobles, not all of whom were lacking in expertise. For example, Privy Councillor, President of the Admiralty College, General-Admiral Count Fedor Matveevich Apraksin had studied shipbuilding in Amsterdam with Peter in 1697. Fedor Ivanovich Soymonov, of humble origin, attended the Moscow School between 1708 and 1712 and was then sent to Holland for his naval apprenticeship. Eventually he became a vice-admiral, a vice-president of the Admiralty College, Governor of Siberia and a Senator.

The success of the St Petersburg Naval Academy was largely due to two officers trained in Europe. Grigori Grigorievich Skornyakov-Pisarev joined the staff of the Academy in 1719 and published the first book on mechanics in Russian. He was joined in 1722 by Aleksandr Lvovich Naryshkin, one of Peter's nephews, whose foreign education had been carefully planned in 1708. Together they were responsible for restructuring the curriculum of the Academy to make it a more practical prelude to naval apprenticeship. Together these two men transformed the Naval Academy of the 'twenties into the kind of school Peter had envisaged.

It is therefore obvious that when Samuel Greig entered the Russian naval service in1763 he was by no means filling a void; and that there was a sufficient number of experienced Russian senior ranks to resent the intrusion of foreigners into a service which had already had about sixty years in which to build a proud tradition.

After the death of Peter I in 1725 until the accession of Catherine II in 1762, Russia participated in five wars, while six rulers occupied the throne in rapid succession. Two of these, Anna I (1730-1740) and Elizabeth I (1741-1761), reigned for thirty of these thirty-seven years.

Some, like Elizabeth, were able rulers, some were imbeciles, but with the exception of Elizabeth, none was interested in the navy, which was allowed to deteriorate.

In the naval officers' corps at Peter's death, of 243 top officers, at least 75 were foreigners. These men respected Peter; their loyalty was personal and did not extend to his successors or to the state. The practice of employing foreigners, and of sending young men abroad for training, declined. Many left the service or, if they remained, lapsed into sloth. Many grew senile and incompetent; some frankly venal. At Peter's death the Baltic fleet consisted of 34 battleships, 9 frigates and numerous smaller vessels, manned by some 25,000 officers and men. In the Caspian Sea were 17 sailing vessels and 38 rowing vessels. The White Sea also had a small fleet of larger vessels, based on Archangel. For seven years no new ships were built and many, especially those built of soft woods, rapidly rotted.

Catherine I (1725-27) laid down no new ships, but five battleships and some eighty galleys which were on the stocks at Peter's death, were completed. Apraksin was unable to obtain funds even for the upkeep of the fleet; some men were naked and unshaved, some officers had no uniforms. Apraksin gave 2000 roubles out of his own pocket for the careening of bottoms, but no one else followed his example.

During the reign of Peter II (1727-30), all ship-building ceased and naval funds were slashed by a further fifty per cent. Several officers were caught stealing and demoted.

In the reign of Anna (1730-40), some improvements were attempted but did not go far, and work progressed only slowly. Admiral Sievers retired and his successor, Admiral Golovin, was found guilty of misappropriation of funds.

In 1734, however, the first marine force was reorganised into regiments consisting of 1800 to 2000 men, each regiment comprising three battalions of four companies. Because the wars of Anna and her successor, Elizabeth, involved many landing operations, the marines became the most essential and efficient part of the navy.

Elizabeth, as befitted a daughter of Peter the Great, appreciated the necessity for a strong navy and started to do something about it. The Naval Academy was moved from Moscow to St Petersburg. She appointed a commission to investigate naval needs; and 36 new battleships, 8 frigates and many smaller vessels were built during her reign. However, the standard of shipbuilding had declined sadly since the days of Peter's personal supervision; many had weak rigging and many leaked. Elizabeth was also unfortunate in her admirals.

During the Seven Years' War (1756-63), England and Prussia were arrayed against France, Russia, Austria and Sweden. In the Baltic Sweden with 26, and Denmark with 27, opened the war with more battleships than Russia's 20. Between 1750 and 1756 no less than 21 Russian battleships had to be scrapped. However, since Russia and Sweden (and for a time Denmark) were on the same side, their relative strengths were unimportant. Prussia had no navy and England never sent her fleet into the Baltic. Although the Russian navy did almost no fighting, a number of ships were lost from other causes, amongst which were rotten hulls, poor rigging and deplorable seamanship.

Finally, when Prussia was worn out and all but bled white, fortune played into Frederick the Great's hands. Elizabeth died and was succeeded by Peter III, who at once allied himself with Frederick whom he had always admired. However, Peter was quickly deposed (and died in prison a week later), to be succeeded by his wife Catherine. A year later the Treaty of Paris ended the war.

It is a remarkable tribute to Peter the Great that much of his work survived the neglect of the six mediocrities who followed him. When Catherine II came to the throne, the fleet was weakened in size and quality, but had suffered no great defeats. The Baltic Fleet retained both its identity and its prestige. The scene was set for the Russian navy's greatest hour.

When Catherine had been on the throne but a year, Samuel Greig joined the Russian navy as a lieutenant. He was born at Inverkeithing, Fifeshire, on November 30, 1735, the son of Charles Greig, a shipowner. After serving several years at sea in merchant ships, he entered the Royal Navy as master's mate on board the *Firedrake* bomb; served in the *Royal George* during the blockade of Brest in 1759; was present at the battle of Quiberon Bay and at the reduction of Havana in 1762.

Though only a lieutenant, the handsome young man of 27 could not fail to respond to the glamour which surrounded the young queen. Though there was never a hint of romantic attachment, Catherine held the young naval officer, who remained in her service for twenty-five years, in the greatest affection, and his untimely death at the age of fifty-three caused her the greatest grief in her own declining years.

His promotion in the Russian navy was rapid and well-deserved; from lieutenant to rear-admiral in seven years!

His career ran parallel to, and was complemented by, that of another eminent Scots naval officer, John Elphinston, who, born in 1722, was thirteen years Greig's senior, and had had more experience in the British Navy. Elphinston also started his career in the merchant navy where he spent six years, being commissioned in the Royal Navy in August 1746. In 1757 he commanded the fireship *Salamander* and in 1758 served under Commodore Howe in expeditions against St Malo, Cherbourg and St Cas, at which he was taken prisoner. On being exchanged he was promoted to post rank and command of the *Eurus* of 20 guns (Feb. 1, 1759), in which he accompanied Sir Charles Saunders' fleet to North America and took part in operations which led to the capture of Quebec. He commanded the guardship *Firm* (60 guns) at Plymouth from 1764 to 1767.

In 1769 he accepted a commission as rear-admiral in the Russian navy, arriving at Kronstadt just in time to take a prominent part in the greatest adventure of the Russian navy to date.

Catherine was determined to make the Black Sea, as Peter had made the Gulf of Finland, a Russian sea.

The idea of an attack on Turkey through the Mediterranean occurred initially to Count Aleksei Orlov, who was Catherine's lover as well as adviser. He and his brother, Grigory, who was then stationed at Leghorn, proposed the dispatch of eight or ten warships from the Baltic to the Aegean. Catherine approved. The plan was at that time without precedent and, considering the limited experience of Russia's navy in long ocean voyages and the poor condition of its vessels, decidedly risky.

On August 23, 1769, nine battleships and several large vessels of the Baltic fleet with Rear-Admiral Spiridov in charge left the Baltic and were followed shortly after by a second squadron under Rear-Admiral Elphinston. One ship, the *Lapomnik* 22, was wrecked in the Skaw off Jutland, and the crews of all ships suffered severely from the late autumn and winter weather; they would have suffered more had not the British Government permitted them to rest in British ports. As it was, 332 men died and 600 were sick by the time the squadrons reached England. Elphinson, being but newly appointed to the command of a squadron, was subjected to considerable insubordination by some officers, and was delayed at Copenhagen into winter; in fact he left only just in time to avoid being iced in. His squadron consisted

of four battleships, some frigates and smaller vessels. They were
badly found and were damaged by severe weather in the North Sea.
He put into Portsmouth, permission to do so being readily granted;
but Elphinston's pretensions to fire morning and evening guns in
Portsmouth harbour were resented by Vice-Admiral Geary,
Commander-in-Chief Portsmouth, who refused to allow foreign ships
to set the watch in this manner. Reported to the Russian Minister,
Count Vorontsov, Elphinston was ordered to desist the practice or
quit Portsmouth. He remained in Portsmouth until the middle of
April, 1770.

Towards the end of May the squadron was off the island of Cerigo
(now Kithira, off Cape Matapan); and having learned that the Turkish
fleet had gone to Nauplia in the Gulf of Argolis, Elphinston decided
to pursue it. He met it in the mouth of the Gulf on May 27 and,
although an inferior force, decided to attack instantly. Elphinston's
force of three battleships and five smaller vessels attacked a much
larger Turkish fleet of thirteen battleships, of 50 to 84 guns each, and
some smaller vessels. His own flagship, the *Sviatoslav,* 80, and the
Afrika, 32, were slow getting into action. After a few desultory shots
the Turks declined battle and retired to anchor under the shore
batteries of Nauplia. A Russian attempt on May 28 failed because the
wind had died down and some of Elphinston's captains objected that
the shore batteries would give the Turks additional strength.

Elphinston's advantage mainly depended on the use of shells, used
for the first time in a purely naval action, which struck terror in the
Turks. The Turkish vessels were manned to a large extent by Greek
impressed men, who were disinclined to sacrifice their lives for Allah
or the Sultan.

When, on June 2, Spiridov joined Elphinston, their combined fleets
stood at seven battleships, three frigates and two storeships. "From
the first, command relations between the two men were strained
because of decided differences in personality. Spiridov, whose record
during the Seven Years' War had been excellent, was fifty-four years
old and in poor health. His lethargic and somewhat over-cautious
nature tended to hold back and irritate his more energetic but
frequently rash colleague."[5] Both moved their squadrons to Navarino
where they came under the command of Admiral Count Aleksei
Orlov. Their arrival increased the Russian fleet at Navarino to nine
battleships, three frigates and eighteen lesser craft, some thirty in all.

On the approach of the Russian fleet, the Greeks were supposed to rise against their Turkish masters, but their insurrection was ill organised and quickly suppressed by janissaries. The Russians were ill-prepared to give real support to the rebels, and, after blowing up the fort at Navarino, they put to sea again, making for the north of the Aegean towards the Dardanelles. Off Lemnos the Turkish fleet appeared, compelling the Russians to retire; but although the Turks were far stronger in ships and guns, the Russians attacked them off Chios. This action was indecisive and the Turkish fleet took refuge in Chesme Bay. The Turkish fleet, of sixteen battleships with frigates and lesser vessels totalling seventy-three ships, then anchored north of Chesme harbour, between the island of Chios and the Anatolian mainland.

The battle of Chesme was fought in two stages. The first stage started at 1.30 a.m. on July 5th. Spiridov's ship, the *Sv. Yevstafy,* closed with the Turkish commander Hassan Pasha's *Real Mustafa.* Both ships caught fire and blew up, killing all but sixty-three of the crew of the *Yevstafy;* aboard the *Mustafa* the loss of life must have been equally high; the Russians lost 636 men in the *Yevstafy,* but other casualties were low; 14 dead and 30 wounded in the rest of the fleet, due to poor gunnery on the part of the Turks. Miraculously both admirals survived.

The Turkish fleet retreated into the harbour of Chesme, about two miles deep and one mile wide. It consisted of fourteen ships of the line, several frigates and a vast number of transports and storeships, totalling about 200 craft in all. The wind was blowing fresh on shore and Elphinston, going on board the admiral's flagship, offered to lead in, and proposed that they should anchor with springs on their cables on the bow and quarter of the weathermost Turkish ships. "By this arrangement our nine line-of-battle ships would have been engaged against only five or six of the enemy, and the rest of their numerous fleet would have been rendered useless, as they could neither come to the assistance of those ships engaged nor attempt to get out of the situation they were in without the greatest danger of running ashore."[6]

Jealousy on the part of the Russian officers prevented the adoption of this plan; but it is nevertheless worth drawing attention to as a first-class exposition of the great tactical rule of establishing a local superiority, identical in principle to that which Nelson carried into effect at the battle of the Nile.

A large fleet anchored under friendly shore batteries generally discourages direct attack. However, it scarcely needed an experienced officer to see that it could be destroyed by fireships. This terrible work was carried out on the night of July 8th under Elphinston's supervision, the fireships being commanded by two Scots lieutenants, Robert Dugdale and Thomas Mackenzie. Of the mass of Turkish ships only one of 64 guns and a few galleys were saved and brought out of the bay; the rest were all destroyed. The Russians lost only eleven men in this encounter; no reliable figures are available for the Turkish losses which have been variously estimated at between eight and eleven thousand.

The destruction of Turkish naval power was complete. Mopping up operations in the Aegean continued until 1773. In 1772 Orlov raided Mitylene, overran the dockyard, burnt two 74s and a shebek on the stocks, captured some twenty smaller vessels, and retired. On Nov. 4th, 1772, an attack by Greig on the town of Chesme was also successful; part of the town was burned and the ships in the harbour captured.

The battle of Chesme was rightly hailed as the greatest triumph of the Russian navy. It is understandably difficult for any nation to attribute responsibility for its victories, if not for its defeats, to the actions of foreigners; and from the beginning mutual recriminations between British and Russian officers and considerations of national pride distorted assessments of their respective contributions.

Catherine, forgetting the battle of Hangö, described the battle of Chesme in a letter to Voltaire in June 1771[7] as "la première victoire que la flotte de l'empire de Russie ait gagnée depuis neuf-cent ans." She attributed the victory wholly to the leadership of Aleksei Orlov: "Was I wrong," she wrote to Voltaire, "when I said these Orlovs were forged for great things?" Intent on making it a Russian victory, she did not mention Elphinston, Greig, Dugdale, Mackenzie or other foreign officers; but the British officers who took a prominent part in the destruction of the Turkish fleet were nevertheless thanked, decorated and rewarded.[*]

In the first place, the overall strategy was undoubtedly the brainchild of Count Orlov, ably supported by his brother, Grigory, and his sovereign. Elphinston was undoubtedly a brilliant, impetuous and somewhat rash thruster who, as a newcomer and a foreigner, irritated by his tactlessness and brashness his Russian colleagues who had not

*See also Catherine's letter to Voltaire dated 16/27 Sept. 1770, Reddaway, pp. 74-76

had time enough to evaluate his qualities in command. Greig, though generally given credit for a larger part in the victory than the facts warrant, achieved his reputation more by his subsequent career than by his limited role in the battle of Chesme.

Yet there seems little doubt that British expertise and discipline were essential to the ultimate success of the enterprise. Of the nineteen ships of the Russian navy engaged at Chesme, six, including two of the four fireships, were commanded by British officers (John Elphinston, Samuel Greig, William Roxburgh, George Arnold, Robert Dugdale and Thomas Mackenzie). Throughout the campaign British officers complained of the incompetence and insubordination of the Russians, and their side of the story is preserved in contemporary accounts. In 1772 an unabashed eulogy of Elphinston, written by an unknown fellow officer, was published in London and accepted predictably as "a just representation of the facts."[8] Greig's more balanced account of the campaign was published much later; and James Trevenen's only recently. Trevenen described Greig as "my third tutelary genius, my household god, my successor to Cook and King."[9]

Both Czarist and Soviet writers regard Chesme as the greatest naval victory of all time. Most fail to give the British officers any credit at all, or even to mention their names.

The firing of the Turkish fleet offers an example of chauvinistic distortion. It is generally ascribed to the two Scots lieutenants, Dugdale and Mackenzie; but, according to Mitchell (6), the facts are somewhat different. Four fireships (or "branders," as they were called in Russian accounts), were to be towed by ten-oared boats alongside four Turkish ships, skeleton crews were to set fire to the ships and escape by row-boats. These fireships were under the command of Admiral Greig, who sent in Dugdale with Mackenzie as second in command. The first fireship was intercepted and sunk by two Turkish galleys. The second reached a ship already on fire. The third, commanded by a Russian lieutenant, Dimitri Illyin, fired a Turkish ship and the wind rapidly spread the flames down the Turkish line. The fourth never went in, because there was no need for it. Perhaps the greatest credit should go to the unnamed gunner on the *Grom* whose shot started the first fire.

British accounts similarly fail to give sufficient credit to the many Russian officers, such as Admiral Spiridov, Captains Khmetensky,

Klokachev and Lupardin, and Lieutenant Illyin.*

Peace between Russia and Turkey was arranged in 1774, both sides being tired of fighting.

Elphinston's career with the Russian navy was nearly over. He was thwarted in his impetuosity by the caution of Orlov, whose vacillation in attacking the Dardenelles after Chesme was one of the few serious acts of omission in the campaign. In Sept. 1770 he had grounded the *Sviatoslav* on a reef near Lemnos during a voyage not authorised by Orlov, and the ship was eventually lost. Orlov ordered Elphinston to Kronstadt where he was court-martialled for the loss of the ship. Though not convicted, he was rusticated to Leghorn under a cloud, and was instructed to go under an assumed name, Howard. He returned to St Petersburg in 1774 and was favourably received by Catherine, but the war being ended, he shortly after left the Russian service and returned to England in 1775.

His subsequent career was mostly conducted in the West Indies, in command of *Egmont* 74 and *Magnificent*. Towards the end of 1782 he was appointed to *Atlas* 90, but peace was signed before she was ready for sea and she was put out of commission. He died on April 28th, 1785. He had three sons; the third born on May 4th, 1773, being christened Howard in celebration of his sojourn in Leghorn where he was conceived.

Samuel Greig's greatest contribution to the Russian navy was subsequent to the end of the Turkish war in 1774. During the next few years he spent his time improving and developing the Russian navy.

His career reached its zenith in 1776 when his great services were acknowledged by Catherine, who appointed him Admiral, Governor of Kronstadt, and Knight of the Orders of St Andrew, St George, St Vladimir and St Anne; and on July 18th, 1776, his sovereign did him the signal honour of paying him a state visit on board his flagship, dined in his cabin, reviewed the fleet and placed on his breast the order of St Alexander Nevski.

By this time Greig had recruited a considerable number of British officers into the Russian navy, principally Scots, of permanent benefit to the service, but at the same time of some embarrassment to the country, as rendering its foreign policy dependent on the good will of

---

*"He (Orlov) had under him three able admirals in the Russian, Spiridov, and two Englishmen (sic!), Greig and Elphinston," *Catherine the Great,* by Ian Gray. p. 155.

foreigners. In 1780 the "armed neutrality" had virtually become the "armed nullity" by reason of the fact that the navy was not available for service against England.

It was as Governor of Kronstadt that he saw the fulfillment of his plans, where he was instrumental in reorganising the port and built, among other things, a new prison which brought praise from John Howard, the prison reformer.

There was considerable activity at Kronstadt, much of it carried out by British advisers and technicians under contract to the Russian government. In July 1782 Catherine described to Baron Grimm how, during her visit to Kronstadt, "Nous avons été voir la machine à feu qui vide le canal."[10] This was the scientific wonder of the age, the fire engine which was built in the period 1775 to 1777 with British materials and by British experts.

Soon after their arrival in St Petersburg in 1770, Admiral Sir Charles Knowles, whose brief was to supervise ship-building and naval administration, and his secretary, John Robison,[11] had conceived the idea of replacing the antique windmills used to empty the dry docks by fire engines imported from Britain. An order was placed eventually with the Carron Company, whose managing director, Charles Gascoigne, with the help of John Smeaton, had produced a "Grand Plan for converting the Mill into a fire engine for draining the docks of Cronstadt;" This, however, was only after Robison had made unsuccessful attempts to bring his friend, James Watt, the inventor of the steam engine, to Russia. By the time the group of fourteen workmen under the chief engineer, Adam Smith, had arrived from Scotland late in 1774, Knowles and Robison had left Russia; and Greig, who had returned from the Mediterranean in the middle of 1773, was now in command of Kronstadt. The first tests of the fire engine were run in June 1777, five years before Catherine's official visit. The majority of the workmen then returned to Scotland, but Adam Smith remained to supervise the working of the machine and was joined, in 1783, by his son, Alexander, who was himself a highly skilled engineer and produced an engine of his own design in 1792.

Greig, who was most impressed by the original fire engine, ordered another from the Carron works shortly before his death, but this never became operational. He was also instrumental in securing for Catherine the services of Charles Gasgoigne, the inventor of the new light gun called the gasconade or carronade, who arrived in Russia in 1786. The Russians had been ordering large quantities of guns from the Carron Company in the 1780s, as well as requesting machinery to cast the guns themselves; so the engagement of Gascoigne to establish an artillery foundry in Russia was a logical outcome.

Charles Gascoigne was not the sole inventor of this gun. Three main claimants have been suggested: General Robert Melville, Patrick Miller and Charles Gascoigne; but the gun was probably the result of many years of experimentation. The name, gasconade, was dropped fairly soon; this however did not prevent Gascoigne from trying to get the patent for the gun registered in his name, in which he did not succeed.

Gascoigne left Scotland as an undischarged bankrupt, escaping from both his creditors and a flock of lawsuits, and from perpetual conflict with his co-directors, which included his father-in-law, Samuel Garbett. Their feuding raged loud and long, and involved the Lord Advocate and even the Prime Minister, William Pitt.

Gascoigne was what was called at the time a "thruster"; dynamic, hard-working, egotistical and overbearing. His reputation reached Russia with him and for a time both he and his sponsor, Admiral Greig, were ostracized by the British community in St Petersburg. Clarke, who met him in 1800, voiced the opinion of many of his fellow countrymen in calling him an "outlaw".

In Russia he started with a salary of £2000 per annum as manufacturer of ordnance to Catherine, achieving rank and wealth. In 1803 Matthew Boulton, one of his ex-partners in Carron Company, wrote to Samuel Garbett:

> "I am persuaded that he has no motive for quitting Russia, where he has a good income, lives in more splendour, and has greater connections than he can ever have in this country. I have had three different parties of Russian nobility at my home within these 2 or 3 weeks; they all spoke of Gascoigne's income and the riches and power he has acquired and continues to acquire; hence I conclude it would be folly in him to think of returning."[12]

About the same time Gascoigne tried to obtain a discharge from his creditors in Scotland and offered £10,000, which was refused. He died in 1806, still a bankrupt in Scotland but a very wealthy man in Russia; and it was not until 1827 that his daughter, the inheritor of his estate, finally obtained a discharge from her father's creditors.

Scots were in favour at Catherine's court in a number of roles: Richard Sutherland (1739-91) was for many years her "banker," i.e. financial adviser, and was made a Baron of the Russian Empire for his services. Another of her "bankers' was Robert Rutherford, who had made his fortune as a "Turkey merchant" in Leghorn, and was similarly ennobled by Catherine. One of the Court painters who accompanied Catherine on her celebrated progress to the Crimea was a Scot, John Lindsay.

With the outbreak of war with Sweden in 1788, Admiral Greig was recalled to active service. Sweden, under Gustavus III, opened with a surprise attack, hoping to destroy the Russian fleet, retake Finland and capture St Petersburg. Sweden had twenty ships of the line in good condition and superiority of frigates. Russia had fifty-four battleships, but many of these were unserviceable and dispersed between the White Sea, the Baltic and Black Seas.

On July 3rd, 1788, Admiral Greig put to sea with seventeen battleships and eight frigates. The fleet was divided into three squadrons; the first was under the command of Rear-Admiral von Dessen, the second under Admiral Greig, with Admiral Spiridov as second-in-command; and the third under Admiral Koslyaninov. Five out of the seventeen battleships were commanded by British commanders (Frank Denison, Samuel Elphinstone, Stephen Scott, George Tate and James Trevenen).

The battle of Hogland took place on July 17th, 1788. In fighting strength there was little to choose between the two fleets. The Swedes had twenty ships of the line to the Russians' seventeen. Gunpower favoured the Russians by 1450 guns to 1299. Each side lost one battleship captured, both fleets were badly battered, and the Russians suffered some 1800 casualties, the Swedes about 1350. Neither side tried to renew the action and honours were about even. Strategically, however, the fight was a Russian victory, since it defeated the plans of the Swedish attack.

During the battle of Hogland, Greig felt he had not been properly backed up by the Russian officers under his command, and sent seventeen of them to St Petersburg as prisoners charged with dereliction of duty. They were all, it is said, condemned to the hulks.

The force displayed by the Russians dismayed the Swedes, who were thereafter on the defensive. Throughout that autumn Greig kept them bottled up in Sveaborg; but his health gave way under the strain and on October 6th, worn out with his exertions, he died on board his flagship, the *Rostislav,* attended by his physician, Robert Simpson, whom he had recruited into the Russian service fourteen years before.

His death occasioned national mourning on an unprecedented scale.

Of all the British officers serving in the Russian navy, Samuel Greig was the only one held in universal esteem by both his Russian and British colleagues; even when, as indicated above, he could be severe in the maintenance of discipline. The Comte de Ségur, an impartial observer, wrote: "l'empératrice fit une perte qui lui coûta de larmes justes: L'amiral Greig mourut. Chef actif, administrateur éclairé, habile amiral, guerrier intrépide et modeste, il emporta au tombeau l'estime de ses ennemis, et les regrets de tous ceux qui l'avaient connu."[13]

He did not exaggerate Catherine's grief. Greig had served her brilliantly and loyally for twenty-five years. She was six years older than Greig, very corpulent and suffering from dropsy; maybe she paused before her mirror and wondered if the hour-glass was not running out for her too.

Admiral Sir Samuel Greig was given a state funeral in Reval Cathedral where his monument remains, unless Soviet revisionists have decided to deny that he ever existed. He left two sons: Aleksei Samuilovich Greig (1775-1845), who became a Russian admiral (as did his son in his turn); and Samuel who married Mary, daughter of Sir William George Fairfax.

Few men have contributed their talents so richly in the service of a foreign sovereign. Peter the Great is justly awarded the title of "Father of the Russian Navy": to Samuel Greig must go the honour of being its most brilliant tutor, developer and benefactor.

One of Admiral Greig's sons, Aleksei Samuilovich Greig, (1775-1845), was enrolled at birth as a midshipman in the Russian Navy. In 1801, for remonstrating with Czar Paul against the latter's severity towards some British seamen, he was exiled to Siberia for a while, but later pardoned. He first distinguished himself in the war between Russia and Turkey in 1807, the year he attained the rank of rear-admiral.

During the Russo-Turkish War of 1828-29 he was in command of the Russian fleet at the siege of Varna; and in June 1828 was promoted to full admiral.

After the Peace of Adrianople in September 1829, he devoted his energies to the reorganisation of the navy, especially of the Black Sea fleet. He was appointed Admiral in attendance on the Czar, a member of the Imperial Council, Knight of the Order of St George, and received numerous other decorations. He died in January 1845 and was buried in the Smolensk Cemetery of St Petersburg.

One of his sons, Vorontsov Greig, distinguished himself against England at the siege of Sebastopol, and was killed at Inkermann.

Another distinguished Scots naval officer was Admiral Thomas Gordon (1662-1741), who had had a long record of command (some thirty-nine commissions all told) in the British Navy before being appointed rear-admiral in the Russian Navy in 1719.

He is an early example of the serviceman who was also used as a diplomat. In the Scottish Record Office is a paper,[14] in French, headed "Articles du Paix" (probably a draft or copy of terms to be presented to the King of Sweden). Although undated, it obviously preceded the Peace of Nystadt in 1721. It reads:

"1. Of the conquered countries, the provinces of Ingria, Livonia, Esthonia, with the town of Reval, and Karelia, should remain with the Czar; also the town of Viborg.

2. The Czarian Majesty will restore to the Crown of Sweden the Grand Duchy of Finland with dependencies as far as the boundary of Viborg.

3. King August(us) the Second shall remain on the throne of Poland, and shall be recognised by his Swedish Majesty as lawful king.

4. In the same treaty of peace the King of Prussia ought to be comprehended that he might have satisfaction for his pretensions.

Further, if his Swedish Majesty wishes to enter on negotiations he is desired to send one with full power some place as near as possible to the territories of the Czar" . . . etc.

In July 1740 he applied for permission to retire to Britain on account of ill-health (he suffered from asthma). His health did not improve and he died in Russia in 1741.

It is not generally known that the American folk-hero, Paul Jones, was not only a Scotsman but was, for a time, a rear-admiral in the Russian Navy.

Born at Kirkbean, Kirkcudbrightshire, in 1747, he was a seaman from the age of 12, engaged in the slave trade and smuggling. He went to America in 1773 and found fame as a harasser of British shipping in the War of American Independence. He left American service in 1781, first tried France, and then joined the Russian Navy as a rear-admiral. In June 1788 he was in command of a division of the Black Sea Fleet at Liman in the Crimea but took no active part in the battle. He quarrelled with his superior officer, Count Nassau-Siegen, and was unpopular with his commander-in-chief, Prince Potemkin, and with the numerous Scots community in Russia; so that Catherine was obliged to dispense with his services.

John Paul Jones (to give him his full name) is the only example I can find of a Scots renegade taking up arms against his own country. Mercenaries sold their services to the highest bidder, whether of Sweden, Russia, Poland or Prussia, but did not fight against Britain. Hence his unpopularity with the Scots in Russia.

The presence of so many Scots in the Russian forces also had an inhibiting effect on Russian foreign policy (see "armed neutrality" and "armed nullity" in the account of Sir Samuel Greig); and it helps to explain why there was no war between Russia and Britain until the Crimean War of 1854.

Paul Jones retired to Amsterdam and, in 1790, to Paris, where he died in 1792 of cirrhosis of the liver.

The DNB says of him "Jones was a man of distinguished talent and originality, a thorough seaman, and of the most determined and tenacious courage. His faults were due to defective training. Excessive vanity, and a desire for "glory," which was, as he wrote, "infinite," and recognised no obstacles, made him a traitor to his own country, as it made him quarrelsome, mean and selfish."[15]

CHAPTER 5 — BIBLIOGRAPHY

1. See p. 62.

2. Garrard, J. G. Ed., *The Eighteenth Century in Russia,* Clarendon Press, Oxford, 1973, p. 133. Cf. especially pp. 131-145. Chap. 5: "Russian Students in Europe in the Age of Peter the Great" by Max J. Okenfuss; also pp. 233-263, Chap. 9: "The British in Catherine's Russia" by Anthony G. Cross.

3. Garrard, *ibid.,* p. 134.

4. Garrard, *ibid.,* p. 136.

5. Mitchell, Donald, W., *A History of Russian and Soviet Sea Power,* Andre Deutsch, London, 1974, pp. 58-64.

6. *Beatson's Naval and Military Memoirs: An Authentic Narration of the Russian Expedition against the Turks by Sea and Land; compiled from several authentic journals by an Officer on board the Russian Fleet* (1772), p. 56.

7. Reddaway, W. E. Ed., *Documents of Catherine the Great,* Cambridge University Press, 1931, p. 115.

8. *Critical Review* xxxiii (1772), p. 138; of *An Authentic Narration. . .* See also Garrard, op. cit., p. 257 fn.

9. Garrard, *ibid.,* p. 258, quoting from Christopher Hill and R. C. Anderson edd., *A Memoir of James Trevenen,* Publications of the Navy Records Society, ci, London, 1959, p. 156.

10. Garrard, *ibid.,* p. 258.

11. See below, Chap. 7.

12. Campbell, R. H., *Carron Company,* Oliver & Boyd, Edinburgh, 1974, p. 153.

13. Garrard, *ibid.,* p. 258.

14. *Scottish Record Office. GD24. Sec. 1. 854/284.*

15. For biographies of Greig, Elphinston and Paul Jones see the *Dictionary of National Biography.*

CHAPTER 6

Field-Marshal James Francis Edward Keith (1696-1758)

James Keith was a classical example of a Scots "lad o' pairts" who had "a guid conceit o' himsel'."

He came of that family which, from the twelfth century, had held the hereditary office of Earl Marischal of Scotland; Marischal College, Aberdeen, being founded in 1593 by George, fifth Earl Marischal. It appears that James Keith was not the first Keith to serve in the Russian army. According to Steuart[1], quoting from Birth brieves, there was a "Lieut. George Keith, who did serve under the Lord of —— as levtenant Colonell in Ireland and is now certanely informit to be departit this lyff in Muscovia some years ago." He left an heir, Alexander Keith, who claimed to be the only lawful son of Major William Keith, only son of Robert Keith of Kindruct.

James Keith was born at Inverugie Castle, near Peterhead, on June 11th, 1696, the younger son of William, 9th Earl Marischal of Scotland, and his wife, née Lady Mary Drummond. His elder brother, George, the last Earl Marischal (1693-1778), was one of those Tory nobles who signed the proclamation of George I, but, being disappointed in their hopes of advancement, the brothers declared for the Pretender in 1715. What they expected from George is not known: they were 22 and 19 years of age in 1715, which is a bit early for the iron of disappointed ambition to enter their souls. With their cousin, the Earl of Mar, they were routed at Ruthven in Badenoch and escaped to the Western Isles, whence they made their way to France, arriving there in May, 1716.

With the failure of the '15 uprising they were attainted, lost all and were forced to seek service in foreign parts. In France James Keith's offer of his tyro sword was countered with the suggestion, very sensible in view of his tender years, that he should give up his military ambitions and study for the law, which had been his father's original intention for him; but in 1717 he received a commission as Colonel of Horse in the service of the King of Sweden. In the same year he was presented to Peter the Great on the occasion of the latter's visit to Paris, but nothing came of the introduction at that time.

In 1718 Spain formed the intention of attempting the restoration of James II to the English throne. James Keith and his brother had several interviews with Cardinal Alberoni, then Prime Minister of Spain, and met at Le Havre de Grace with several other exiled Scottish leaders. They were led to expect that there was to be a landing in Scotland under James Butler, second Duke of Ormonde (1665-1746). Accordingly, in March they embarked on a small vessel of 25 tons and, after a hazardous voyage, reached the island of Lewis on April 4th, 1718. However, it all fell apart: Ormonde's fleet was dispersed; the Highlanders refused to rise; the Spaniards surrendered and such adherents as they collected were soon scattered. Thus the rebel officers were left to make their escape as best they could. James was again an outlawed fugitive, without means or a home. He found his way to Peterhead and from there to Holland and on to Madrid, where he stayed until 1721. He remained in the service of Spain until 1728.

Their mother was a Catholic, but the boys were brought up in the Protestant faith. "Thinking himself, however, rather overlooked, he in this year addressed a letter to the King (Philip V) soliciting his patronage and requesting that he might be appointed to the command of the first Irish regiment that should become vacant. The answer of his Majesty to this application was that so soon as he knew that he was a Roman Catholic he should not only have what he asked, but that his future fortunes should be cared for."[2] Finding all hope of promotion in the Spanish service cut off on account of his religious beliefs, James solicited a recommendation from the King of Spain to the Czar of Russia. This recommendation was promptly granted and forwarded to Czar Peter II, who soon after invited him into his service. He was now 32, and it is difficult to see, beyond ambition, why he should expect instant and rapid promotion. He had never been in action, though he had proved himself diligent in the discharge of his duties.

Peter II died in 1730, and James Keith immediately took the oath of allegiance to his successor, the Empress Anna Ivanovna, and was made lieutenant-colonel of her bodyguard.

In 1733, on the death of the King of Poland, the Russian army invaded Poland in support of Russia's claimant to the Polish throne, Augustus, Elector of Saxony. The Russian force consisted of six

Statue of Marshal Keith.

battalions of foot, 600 dragoons and 4000 Cossacks. Keith, who was serving under the Irish Catholic, General de Lacy, was ordered by his commander-in-chief, Prince Shakhovsky, to ravage the country. He endeavoured to evade this painful and dishonourable action; only by appealing to Prince Shakhovsky's interests, that the Russian army would be reduced to starvation if his intentions were carried out, did he succeeded in getting this savage order repealed.

Between 1733 and 1737 he fought in the German wars and against the Turks in the Ukraine where, in July, 1737, he was wounded in the knee at Ochakov and incapacitated for the rest of the campaign.[3] After his recovery he visited London, not as a Jacobite exile, but as a renowned general. On his return to Russia he was appointed Governor of the Ukraine, where his humane rule made him considered the best Governor the Ukraine had ever had.

On the death of the Empress Anna (October 3rd, 1740), her grand-nephew, Ivan Antonovich of Brunswick, was declared Emperor. For 22 days Anna's favourite, Johann Ernst, Duke of Courland, acted as regent, but by a palace revolution the boy Czar's mother, Anna Leopoldovna, was declared regent. Her rule was weak and ended suddenly on November 25th, 1741, when her mother's cousin, Elizabeth, younger daughter of Peter I, assumed the title of Empress and sent the deposed royal family to Kholmogory and lifelong exile.

Whilst this was going on, James Keith was fighting in Sweden and helped in the reduction of Willmanstrand. It was here that he met an orphan prisoner, Eva Merthens, whom he took under his protection and educated. To her and her children by him he left all his money. She died in 1811.

The Swedish campaign continued into Elizabeth's reign, and did not finish until the capture of Helsingfors and the Åland Islands forced the cession of Karelia to Russia in 1743. There seems to have been some general dissatisfaction amongst the foreign generals in Elizabeth's service; and Generals Keith, Lowendahl, Lieven and Douglas all wished to retire. Keith was offered the chief command in a campaign against Persia and the Order of St Andrew; he declined the first and accepted the latter.

War against Sweden again broke out, in which Keith was employed as commander-in-chief. After peace had settled again, he was appointed minister-plenipotentiary to Sweden and became the recipient of numerous swords of honour. He was again employed on active service in the Prussian campaign of 1745, and in 1746 received the Empress at Narva when she reviewed his troops. This was the zenith of his career in Russian service. He was now 50 years of age: honours and commands had been heaped upon him; but now a decline set in: a command to which he felt entitled was given to another. One by one his commands were taken from him, and the royal favour was no longer extended to him. His brother, still considered a Jacobite, was refused permission to visit him in Russia. It is difficult to explain this sudden reversal of his fortunes; rumours had it that the amorous Empress wished to marry him, and he feared exile to Siberia if he refused.

His military fame had by now extended all over Europe. To him is ascribed the origin of *kriegspiel* (war exercises or manoeuvres) and he was the recipient of offers from many European princes. He was not likely to be permitted to leave Russian service for that of any potential enemy of Russia, which somewhat limited the scope of his employment. However, eventually, in 1747, he obtained his dismissal and was eagerly received by Frederick of Prussia. Frederick had previously accepted his elder brother, whom he had made Governor of Neuchâtel, where George Keith and his royal master exchanged ideas with French philosophers like d'Alembert and Rousseau, "who was snarling at all the world, and biting those who comforted or caressed him, licked one hand alone, that of his venerated and patriarchal patron, le bon Milord Maréchal."[4]

Frederick welcomed James Keith with open arms; he was made Field-Marshal and Governor of Berlin, with ample means to support the dignity of his appointments. He became military advisor to Frederick, whose life was dedicated to militarism and who regarded intervals of peace as periods of preparation for the next outbreak of hostilities, which were often provoked by him; such as his cowardly attack on the young Maria Theresa of Austria, whom he had promised to support and defend on the death-bed of her father, the Emperor Charles VI, in 1740. His actions precipitated the War of the Austrian Succession, which later almost imperceptibly merged into the Seven Years' War (1756-1763).

The year 1757 was Frederick the Great's *annus mirabilis*. Faced with the combined forces of France, Austria, Russia and Sweden, Frederick, with Field-Marshal Keith as his second-in-command, may well have been daunted by the odds stacked against him. Early in the year his invasion of Bohemia had proved a catastrophic failure in which he had lost a third of his forces and was compelled to retreat north of the Erz Gebirge: but in the same autumn he inflicted a crushing defeat on the French under the Prince de Soubise at Rossbach; and a month later he routed the Austrian general Daun at Leuthen, which Napoleon described as "a masterpiece of movements, manoeuvres and resolution."

In September 1757 Keith informed the King that a formidable army of French and Imperialists was advancing on Leipzig, and that it appeared impossible, with the meagre forces at his command, to hold the town against such a superior army. Frederick wrote from Gröschwitz on the 23rd; "You will not be attacked by these people at Leipzig; they fear destroying the town; but as they are growing audacious now, I flatter myself that, in marching towards them, a battle may ensue which will rid me of them."[5] Keith promised to hold out, but was well aware that, in the case of a serious attack, he would be unable to sustain any defence for long, as the place had scarcely any fortifications left and he was almost entirely out of ammunition. Nevertheless, when, on October 24th, a force of Austrian hussars appeared, Keith sent out a skirmishing party which harassed them for three hours. Later on the same day a division of the enemy's troops appeared, numbering some 8000 men, and called upon Keith to surrender in the name of the Prince of Hildburghausen, Commander of the Imperial Army. Counting all the men hurriedly collected out of Halle, Merseberg and Weiszenfels, Keith's forces scarcely amounted to 4000 men, mostly exhausted, ill-equipped and out of even cartridges. The Prince knew this and scarcely expected any resistance; but Keith replied to the surrender demand: "Let your master know that I am by birth a Scotsman, by inclination as well as by duty a Prussian, and shall defend the town in a manner that neither the country that gave me birth, nor that which has adopted me, shall be ashamed of me. The King, my master, has ordered me to defend it to the last extremity, and he shall be obeyed."[6]

Then, remembering Frederick's advice in the letter quoted above, he informed the town council that if the prince attacked he would burn the town rather than surrender, starting with the suburbs, "and, if that will not stop him, I shall go on and not even spare the town." The Prince was enraged when he received this challenge and sent a message that, if Leipzig was burned, he would lay Berlin and Potsdam in ashes. Keith made no reply, but made every preparation to withstand an attack.

Keith was well aware of the vulnerability of his position. The

Austrian commander, General Daun, had over 70,000 troops under his command. Frederick had 30,000 and Retzow, who was separated from Frederick's army, possibly 10,000 more. Against this advantage, Daun was known as the most dilatory and pusillanimous of commanders, but even this most unenterprising of Frederick's adversaries was forced, for very shame, to act in such an advantageous position; especially as he could appreciate that Frederick had placed the Prussian army in an indefensible position.

The battle of Hochkirch began at 5 a.m. on the morning of October 14th. The Austrian attack emerged suddenly from the morning mist. The Prussians had not posted outposts and complete surprise was effected. Frederick was slow to appreciate that he was under attack and it was not until cannon shot began to fall about him that he was moved to action. The main Austrian attack was concentrated on Keith's forces. Keith was killed by a cannonball in the chest and his regiment virtually annihilated. By 7.30 a.m. Hochkirch was in Austrian hands and Frederick began to withdraw his badly mauled forces to a new position of defence on higher ground in the rear. The failure of Daun's second-in-command, General Durlach, to keep up the pressure on the defeated enemy allowed Retzow, who had taken almost no part in the action, to retire unmolested, thus protecting Frederick's army from total destruction. The combined Prussian forces then retreated to Doberschütz where a strong position was taken. Daun forbade all pursuit, contenting himself with some desultory artillery fire at the retreating enemy's back.

As well as James Keith, whose death affected Frederick badly, Prince Francis of Brunswick was killed and Prince Maurice of Anhalt-Dessau was severely wounded and fell into enemy hands. Frederick's cup of bitterness was filled when, that evening, he received news of the death of his favourite sister, Wilhelmina, who was married to the Margrave of Bayreuth.

Keith was buried next day with full military honours, the curate of Hochkirch village officiating. In January, 1759, Frederick had his body removed to Berlin where it was placed in the crypt of the garrison church. In 1776 Keith's distant cousin, Robert Murray Keith, British Ambassador in Vienna, caused a memorial urn to be placed in Hochkirch church.. There is (or was) a street in Berlin, Keithstrasse, named for Frederick's Scots friend, who was never far from the King's mind until his own death in 1786.

Keith was 62 when he died and never married. While in Paris in 1718, he refused a commission for Spain in Sicily because "I was then too much in love to think of quitting Paris, and, altho' my friends forced me to take some steps towards it (the Spanish commission), yet I managed it so slowly that I set out only in the end of that year; and had not my mistress and I quarrelled, and that other affairs came to concern me more than the conquest of Sicily did, it's probable I had lost many years of my time to very little purpose—so much was I taken up with my passion."[7]

We are curious to know the recipient of so much ardent worship, but James Keith, as a gentleman should, never revealed her name. Nor is he known ever again to have experienced so strong an attachment.

Many were the eulogies that followed this flower of Scottish chivalry to the grave. His biographer in *Eminent Scotsmen*[8] wrote: "If anything were wanting to complete the illustrious character of this man, it is to be found in the circumstances of his death having been nearly as much lamented by the Austrians, then the enemies of Prussia, as by the Prussians themselves. His humanity was ever on the alert to protect even those against whom he fought from any unnecessary violence, and the Austrians had, in a thousand instances, been indebted to this ennobling trait in his character, admirably calculated in all its parts to gain the esteem and admiration of mankind."

Carlyle[9] wrote of him: "Highly respected, too, and well worth talking to, though left very dim in the books, is Marshal Keith; who has been growing gradually with the King, and with everybody, ever since he came to these parts in 1747. A man of Scotch type: the broad accent, with its sagacities and veracities, with its steadfastly fixed moderation, and its sly twinkles of defensive humour, is still audible to us through the foreign wrappings. Not given to talk unless there is something to be said, but well capable of it then. On all manner of subjects he can talk knowingly and with insight of his own."

"The friendly intimacy between Keith and the King was never shaken," wrote von Ense.[10] "All Frederick's generals had to suffer from his bad humour, but he no less from their touchiness and jealousy.

Winterfeldt and Keith were exceptions; and Keith was the least burdensome to the King through discontent and ambition, agreed with his brother officers, obeyed and commanded with the same zeal, and led the smallest corps as willingly as he would a whole army. He stood on amicable terms with Schwein; Schmetter was devoted to him; Winterfeldt enjoyed his esteem; Seydlitz and Zieten seemed, without any near personal relationship, to hold with him. The only person spoken of as really an enemy of Keith is Prince Maurice of Dessau, who tried secretly to slander him to the King . . . But as that reckless and unsociable Prince could not speak French and could only stutter in German, he had few chances of collision with Keith."

He could converse with monarchs and generals, diplomats and philosophers in six languages. As A. Francis Steuart wrote:[11] "He had seen all the courts of Europe, great and small, from that of Aragon to the residence of the Khan of Tartary, and accommodated himself to every place as if it had been his native country. General, minister, courtier, philosopher—all these characters, however different in themselves, were in him united."

CHAPTER 6 — BIBLIOGRAPHY

1. Steuart, A. F., *Scottish Influences in Russian History*, p. 40.

2. *Biographical Dictionary of Eminent Scotsmen*, Vol. ii, p. 423.

3. See p. 113.

4. Burton, J. Hill, *The Scot Abroad*, Vol. ii, p. 164.

5. Burton, *ibid.*, Vol. ii, p, 345.

6. Burton, *ibid.*, Vol. ii, p. 345.

7. *Biogr. Dict. of Emin. Scots.*, Vol. ii, p. 425.

8. *ibid.*, p. 424.

9. Carlyle, Thomas, *Life of Frederick the Great*, Vol. iv, p. 389.

10. von Ense, Varnhagen, *German Lives*, 1844, quoted in *The Scot Abroad,* Vol. ii, pp. 177-8.

11. Steuart, A. F., *ibid*, p. 112.

CHAPTER 7.

Foreign Doctors in the Russian Service

Dr Robert Erskine was the first British doctor in Russia who is identified as undoubtedly a Scot. He arrived in Moscow in 1704 to take up a Court appointment and died in Russia in 1718, aged 41.

According to the Diary of Patrick Gordon[1], in 1665 a "Doktor Thomas Wilson came to Moscow and lodged with Doktor Collins." Dr Wilson was probably a Scot, but nothing seems to be known about him, except that he qualified M.D. Leyden and was awarded an honorary F.R.C.P. Leyden in December, 1664. Dr Samuel Collins was physician to Czar Aleksei Mikhailovich; on his return to England he wrote a book on "The Present State of Russia," which was published posthumously and remained the most reliable source of information about Russia for many decades.

However, foreign doctors had been employed at the Russian Court since at least 1533; the Grand Duke Vasili III was attended by one such as he lay dying in 1533; and there were English doctors at the courts of Ivan IV and Boris Godunov.

Three national periods of doctors are apparent: English doctors in the sixteenth century (1553-1633), German in the seventeenth century and Scots from 1704 up to the Crimean War.

English doctors were sent to Russia soon after the arrival of the first Russia Company expedition in 1554. According to Hamel[2]: "There came moreover a physician, Doctor Standish, an apothecary, and several persons besides . . ." They arrived in Moscow on September 12th, 1557, were admitted to an audience with the Czar on the 14th, and "two days later, the Czar sent Dr Standish, as well as each of the other newly-arrived Englishmen, a horse to ride about the town." On September 18th, Dr Standish received a gift of some sable furs, and on October 1st he dined with the Czar. On October 11th he received seventy roubles, and the apothecary and the others each thirty. Five times between October, 1557, and April, 1558, he was invited to the Czar's table .

In 1567 there arrived another, Dr Richard Reynolds, an apothecary (Thomas Carver), an engineer (Humphrey Lock), his assistant (John Finton), a "goldsmythe and goldfyner" (assayer) (Thomas Green), and other professional men.[3]

At the end of May, 1568, a doctor, an apothecary and a surgeon had arrived; "the doctor was jolyvated" (he makes an English word out of *jalovat*=to pay) "with 200 roubles, the apothecarie with 100, and the surgeon with 50 roubles"; which gives a clear impression of the relative standing and pay of the various branches of the medical profession. In 1580 Dr Robert Jacob was brought to Moscow by Sir Jerome Horsey, the resident director of the Russia Company.

From the first arrivals of foreign doctors in Moscovy, there was a tendency to use them for diplomatic and other purposes. Steuart[4] says that the idea that Ivan IV should marry Lady Mary Hastings, one of Queen Elizabeth's ladies-in-waiting, "appears to have been suggested to the Tsar by his physician, Dr Bomel (educated at Cambridge), whom he so cruelly put to death." And, later, "She (Elizabeth) sent a physician, Dr Robert Jacob, who favoured the English match."

The first known and named doctors at the Russian Court, then, were Dr Ralph Standish and Dr Reynolds, who went out with the Russia Company in 1557.[5] In the reign of Boris Godunov there was the scholarly Dr Mark Ridley[6], who presented a Slavonic Book of Hours to Trinity College, Cambridge, and who compiled a Russian-English and English-Russian dictionary which exists in manuscript in the Bodleian Library. He was succeeded by a Dr Joseph Jessop, who, however, died before he could take up the appointment. Instead a Dr Timothy Willis was sent: a most unfortunate choice. His medical qualifications were slight. He had been expelled from St John's College, Oxford, and denounced as a "corrupter of all the scholars", and had failed an examination at the Royal College of Physicians in 1586. Indeed, his sole qualification appears to have been that he was willing and eager to go to Moscow where, presumably, he thought he could make his name and fortune. Also Elizabeth and Cecil were desperate to have some representation at the Russian Court and no one else seems to have volunteered. So, on June 24th, 1599, the Queen signed a letter recommending "an especial choice amongst our learned physicians of him to be used in your service; being in degree a Doctor of Physic and of great experience, not only in that profession but in all liberal sciences, fit for any Prince's service." The unfortunate Willis was not only inadequate, but was not properly briefed; and after failing to impress the Czar and his advisers, was given his *congé* after a stay of just three weeks.[7]

Apart from looking after the health of the monarch and his court, some curious part-time activities were expected of the Court physician. In 1600 Bogdan Belsky was summoned to the court of Boris Godunov for interrogation and found guilty of *lèse majesté*. "The extent of Boris's anger was demonstrated by the fact that he ordered one of his doctors, a Scot, to pluck out Belsky's beard. This was a fearful humiliation. Orthodox Russians tended their beards with almost religious fervour. In the case of Belsky the humiliation was all the greater because he had a passionate hatred of foreigners."[8]

Who this doctor was is not stated: Dr Ridley, an Englishman, was the official court doctor at the time; the job was probably given to some more menial attendant at court, such as one of the "surgeons" who, almost entirely untrained and unskilled, ranked very low in the professional hierarchy.

Olearius,[9] a Holsteiner, in his *Travels*, records several German doctors: Dr Wendelin Sybelist, formerly employed by the Holstein Court, replaced an Englishman, Dr Arthur Dee,* who retired in 1634. Sybelist was Court Physician from 1633 to 1642, and again from 1644 to 1646. In his absence Dr Johann Balau (or Belau) of Rostock stood in for him. Dr Hartmann Gramann, a German from Thuringia, who had studied medicine at Jena, Leipzig and Wittenberg, and had practised in Halle, was engaged in 1633 as the Holstein Embassy's doctor, but entered the Czar's service in 1639 where he remained for several years.

The first Russian doctor who obtained a degree was probably P. B. Postnikov,[10] who graduated from Padua in 1695; it was not until the nineteenth century that the first Russian doctor graduated in Russia.

There was no private medical practice in Russia before about 1677 or 1681, when retiring foreign doctors were first permitted to remain in the country and continue their practice, free of the jurisdiction and control of the Aptekarskii Prikaz. This body, which can be loosely translated as the Ministry for Medical Affairs, was started in 1591 by an Englishman, James Frencham, one of the many English apothecaries

---

* Dr Arthur Dee ("Artemy" Dee in Russia), 1579-1651, was the son of Dr John Dee (1527-1608), alchemist, astrologer, astronomer and mathematician.

at the court of Ivan IV, who arrived in Russia with Robert Jacob.

In the sixteenth and seventeenth centuries at least, foreign doctors were paid by salary and were not permitted private practice. Olearius[11] says that Gramann "is in high favour, and not with his Tsarist Majesty only, for boyars, princes and magnates also greatly admire and respect him, and bring him gifts. He receives a monthly salary of 62 roubles, besides an annual sum of 300 for a total of 1044 roubles, in addition to bread, grain, salt, honey, and other things for the household. When he has to bleed someone or give other medical treatment, he receives an extra payment of 50 roubles in cash, and also a piece of satin or damask, a timber of sables, and the like. The physicians rarely receive cash payments from the boyars, princes and other magnates, but are given sables, bacon, vodka, or other provisions instead. They must appear at the Court daily, and beat their heads to the magnates, especially to their superior, the inspector of the Tsar's apothecary, (which, incidentally, is very well supplied)."

Foreign doctors were the highest paid persons in the Czar's service around the middle of the seventeenth century. Prince Cherkassky, the highest paid Russian official, received 850 roubles a year; but, of course, his income was greatly increased by what his estates produced. Foreign officers of the rank of colonel received 30 to 40 roubles monthly, as against 60 or so for the doctors.

Dr Robert Erskine,[12] or Areskine, as his name appears in documents of Russian origin, arrived in Russia in 1704. He was the sixth surviving son of Sir Charles Erskine of Alva, Bart., and great-grandson of John, 7th Earl of Mar. He was born at Alva in 1677 and educated probably by a tutor until he started his medical studies at Edinburgh in 1692, at the tender age of 15. There was as yet no medical school in Edinburgh so he was apprenticed to Hugh Paterson, surgeon-apothecary. It was usual for Scottish students to go abroad, to Paris or Leyden, to further their education and to obtain a degree. Between 1694 and 1739 no fewer than thirty Scots students received their M.D. from the Continent. Erskine went to Paris in the autumn of 1697.

The time of his arrival in Paris was one of considerable political excitement. The long war between France and England and her allies had terminated with the Peace of Ryswick in September, 1697, and was followed by a season of great want and poverty in France; whilst the cruel persecution of the Huguenots persisted intermittently since the revocation, in 1685, of the Edict of Nantes removed from non-Catholics the freedom of worship and freedom from persecution they had enjoyed for nearly ninety years. Erskine remained in Paris probably for two years and obtained degrees in philosophy and medicine. From Paris he proceeded to Holland, graduating M.D. Utrecht in 1700. He then returned to London where he gained a reputation as a skilful anatomy dissector and lecturer at a hospital school or college, and was elected a Fellow of the Royal Society of London in November, 1703.

In June, 1704, he set off for Russia, probably due to some influence or with some promise or prospect of employment. All Europe was ringing with the fame of Peter I of Russia, who was working as a shipwright at Zaandam, near Amsterdam. Peter spent three months in England in 1698 (where he did severe damage to John Aubrey's holly hedges by pushing members of his staff through them in a wheelbarrow), where, with the permission of King William III, he recruited nearly 500 skilled mechanics, seamen, engineers, gunners, etc.—including thirty surgeons—into the Russian service. Erskine is not known to be among those thus recruited, but must have had some recommendation or introduction; he could not just go to Russia and set himself up in practice.

He evidently arrived at Archangel, at that time the only seaport in the Muscovite realm, and then by horseback or carriage over six hundred miles to Moscow. He must, very soon, have been received into the Czar's service, as in a letter from Peter to William III in March, 1717, Peter mentions "Areskine" as having been in his service for thirteen years. He would come under the jurisdiction of the Archiator of the Aptekarskii Prikaz.* Soon after commencement of his service he was appointed Archiator at an annual salary of 1500 ducats (=£700 sterling), and continued to serve the Czar until his death, high in the Czar's affection and regard.

Erskine travelled frequently with the Court. In 1716 he accompanied Peter and his wife Catherine on a tour of Denmark, Germany, Holland and France. They remained at Danzig for three months from February to April, 1716, during which Peter conferred on him the distinction of

---

* Steuart, op. cit., p. 79. The Aptekarskii Prikaz was transferred from Moscow to St Petersburg in 1712, and renamed the Medicine Chancery. It supplied the Army and the Navy, and indeed the whole Empire, with drugs, and incidentally made a considerable contribution to the Czar's revenue. George Mackenzie described the new capital in 1714: "Our infant city here is of that extent that, though far from being at the fag end of it, yet have my house at above 2 English miles from that of the Dr's (Erskine's), so that my letter found him all ready gone abroad with the Czar, though it was with him before 7 o'clock."

Counsellor of State, which carried with it the privilege of being addressed as "Your Excellency," and confirmed his appointment as Court Physician and Chief Archiator.

It was during a stay at the Hague in 1716 that serious charges were preferred against Erskine. Görtz, chief minister of Charles XII of Sweden, at that time acting as Swedish Ambassador at the Hague, had concocted a plan to reconcile Peter and Charles, drive George I from the English throne, and set the Pretender on it. He was in communication with Baron Spaar, Swedish Minister in Paris, and Count Gyllenborg, Swedish Minister in London, whose letters were intercepted; both were arrested and kept in confinement for six months. Several letters referred to Peter and there were repeated allusions to his Chief Physician as a likely and suitable intermediary who might be used to win over Peter. Peter wrote to Lord Stanhope, British Secretary of State, denying all complicity in, or knowledge of, the plot, as did Erskine also. Subsequent correspondence, however, has shown that Erskine was not only sympathetic to the Jacobite cause, but had been fully conversant with the plot, and had approached Prince Menshikov. He undertook to interest Peter who, by his continued favour of and friendliness towards Erskine, showed considerable sympathy with the Jacobite cause.

Erskine returned with Peter to St Petersburg in October, 1717. During 1718 his health became seriously impaired and he retired to Koncheserski (now Konchesevo), a health resort on the western shore of Lake Onega, to recuperate; and there, in a residence the Czar had built for himself when he went to drink the waters, Robert Erskine died in December, 1718, at the age of 41. His body was brought to St Petersburg and buried with full honours in the churchyard of the Alexander Nevsky Monastery. Always well treated by the Czar and handsomely paid (and even promptly, which was most unusual), he returned the Imperial kindness in his will. He left all his money in Britain to his mother, that in Russia to necessitous families. He ordered his library to be sold for the benefit of his heirs, his medals, coins, curios and surgical instruments to be sold and the money given to orphanages and hospitals in Scotland. He gave certain porcelain and furniture to members of the Imperial family.

He also recommended "Thomas Garvine, who is now a surgeon in the Hospital of Petersburg, who was later sent by Peter I to Peking at the request of the Chinese Emperor Kang Hsi, on one of those Oriental missions which owe so much to Scottish leaders."[13]

Thomas Garvine had been apprenticed to John Marshall, surgeon of Kilsyth, who was in charge of the Glasgow University Physick Garden in 1704. When Garvine arrived in St Petersburg is not known, but he was working at a hospital there before 1713. In 1715 the Chinese Emperor, Kang Hsi, requested the Czar (Peter I) to "send an able physician, and some Medicines that would provoke the Venery . . .";

Dr Thomas Garvine.
(By kind permission of the Wellcome Institute.)

as a result of which Garvine was attached to a mission to China headed by Lorenz Lange (fl. 1715-38). The latter was a Swedish architect in charge of the Czar's building at Peterhof and was also employed as a diplomatic agent. Together they left Moscow in August, 1715, and arrived in Peking in November, 1716. Brought before Kang Hsi's throne, the doctor was asked about his medicines. Next day Lange and Garvine again appeared before the Emperor; after much kneeling and bowing they were given two damask coats with fox fur and had to put on gloves. The surgeon was then directed to feel the

Emperor's pulse. His pronouncement that the Emperor "was very well" pleased the Emperor. This appears to have been the sum total of Garvine's medical activity in China. After receiving more presents and attending the Chinese New Year celebrations on February 2nd, 1717, they left Peking about the beginning of June and reached Moscow early in February, 1718.

Another Scots doctor employed on a similar mission was John Bell of Antermony, who went to Russia in 1714 and was received by Erskine "in a very friendly manner." As Bell was desirous of travelling, Erskine recommended him, as having some knowledge of surgery, to the College of Foreign Affairs in St Petersburg, where he entered the Czar's service. He first went in the suite of Artemy Petrovich Valensky on an embassy to the Sophy of Persia from 1715 to 1718, and next year set off in the train to Lev Vasilievich Izmaylov, Ambassador from the Czar to Kang Hsi. Bell again went to Persia and then, in 1737, on a mission to Constantinople. He married in 1746, a Russian lady, Marie Peters, left the Russian service and, after a career as a Turkey merchant, retired to his native land and died at Antermony in 1780, aged 89 years.[14]

Two excellent volumes, published later by subscription, were the fruits of his observations during his travels in Asia from 1718 to 1721.[15]

Between 1730 and 1762, during the reigns of Anna and Elizabeth, Scots doctors continued to be in favour in Russia, and indeed not with the Court only. They now became doctors to the services and employed in military and civil medical establishments.

John Cook went to Russia in 1735. In his book he mentions several Scots doctors in St Petersburg, such as Lewis Calderwood, who went to Russia in 1728 as surgeon to the Preobrazhensky Guards, and was employed in hospitals in Moscow and St Petersburg. He also mentions meeting Dr James Mounsey (see below), a Mr Selkirk, "surgeon to the Guards," and a Mr Sylvester Malloch who was chief surgeon to the port of Astrakhan and died in Russia on November 13th, 1742.

We are also indebted to Dr Cook for a portrait of the Empress Elizabeth, "whom the deluded Jacobites so fondly hoped Prince Charlie would marry." "She was of large stature, and inclineable to be fat, but extremely beautiful; and in her countenance I saw so much mildness and majesty, that I cannot in words express them. Her hair was black, and her skin white as snow untann'd . . . At this time Count Razumovsky (Aleksei Grigorievich) was attending her Majesty. It is really surprising that a fat, though young woman, could move so cleverly as the Empress did, in so much as I could scarce hear her feet upon the floor; but indeed her august presence had much disconcerted me."[16]

In his book John Cook records the gruesome story of the execution of Mary Danielovna Hamilton in 1719. She was descended from the "Swedish Hamiltons" who gave Peter the Great his tincture of western freedom and culture, and was introduced to his dangerous court to wait upon the Empress Catherine. The Czar fell in love with her, but she favoured others, especially a certain Orlov. Children were born of this guilty association whom she quietly disposed of. Russian custom at the time regarded infanticide lightly; and it is more likely her rejection of Czar Peter than her infanticidal habits which eventually led to her trial and condemnation to death.* Catherine, whom she had taunted and ridiculed, interceded on her behalf; but Peter was immovable. She mounted the scaffold on March 14th, 1719, dressed "in a silk gown trimmed with black ribbons." Peter supported her at the scaffold and after she was beheaded , lifted the head and touched the pale lips with his own, dropped the head, crossed himself and departed.

In 1735 Dr Cook, visiting the Academy of St Petersburg, writes:[17] "Here I saw the head of the unfortunate Miss Hamilton, a Swedish lady, who lost it for having murdered her child, unlawfully begotten; and this is the only murder of that kind that I heard of in Russia. This lady was maid of honour to the Empress Catherine. It is said that Peter went and saw her executed. He wept much, but could not prevail with himself to pardon her, for fear, as is said, that God would charge him with the innocent blood she had shed. He caused her head to be cupped and injected. The forhead is almost compleat; the face is the beautifullest my eyes ever beheld; the *dura mater* and brain are all preserved in spirits in their natural situation. This is kept in spirits in a large chrystal vessel."

There it remained, in company with the head of William Mons, supposed lover of Peter's wife, also executed by Peter the Great, until they were removed by Princess Dashkova about 1784, when she became director of the Russian Academy.[18]

By the time of the accession of Catherine the Great in 1762 British doctors were becoming numerous in Russia. John Richard, an English

---

* Her story is thought to be the origin of the ballad, *The Queen's Marie.* Sir Walter Scott recorded the analogy in his *Minstrelsy of the Scottish Border.*

traveller in Russia in 1775, however, exaggerated when he stated that doctors "were scarce and generally Scotch"; he probably meant that, of the few doctors he encountered, one or two were Scots.[19]

A Russian historian, Y. Chistovich, lists 511 doctors who were given the right to practise by the Medical College in the eighteenth century; of these only 19 were British and of these only 14 practised in the reign of Catherine. It is true, however, that of these 14, 12 were either Scots or trained at Edinburgh University.[20]

There were tremendous advances in medical services in Catherine's reign, and it is difficult to evaluate how much was due to Catherine herself and how much to the able men with whom she surrounded herself. Peter the Great had founded good military hospitals; it was left to Catherine to found civil hospitals, not only in the main cities, but throughout the country. In 1763 Catherine founded Russia's College of Medicine, comprising a director, a president and eight members. It had an annual revenue of 470,000 roubles, plus one percent of the salaries of all military and civil service personnel, who in return received free medical treatment. The object of the College was to train a sufficient number of Russian doctors and apothecaries to serve all the provinces; and to further medical knowledge. In 1778 the College published its first *Pharmacopoeia Russica*; in 1779 it laid down rules for the conduct of apothecaries and midwives, and a scale of charges for medical treatment; and in 1795 the College was provided with its own printing press.

In 1763, when the document establishing the College of Medicine was presented for her signature, Catherine added in her own handwriting: "The College must not forget to submit plans to me for hospitals in the provinces." In 1775, when she reorganised the provinces, Catherine decreed that each province should have a hospital, and each county—say, 20 to 30 thousand inhabitants—a doctor, surgeon, assistant surgeon and student doctor. Salaries were higher in the remoter areas and state doctors were allowed to treat private patients. Until there were enough native doctors, Catherine attracted many Germans with the offer of an 800-rouble retirement pension. Catherine founded, in the name of her son Paul, a small model hospital in Moscow which the prison reformer John Howard said would do honour to any country. Another visitor, Francesco de Miranda, the future liberator of Venezuela, was struck by the Russian habit of transferring patients to summer hospitals so that the winter ones could be cleaned and disinfected before winter set in.

In 1783 Catherine founded a VD hospital in St Petersburg of sixty beds, thirty male, thirty female. It was not permitted to ask the names of any patient; he or she was issued with a night-shirt and a cap inscribed "secrecy."

Catherine's example was followed by others. Baron von Keichen founded a 300-bed hospital in St Petersburg, to which were added, in 1790, 250 beds in wooden annexes.

Catherine gave special attention to orphans, foundlings and unwanted babies. She built a five-storey foundling home in Moscow, superior to anything in Europe, which included a lying-in hospital, a church and a dairy farm. Mothers wishing their babies to be accepted had only to ring the bell, a basket would be lowered in which to place the baby, state its name and whether or not it had been baptised, and the basket was drawn up again. The Moscow Foundling Home took in two thousand infants a year and became the model for similar houses in St Petersburg, Tula, Kaluga, Yaroslav and Kazan.

Heinrich Storch in 1796 gave the following figures for infant mortality, which speak for themselves: London 32 per cent, Berlin 27.6 percent, St Petersburg 18.4 per cent.*

One of the most important medical events of Catherine's reign was the visit to Russia of Dr Thomas Dimsdale (1712-1800). He arrived in St Petersburg with his son and assistant, Nathaniel, in 1768 and inoculated the Empress, the Grand Duke and about 140 gentry against smallpox; then moved to Moscow and did fifty more. He returned to Russia in 1781 and inoculated the Grand Dukes Alexander and Constantine and other members of the royal family.[21] For his services Dr Dimsdale was created a Baron of the Russian Empire and a Counsellor of State, and given a gratuity of £10,000 and an annuity of £500. Britain also was praised as "that island of wisdom, courage and virtue." Catherine, hitherto rather sceptical about the value of doctors in general, rarely having any need of their services personally, began to appreciate their value; their careers prospered accordingly.

Before Dimsdale left St Petersburg in 1768, an inoculation hospital was set up under the supervision of Dr Matthew Halliday (1732-1809), who had arrived in Russia in the reign of the Empress Elizabeth, and whose career is invariably confused with that of his son William.

---

* For all these details of medical progress in the reign of Catherine II the author is indebted to Vincent Cronin's *Catherine, Empress of All the Russias,* Collins, London, 1978, pp. 169 ff.

In 1771 Matthew Halliday was sent to Moscow to assist in containing an outbreak of the plague and was rewarded with a life pension for his services. He continued to administer free inoculation to the poor at his hospital in St Petersburg into the 1790s, and inherited Dimsdale's mantle by inoculating Paul's other children, Grand Duke Nicholas and Grand Duchess Anna, for which he was promoted by imperial decree in May, 1799. He also established a merchant firm in St Petersburg and bought the large island separated from Vasili Island by the River Smolenka, which was known up to the Revolution by a Russified version of his name, Golodai Island. It is now the Island of the Decembrists.

The eldest of Matthew Halliday's children, William, was born in St Petersburg soon after 1766 and trained at Edinburgh and Tübingen before entering Russian service in 1785. He spent many years at Rylsk, in the province of Kursk, before settling in Moscow in 1792, where he practised until a disagreement over a new appointment led to his dismissal in 1797.

Another family of doctors was the Grieves. John Grieve (1753-1805) was one of the doctors who examined the body of Czar Paul after his murder (see below). James Grieve served nearly thirty years in Russia under Anna and Elizabeth. His sister, Johanna, married Dr James Mounsey. Although they were related they were neither father and son, nor brothers, as can be seen from James Grieve's will.

The long sojourn of Dr James Mounsey (1700-1773), who served in Russia from 1736 to 1762, covered the reigns of Anna, Ivan VI, Elizabeth, Peter III, and just into the reign of Catherine II.

James Mounsey was born at Skipmyre, near Lochmaben, in Dumfriesshire. His father, Thomas Mounsey, a merchant from the south, married Janet, a sister of William Paterson, founder of the Bank of England and originator of the Darien Scheme. He moved to Skipmyre for the good of his wife's health, but Janet died in 1698 and he married Mary Steele, sister of the minister of Lochmaben Parish Church, James being the only issue of this marriage.

It has not been established where he studied, and indeed it is doubtful if he had any medical qualification when, in 1736, he was enrolled by Prince Kantemir, the Russian Minister in London, as a "lekar" to serve in the Naval Hospital in St Petersburg; a "lekar" being a medical man who has no medical degree.*

In Russia, Mounsey met and became very friendly with General James Keith. Shortly after, at the battle of Ochakov, the General was severely wounded in the knee. The Russian surgeon** advised amputation, which Mounsey resisted. After months of invalidism, Keith's brother, the last Earl Marshal, arrived in Russia and removed him to Paris, where surgeons removed bits of cloth which had been

Dr James Mounsey.
(By kind permission of the Royal College of Physicians of Edinburgh.)

* cf. German "feldscher"; today he would be called a "para-medic."

** From a letter from Admiral Thomas Gordon to a Mr Williams: "I have had the honour of a visit from the Earl Marshal; his brother General Keith is under the care of one Horn, an able experienced surgeon. He (Horn) is of the opinion that the General's leg which is wounded is in danger. What the General's fate can be cannot be known for some time." Horn was probably a German. Cf. Scottish Record Office, Sec. 1/855/290.

carried into the knee-joint by a bullet; after this the wound healed promptly and completely. Mounsey accompanied his friend to Paris.

Thereafter he rose steadily in the medical hierarchy and, by the time Keith left Russia in 1747 to serve Frederick the Great, he had been appointed physician to the Repnins Corps and later to the First Medical Division. In 1757, after five years in private practice, he was made First Physician to the Empress Elizabeth, which was no sinecure. The beautiful young woman, "but inclineable to fat," described by Dr John Cook, continued as she was inclined. Later she suffered from frequent nose bleeds, dropsy, and, from 1761, convulsions. She also drank excessively. In 1762 she suffered a haemorrhage, declined into a coma and died—a classic example of hypertension and chronic congestive heart failure.

In the Scottish Record Office is a letter[22] written by Mounsey from Oranienbaum, June 18th, 1762, probably to Provost Drummond of Edinburgh, but not so addressed. It is on black-edged paper as the Court was in mourning for the Empress Elizabeth. As it gives a good picture of medical practice in Russia at the time, here is an extract:

". . . To give you any tollerable account of myself or of my office would be a very long story and of no consequence. But as you take a friendly part in what concerns me I cannot leave it altogether untouched. You know I was settled in Moscow where I had great reputation and no ungratefull Practice. But I was called to the Court without any desire or inclination and appointed first Physician and Counsellor of State to the late Empress (which gave me the rank of General Major). I had the good luck to have her confidence and Grace and if she had lived I am persuaded she would have made the fortune of my family considerable. My conduct during her illness, the success I had in the attempts I made to help her, and the justness of my Prognostick, encreased my reputation. So I found after her death that I had even gained credit both with the Ministry and Publick. The Present Emperor (Peter III), who had long ago known and Esteemed me, on his accession made me Privy Counsellor, first Physician and Archiater. The last two seem synonymous to you but you must know it is not allways the same Person who is in fact both, for Archiater in this country is the Chief Director of the Medicine Chancery and of the whole Faculty, and of all medical affairs throughout the whole Empire, in a way you can have no idea of. First Physicians of other Monarchs may be great as to themselves by personal merits but the greatness of their office and Power bears no manner of comparison with mine and thank God I am not only Esteemed and beloved by my Master . . . but I have the confidence and friendship of the nation also. Nevertheless I can assure you all this grandure has been forced upon me; nor can I say I feel that Pleasure which the world may think; indeed I am a little flattered as I can do more good to those under me than any of my Predecessors ever could. Still I have not quit thoughts nor hopes of taking a walk with you on the Kirk or Castle lochside. My health is but invalitudinary and my offices will be too heavy for me long to bear, and I have long been troubled with *hame wae* [home-sickness]."

The Emperor Peter III was generally considered mentally defective and reigned only six months. He was deposed on orders from his wife, who usurped the throne as Catherine II, and died a week later "of a haemorrhoidal colic which had affected his brain and brought on apoplexy"; and so it might have done, had he not first been poisoned with arsenic and finally strangled.

One month later James Mounsey applied for his discharge, ostensibly for reasons of health, but really because events were getting too rough for his peace of mind. He returned to Scotland, bought an estate at Rammerscales, and died in Edinburgh on February 2nd, 1773, aged 73.

As well as having a practical genius for his work, he had an enquiring mind, and such was the flow of original contributions from his pen that on March 8th, 1749, he was elected to the Fellowship of the Royal Society of London. In 1739 he had obtained his M.D. from the University of Rheims and on his return from Russia he was elected an Honorary Member of the Royal College of Physicians of Edinburgh. He brought with him from Russia seeds of *Rheum palmatum* which he gave to Dr John Hope, Regius Keeper of the Royal Botanic Gardens, Edinburgh; and thus introduced rhubarb medicinally to the British public.*

Two of the best known doctors of the reign of Catherine the Great were Matthew Guthrie (1743-1807) and John Rogerson (1741-1823). Their careers in many respects ran parallel, though Guthrie's always seems overshadowed by Rogerson's.

---

* Medicinal rhubarb is the powdered, dried root of *Rheum palmatum;* the leaf-stalks of common or garden rhubarb used as a dessert have no laxative action.

Matthew Guthrie was born in Edinburgh in 1743, son of Harie (Henry) Guthrie, a professional writer, and grandson of Gideon Guthrie, a noted Scottish Episcopalian divine. He was educated in Edinburgh and obtained his M.D. in 1763. He is believed to have served as a ship's surgeon with the East India Company in the 1760s. He went to Russia in 1770, probably with Admiral Sir Charles Knowles and the latter's private secretary, Dr John Robison (*vide infra*). He probably served in the Russian Admiralty for a year or two before being posted, in 1772, as a surgeon to Rumyantsev's army in Moldavia and Valachia. Here he spent the next few years and, in the course of his duties, travelled extensively in the Crimea and adjacent lands of the northern coast of the Black Sea, in which he ever after held an abiding interest.

He returned to St Petersburg about 1776 and two years later became Chief Medical Officer to the Land Corps of Noble Cadets, which post he retained until his death.

Professor Papmehl,[23] quoting from one of Guthrie's unpublished works, tells us how Catherine dealt with revolutionary agitators in the 1790s:

". . . indeed the propagand (*sic*) made us but short visits, as they did not like Catherine's jokes, who used to send the Physician of the madhouse to feel the pulse of all those who were found preaching *holy insurrection as the most sacred Duties of her Subjects* . . . The Doctor was commonly accompany'd with a couple of stout keepers from Bedlam who immediately carried the Patient there, and a blister on his head and a few purges and watergrouse (a thin gruel) soon brought him to his right senses, and made him as harmless as a child. For he was so laughed at by his Disciples on reappearing in public that he quickly took the road to Prussia, there to write secret memoirs of the Court of Russia, and abuse the whole Empire by every possible falsehood that rage could invent . . ."

Guthrie was made a Counsellor of State in the reign of Paul, which made him a hereditary noble. In 1781 he married a Frenchwoman, Countess Marie de Romont, by whom he had two daughters, both of whom married Britons. She died in 1800 and, in 1807, Guthrie was laid beside her in the Smolensky Cemetery.

Guthrie was an 18th century eclectic with an omnivorous appetite for almost everything of scientific, cultural, historical or musical interest. He was on intimate terms, or in correspondence with many kindred spirits both in Russia and overseas, and contributed frequently and voluminously to many journals, especially *The Bee*, or *Literary Weekly Intelligencer*, a periodical published in Edinburgh by Dr James Anderson, F.R.S., under the pen-name "Arcticus." During his only visit to Britain, in 1782, he was elected to the Royal Society of London. Subsequently he was a member of the Societies of Antiquities of London and Edinburgh, and of the Philosophical Society of Manchester. He was also an original member of the Musical Club of St Petersburg,

He wrote on everything: the treatment of scurvy; plague and quarantine; the climate of Russia; White Sea fisheries; and many other medical and ecological subjects; but especially on Russian folklore, customs and music, in which he performed valuable services in rescuing many old fables, songs, dances, costumes and musical instruments from oblivion.

In 1795 he published in St Petersburg his best known book, *Dissertations sur les Antiquités de Russie . . .* ; and in London, in 1802, *A Tour Performed in the Years 1795-6 . . .* by Mrs Maria Guthrie . . . Described in a Series of Letters to her Husband, the Editor, Matthew Guthrie, M.D. The book, in the fashionable epistolatory form of the day, contained translations of Mrs Guthrie's letters from the French, but owes as much, or more, to the "editing" of her husband, as the copy in the British Museum, copiously annotated in Guthrie's handwriting, shows.

His last work is his *Noctes Rossicae*, on which he spent ten years of dedicated research and which comprised over 600 folio pages. It was "finished" in 1806, but from additional notes written in 1806 and 1807 it appears that Guthrie had yet more to say on the subject, but was cut short by his death in 1807. This mammoth work was on the national music of Russia, dances, choruses, songs, ballads and festivities—a field hitherto largely neglected by Russian writers, who were not interested in the peasants. Guthrie, on the other hand, regarded them as the "true Russians," in contradistinction to the Francophone nobles who despised their own language and customs. Guthrie himself remarked that "the modern Russians are not much pleased to see them (the folk songs) appear in a Collection, from the idea that they are such nonsense as must make them appear ridiculous in the eyes of foreigners . . ." Nevertheless many subsequent Russian writers are indebted to him for his long and original labours in a field that their predecessors had neglected.

In all, he served his Sovereign and his adopted land well over a period of nearly forty years as an interpreter of Russian history, culture, customs and music, to the western world; and maintained his exalted position as one of the leading personalities in St Petersburg society under three sovereigns.

It is remarkable that three well-known Scots doctors in Russia all came from one small town in Dumfriesshire: Lochmaben. They were Matthew Halliday and James Mounsey (whom we have already considered) and John Rogerson; and it is thanks to the diligent research of a Lochmaben doctor, Dr John B. Wilson, that we have a full account of the last two of this colourful group.[24]

Dr John Rogerson.
(By kind permission of the Scottish National Portrait Gallery.)

John Rogerson was born in 1741 at Lochbrow, four miles north of Lochmaben. One half of Lochbrow was farmed by his father, Samuel, and the other half by William Halliday, whose son Matthew preceded Rogerson as one of his Imperial Majesty's Court Physicians and on whom the mantle of Dr Thomas Dimsdale, the inoculator against smallpox, descended.

Rogerson received his medical training at Edinburgh University and was recommended to the Russian Court by James Mounsey, whose half-brother married Rogerson's father's half-sister. He went to Russia in 1765 and gave immediate proof of his medical skill by saving the life of Princess Dashkova's son who was suffering from croup (diphtheria?). Shortly after he was appointed Physician to the Court and Counsellor of State, a position he held for nearly fifty years. He accompanied Catherine on most of her travels, notably on her progress to the Crimea in 1787, and attended her in her brief final illness in 1796.

He became a close friend of the Empress, who appears to have preferred him as a friend and adviser than as a physician. She treated Rogerson as a kind of Molière charlatan: "You couldn't cure a flea-bite!" she would say to him. Rogerson, good-natured, continued to urge her to take this or that pill, and on the rare occasion when he succeeded, he would pat on the back the Empress of All the Russias, saying in a jolly tone: "Well done, Ma'am, well done!"[25]

He was a jolly, sociable man, the sort about whom anecdotes abound. He was fond of whist which he played very badly; and on one occasion Count Bezborodko enraged him by ordering a battery of cannon to fire a salvo every time he revoked.

Rogerson was more of a diplomat than Mounsey or Guthrie. He made no original contributions to medical science. He acted for Catherine in negotiations with the Imperial Austrian Court, for which Catherine gave him an estate in White Russia with 1600 serfs.

As has been said before, Court Physicians were permitted to attend private patients, but not to receive fees: there was, however, nothing to prevent them from receiving presents, the exact value of which was understood amongst his patients. Dr Rogerson was usually paid with a silver snuff-box; Dr Clarke[26] tells the story:

> "The method of paying their physicians by trinkets, which I before mentioned, might seem an inconvenience to the faculty; but it is not so. Dr Rogerson, at St Petersburg, as I am informed, regularly received his snuff-box and as regularly carried it to a jeweller for sale. The jeweller sold it again to the first nobleman who wanted a fee for his physician, so that the doctor obtained his box again; and at last the matter became so well understood between the jeweller and the physician, that it was considered a sort of bank-note, and no words were necessary in transacting the sale of it."

One of Rogerson's duties was examining Catherine's favourites for V.D., a disease she dreaded, and not without reason. It was said that two noble ladies of the Court were employed to carry out tests of a more practical nature, and were known as *les éprouveuses*. This gave him access to many court secrets, which remained such in his canny keeping.

In 1786 he went on a six-months' leave to Scotland. During his absence the Comte de Ségur visited Russia and noted his absence with satisfaction: "As he dabbles in politics as much as in medicine, and as it is through his hands that bribes are supposed to pass, I cannot but be very pleased at his absence."[27]

Rogerson outlived Catherine by many years and was equally favoured by her son and successor, Czar Paul, who made him a Privy Counsellor in 1797, the first year of his reign. Rogerson was present at the Mikhailovsky Palace when Paul was murdered on March 1st, 1801, and helped the Empress to safety in the Winter Palace, carrying the future Czar Nicholas I on his shoulders. He continued to serve under Alexander I and did not retire until 1816, at the age of 75, when he returned to his native land and bought an estate of Wamphray, a small manor of Dumcrieff. In a letter to Samuel Rogerson,* Thomas Henderson, Jr., wrote (March 27th, 1821):

> "The old gentleman (Dr John Rogerson) is now very stout. He walked with me to Dumcrieff and went thro' the house which is now nearly finished. I can assure you it is a most excellent house, abounding with every convenience. The family expect to enter it about June next."

He was not to enjoy his new house long, but died at Dumcrieff in 1823, aged 82 years.

Dr Clarke,[28] writing in the time of Czar Alexander I, was pretty scathing about the state of medical practice in Russia at the time, and of the qualifications and skill of the British practitioners. "Persons calling themselves English physicians are found in almost every town upon the continent. Sometimes they have worked in apothecaries' shops in London or Edinburgh; but generally they are Scotch

---

* Cross, Anthony, "John Rogerson: Physician to Catherine the Great," Canadian Slavic Studies, iv 3 (Fall;, 1970), p. 594, Scottish Record Office, 6D 1, 620/68. Samuel Rogerson could be a son, nephew, grandson, etc.; every generation of Rogersons had Samuels galore. John Rogerson's father was Samuel; and Professor A. G. Cross (Cross, Anthony, *op. cit.*, p. 594) gives Dr Rogerson's name as John Samuel Rogerson.

apothecaries, who are men of professional skill, and of acknowledged superiority. In some places abroad, the practitioners are really natives of England; but whenever this is the case, the traveller is cautioned to shun them, however celebrated they may be, as he values his existence. . . . Without exception I have never met a single instance of a man of talent among expatriated English physicians, neither would such men leave their country, to settle among foreigners, unless compelled by circumstances of misconduct at home. Those Englishmen upon the continent who go by the name of physicians, will generally be found, upon enquiry, to have exercised no such profession in their own country, but to have lived as servants in the shops of apothecaries, chemists and druggists, or to have practised as veterinary surgeons, farriers, or itinerant quacks."

Such scathing criticism stung his editor to riposte: "The sweeping censure is unjust. Beyond all question Russia has benefitted very extensively from the efforts of British physicians. All the three departments into which the medical profession is divided, the civil, military and naval, were, until within a few years, under the presidency of a British subject. Sir Alexander Crichton had the civil, Dr Leighton the naval, and Sir James Wylie the military division. The last named gentleman has had the good fortune to enjoy the sunshine of imperial favour during three successive reigns. Dr Leighton's practice as an accoucheur is stated to be very considerable, for Dr Clarke is in error in his belief that that branch of the profession was practised only by women. In addition . . . very many of the principal Russian nobility maintain English physicians in their families — men certainly far removed from the opprobrious description of Dr Clarke."

Sir Alexander Crichton,[29] son of Alexander Crichton of Newington, was born at Edinburgh in 1763 and entered Russian service as Physician to Czar Alexander I in 1804. He stayed for fourteen years, during which time he was appointed head of the whole Civil Medical Department, in which he worked hard to bring order and discipline to a long-neglected office. He organised the containment of a cholera outbreak in 1809 and encouraged the spread of vaccination against smallpox (which became compulsory in 1804). He died in England in 1856, aged 93.

His nephew, Sir Alexander William Crichton, born in 1791, married, in 1820, a daughter of Dr Sutthoff, another of the Court Physicians. He was knighted by George IV in 1817 and made a member of the Medical Council and a Counsellor of State. He was thirty years in

Russian service, for twenty-four of which he was Physician to the Emperor and his family.

Sir James Leighton was another conscientious administrator who was in charge of the Marine Hospital in St Petersburg and head of the Naval Medical Department. Robert Lee, who knew him well, wrote that Leighton was thoroughly up-to-date with his medical knowledge and that his surgical theatre and indeed the whole Marine Hospital were in excellent order.

James Wylie was born of poor parents at Kincardine-on-Forth in 1768. At an early age he tried to run away to sea, but his mother, a most determined woman, walked 20 miles to apprehend him, grabbed him by the ear and marched him 20 miles home again.

Although Wylie achieved fame in the reigns of Paul and Alexander I, he arrived in Russia in 1790, six years before the death of Catherine II. He was recruited by Rogerson, on whose recommendation he entered Russian service as medical attendant to the family of Prince Golitsyn. Soon after his arrival he was appointed surgeon to the Eletsky Regiment.

Young Wylie was not long in making his mark at Court; in 1798 Kutaitsov, valet and confidant of Czar Paul, developed a large abscess in his neck which was threatening his breathing and indeed his life. Wylie lanced this with immediate and complete relief.

He was the first doctor on the scene after the murder of Czar Paul. Joyneville states that the body of Paul was handed over to three Scots doctors, John Grieve (Mounsey's nephew),* Guthrie and Wylie, for dissection. Wylie signed the death certificate, giving the cause of death as "apoplexy," which must have caused considerable relief and satisfaction to the court camarilla led by Count Pahlen, Military Governor of St Petersburg, who had strangled him; but which caused Talleyrand to remark:"Really, the Russian Government will have to invent another disease!" Next day Wylie was given the task of embalming the body and making the face presentable for lying in state. Alexander was said to have agreed that he would not refuse the crown if Paul was deposed, but hoped "no harm would come to Paul".

Wylie was appointed Body Surgeon and Physician to the new Czar, a position he retained until Alexander's death in 1825. He was present at the battle of Austerlitz in 1805 and at more than twenty other

---

* Not Green, as stated by T. C. Gordon, *Four Notable Scots*, Eneas Mackay, Stirling, 1960.

battles. He is said to have performed more than two hundred operations on the field of Borodino in 1812. "As if this were not enough, he rode with the Cossacks when, under the command of Platov, their giant leader, they drove far into the French lines".[30] Next year, at Leipzig, as General Moreau, the Russian commander, was talking to the Emperor, a cannonball shattered both his legs, which Wylie amputated on August 27th, but he died at Laun in Bohemia on September 26th. He was buried at St Petersburg.

Sir James Wylie.
(By kind permission of the Royal College of Physicians of Edinburgh.)

After Napoleon's defeat, Wylie accompanied the Czar to Paris. On March 30th, 1814, Platov and his Cossacks poured into Paris and bivouacked in the Champs Élysées. Czar Alexander and Wylie occupied a suite in the most fashionable hotel and prepared to discuss terms with Talleyrand. In April Sir Archibald Alison arrived with the British delegation and made contact with the Russians.

In his memoirs he writes:[31] "The extreme kindness shown to us by the Russian generals and officers during our stay in Paris led to our giving them a dinner, which was furnished in handsome style at the Restaurant Mapinot in the Rue St Honoré. Sixteen sat down to dinner and the utmost cordiality prevailed. Count Platov, General Chernikov, General Barclay de Tolly, Sir James Wylie, Sir William Crichton, and many others honoured us with their presence and, contrary to the usual practice, the conviviality was prolonged to a late hour. We then saw what was deeply interesting, Russian bonhomie and abandon; and their manners and usages impressed us with a strong sense of their wealth of feeling and sincerity of disposition. As the evening advanced and the *ponche à la Romaine* and iced champagne began to produce their wonted effect, they became, without being noisy or violent, in the highest degree demonstrative in their exuberance. Everyone drank wine with his neighbour after the continental fashion, touching their glasses before they put them to their lips, and many were the toasts drunk to the 'Eternal Alliance of Great Britain and Russia.' Before parting, the company embraced after the German fashion; and the last thing I recollect is seeing my brother, a man six feet high, lifted up by Platov, who was six inches taller, *and being kissed in the air."*

Alexander, being so near to England, could not resist the opportunity of crossing the Channel and so we find him with Wylie on June 10th at Hampton Court. Later they attended Ascot Races and, at the request of the Czar, James Wylie was knighted on Ascot Heath by the Prince Regent, appropriately using Platov's sword for the ceremony. Nor was this all; before Alexander sailed from Portsmouth on July 2nd, he saw James Wylie kneel again, this time on board a British man-o'-war, to receive the higher dignity of baronet.

It was probably on this occasion that Wylie took the opportunity to invest £60,000 in British funds, intending eventually to return to his native soil. He never married and, a lifelong bachelor, lived frugally— some might say niggardly. He was, however, a very handsome man, as portraits of him show. He was six feet two inches tall, and was said to be an amusing and interesting character. He lived in apartments in the Imperial Palace.

Alexander was very neurotic, religious and introspective. Mystic and paranoiac, he lived in dread of assassination, which, with his family history, was perhaps not unreasonable. "In January, 1824, whilst staying at Tsaskoye Selo, he was caught in a heavy shower of sleet, developed fever and erysipelas which, starting on his leg, spread to his whole body and head, and affected his brain so that he became delirious. Symptoms of gangrene set in and his doctors, with the exception of Wylie, thought it would be necessary to amputate. He, with Scots caution, reflected that if he died of the operation the Russian nation would be more severe in their criticism than if he perished from the disease; accordingly, he took upon himself the responsibility of preventing the amputation. Such was the affection in which Alexander was held that the doctors were threatened by the mob and provided with passports in case the illness ended fatally. At last the complaint yielded to the cautery and lancet . . ."[32] Wylie, even if accused of excess of caution and masterly inactivity, was proved right.

Alexander, however, had only a year to live. Wylie continued to hold a unique place at court under his successor, Nicholas I. He was essentially a practical surgeon and took an interest in training surgeons and in the design of hospitals. The Medico-Chirurgical Academy of St Petersburg and Moscow, at which surgeons were trained, was founded in 1800 by Wylie, who was president of it for thirty years. In his will he left the bulk of his considerable fortune to the foundation of a Medical Clinic and to scholarships for aspiring surgeons.

Paradoxically enough, Wylie was responsible for the discontinuing of the recruitment of foreign doctors as surgeons to the Russian armed forces. Russia, no longer Muscovy, could henceforth stand on her own feet in the matter of medical science. By now he was a Russian himself and, with no near relatives in his old country, he felt no urge to uproot himself from the imperial favour in which he had basked for so long. The shadows were lengthening and not only for James Wylie; he could see war approaching his country and was satisfied that the medical military machine that he had built was ready to prove itself; but that would be for others to discover. He died at St Petersburg on December 2nd, 1854, at the age of 86, just twenty-five days before Britain declared war on Russia.

Robert Lee (1793-1877) was born at Galashiels and took his degree at Edinburgh in 1814.[33] After one year in a country practice and two in Edinburgh hospitals, he set out for London and for five years lived in the household of the Hon. William[*] and Lady Caroline Lamb, looking after their epileptic son. He left the Lambs in 1822 and went to Paris, where he worked in the dissecting rooms and clinics there and was for a time medical attendant to the Bessborough family.

---

* Later Lord Melbourne.

In October, 1824, he entered the service of Count Michael Vorontsov, Governor-General of South Russia, and left it in January, 1827—a bare two and a quarter years later. He reached Odessa after a gruelling eighteen-day journey by coach from Vienna. Odessa was a new city then, barely thirty years old and still a-building. Lee found medical conditions in South Russia primitive in the extreme, with frequent epidemics of cholera, dysentery, dipththeria and cerebro-spinal meningitis. Rheumatism and "intermittent fever" (which probably included malaria, typhoid, typhus and relapsing fevers) were endemic. Lee introduced quinine sulphate to South Russia, where it was so efficacious that the Tartars regarded it as a magic potion.

Czar Alexander I died at Taganrog in November, 1925, of "bilious remittent fever," a term meaningless now, but then variously interpreted as malaria, typhoid or some other disease-entity. The post mortem was performed by Sir James Wylie. Lee was summoned from Odessa, but arrived at Taganrog too late to see the dying Czar, but in time to take dictation of Wylie's notes of the post mortem. The fact that Alexander was ill for three weeks before he died favours typhoid rather than malaria as the correct diagnosis.

After his death strange rumours circulated in Russia that Alexander had not died, but had abdicated his temporal throne and gone to live in Siberia where he died at a great age. So persistent was this rumour that, in 1866, the Russian press announced that Alexander's body was to be exhumed in order to kill the myth. The fact that Wylie was in attendance on the Czar in his last illness was not sufficient evidence that the Czar had in fact died at Taganrog; had he not connived at the falsification of the death certificate of Alexander's father, Paul, when he was murdered in 1801? However, the post mortem of Alexander was attended also by Dr Robert Lee and a German surgeon, Reinhold; and details of the findings are available from Russian sources. There would seem to be little factual support for the hermit story; but well-rooted myths die hard even in the face of subsequent truth.

Lee's subsequent career in England was brilliant. He soon built up a good obstetrical practice in London and published numerous papers on gynaecological and anatomical topics. At the Royal College of Physicians, he was Lumleian (1856) and Croonian (1862) Lecturer; and in 1864 he was the last Fellow to deliver the Harveian Oration in Latin. He died in 1877, aged 84.

It is fitting to conclude this chapter on doctors in Russian service with a brief account of a non-medical doctor, Dr John Robison (1739-1805), for the pleasure of recording a universal scientific genius, Scotland's counterpart to Benjamin Franklin.

John Robison was born at Baldernock, Stirlingshire, and educated at Glasgow Grammar School. He became tutor to Admiral Sir Charles Knowles' son, who as a midshipman was about to accompany General Wolfe to Quebec. Robison saw active service in Canada and was employed in making surveys of the St Lawrence River. He was with Wolfe the night before his death and made the round of outposts with him.

On return to Britain in 1762 he became acquainted with James Watt, then a mathematical instrument-maker at Glasgow University; and it was Robison who suggested to him the idea of applying the power of the steam-engine to the moving of wheeled vehicles; but he was too busy with other things to pursue the matter himself. Watt, however, kept in touch with Robison, whose evidence was useful in a lawsuit in 1796 when Watt defended an infringement of his patent. Robison was appointed lecturer in chemistry in 1766.

In 1770 Admiral Sir Charles Knowles was appointed President of the Russian Board of Admiralty. His service in Russia seems to have been entirely administrative and to have kept him in St Petersburg or its neighbourhood. He took Robison with him as his secretary. In 1772 Robison accepted the Chair of Mathematics at the St Petersburg Naval Academy, and acted as Inspector General of the Corps of Naval Cadets, where he studied the Russian language and instructed his students in shipbuilding, rigging and navigation.

In 1773, from the death of Dr Russel, a vacancy occurred in the chair of natural philosophy in Edinburgh, and Robison was invited to occupy the post. The Biographical Dictionary of Eminent Scots says he left Russia in June, 1771:* This must be a mistake as he gave his first lectures in the winter of 1774, the same year that, Russia having concluded peace with Turkey, Admiral Knowles' commission terminated and he returned to England.

So in 1773 or 1774 John Robison became Professor of Natural Philosophy at Edinburgh University, his subjects embracing mathematics, mechanics, hydrodynamics, astronomy, optics, electricity and magnetism, his lectures being delivered "with great fluency and

---

* A. G. Cross says 1773, which seems much more likely.

precision of language." In 1777 he sealed an old friendship started in Russia by marrying a niece of Dr Matthew Guthrie. In 1783 he became a founder member of the Royal Society of Edinburgh, of which he was the general secretary from then until a few years before his death in 1805, which occurred after an illness of two days only.

In addition to his scientific abilities, he was possessed of no mean skill and taste in music. He performed on several musical instruments; but his "musical lucubrations," as the DNB put it, "proved as useless to the musician as they were valuable to the natural philosopher." He was also the author of several books, an excellent draughtsman and no mean versifier.

The DNB account concludes, almost apologetically: "Although he was a Freemason, Robison published in 1797 a curious work—'a lasting monument to fatuous credulity'—to prove that the fraternity of 'Illuminati' was concerned in a plot to overthrow religion and government throughout the world. The title ran: 'Proofs of a Conspiracy against all the Religions and Governments of Europe, carried on in the Secret Meetings of Freemasons, Illuminati and Reading Societies.'"

Time has revenged Robison of the opinion of his detractors. Long after his numerous tomes on electricity and chemistry have been relegated to the dust-heap by obsolescence, *Proofs of a Conspiracy* remains now the only work by which he is remembered, and has been recently republished in several modern editions.[*]

---

[*] The author's copy was published in 1967 by Western Islands, Belmont, Massachusetts. It is fair to point out that Robison's book is not an attack on Masonry in general, but is a history of the Illuminati, who initially used Grand Orient Masonry for the spread of their revolutionary ideas, were behind the forces that led to the French Revolution, and whose ideology became the basis of the Communist Manifesto of 1848. Robison was a member of the Scottish rite, which had little or no connection with Grand Orient.

CHAPTER 7 — BIBLIOGRAPHY

1. Gordon, *The Diary of General Patrick Gordon*, p. 57.

2. Hamel, J., *England and Russia: comprising the Voyage of John Tradescant the Elder, Sir Hugh Willoughby, Richard Chancellor, Nelson, and others, to the White Sea, etc.*, translated by J. Studdy Leigh, Richard Bentley, London, 1854, p. 158.

3. *ibid.*, p. 177.

4. Steuart, A. F., *Scottish Influences in Russian History*, p. 7 n.

5. Willan, T. S., *The Early History of the Russia Company, 1553-1603*, Manchester University Press, 1956 (reprinted 1968), p. 92.

6. *ibid*, p. 161.

7. Evans, Norman, *Doctor Timothy Willis and his Mission to Russia, 1599*, Oxford Slavonic Papers, New Series, Vol. 2, 1969. Also Willan, *op. cit.*, pp. 231-233.

8. Grey, Ian, *Boris Godounov*, Hodder and Stoughton, London, 1973, pp. 148-50.

9. Baron, Samuel H. (ed. and transl.), *Travels of Olearius in the Seventeenth Century*, Stanford University Press, 1967, pp. 34, 39, 86, 150 n., 201.

10. Mentioned in Baron, *op. cit.*, footnote to p. 34.

11. Baron, *op. cit.*, p. 201.

12. Paul, Robert, ed., "Erskine: Letters and Documents relating to Robert Erskine, Physician to Peter the Great, Czar of Russia, 1677-1720," *Miscellany of the Scottish Historical Society*, Vol. xliv (1904), University Press, Edinburgh, pp. 371-430.

13. Burgess, Renate, "Thomas Garvine: Ayrshire Surgeon Active in Russia and China," *Medical History*, No. 13A, Vol. 19, Jan. 1975, pp. 91-94.

14. Steuart, *op. cit.*, p. 83.

15. Bell, John, *Travels from St Petersburg in Russia in Divers Parts of Asia*, 2 Vols., Glasgow, 1763. A good life of John Bell is given in W. Anderson's *Scottish Nation*, Vol. ii, pp. 273-275.

16. Cook, John, *Voyages and Travels through the Russian Empire, Tartary, and Part of the Kingdom of Persia*, 2 Vols., Edinburgh, 1768, Vol. ii, p. 570.

17. Cook, John, *op. cit.*, ii, pp. 56-57.

18. Londonderry, Marchioness of, and H. Montgomery Hyde, edd., *Wilmot Journals: The Russian Journals of Martha and Catherine Wilmot, 1803-1808*, Macmillan and Co., London, 1934, p. 25 footnote.

19. Cross, Anthony G., *"The British in Catherine's Russia,"* being Chapter 9 of *The Eighteenth Century in Russia*, ed. by J. G. Garrard, Clarendon Press, Oxford, 1973, p. 252.

20. *ibid.*, p. 252.

21. Cronin, Vincent, *Catherine, Empress of All the Russias*, Collins, London, 1978, pp. 169 ff. A full account of Dr Dimsdale's visits to Russia is contained in *Life of Catherine the Great* by E. A. Brayley Hodgetts, Methuen and Co., London, 1914, which also has a portrait of him. Dimsdale also left his own account in *Tracts on Innoculation*, London, 1781.

22. c.f. Scottish Record Office GD 24. Sec. 1/846.

23. Papmehl, K. A., *Freedom of Expression in 18th Century Russia*, Martinus Nijhoff, The Hague., 1971, p. 123.

24. Wilson, J. B., "Three Scots in the Service of the Czars," *The Practitioner,* 210 (April/May, 1973), pp, 569-574 and 704-708.

25. Cronin, *op. cit.*, p. 169.

26. Clarke, E. D., *Travels in Russia, Tartary and Turkey*, William and Robert Chambers, Edinburgh, 1839, p. 25.

27. Quoted in Steuart, *Scottish Influences . . .*, p. 63.

28. Clarke, *op. cit.*, pp. 25-26.

29. Dict. of Nat. Biography: also Anderson, W., *Scottish Nation*, Vol. i, pp. 726-7.

30. Wilson, J. B., *op. cit.*, p. 572.

31. Alison, Sir Archibald, *Some Account of my Life and Writings: an Autobiography,.* 2 vols., 1883, Vol. i, p 93.

32. Wilson, J. B., op. cit., quoting from *Life and Times of Alexander I* by C. Joyneville, 3 Vols., Vol. iii, p. 341.

33. Schuster, Norah, H., "English Doctors in Russia in the Early Nineteenth Century," *Proc. Royal Soc. Med.*, Vol. 61 (1968), pp. 185-190.

For Dr John Robison, Sir James Wylie and Sir Alexander Crichton see the *Dictionary of National Biography.*

See also the *Biographical Dictionary of Eminent Scotsmen.* Cf. in addition Hutchison (Sir) Robert, "A Medical Adventurer. Biographical Note on Sir James Wylie, Bart., M.D., 1758 (*sic*: should be 1768) to 1854," *Proc. Royal Soc. Med.*, Vol. 21 (1928), pp. 1406-8. Wylie was an uncle of Sir Robert Hutchison's paternal grandmother.

For details of Drs Ralph Standish, Richard Reynolds, Eliseus Bomel, Robert Jacob, Mark Ridley, Arthur (*sive* Artemius) Dee and Samuel Collins, see Bishop, W. J., "English Physicians in Russia in the Sixteenth and Sevententh Centuries," *Proc. Royal Soc. Med.*, Vol. 23 (1929), pp. 143-152.

For Dr Matthew Guthrie see Papmehl, K. A.,"Matthew Guthrie—The Forgotten Student of the Eighteenth Century," *Canadian Slavonic Papers,* xi (1969), pp. 161-181.

Further information will be found in the following:

Clemow, Frank G., "Men and Matters in Russia in the XVIIIth Century," Proceedings of the Anglo-Russian Literary Society, xxviii (1900), pp. 15-19.

Robison, J., *Proofs of a Conspiracy*, The Americanist Classics Edition, Western Islands, Belmont, Massachusetts, 1967. Originally published in 1798.

Appleby, John H., "Ivan the Terrible to Peter the Great: British Formative Influence on Russia's Medico-Apothecary System," Medical History 27, 1983, pp. 289-304.

Prince Michael Barclay de Tolly, by George Dawe,
from the Hermitage Gallery, Leningrad.
(By permission of the Novosti Press Agency.)

CHAPTER 8

Napoleon's Invasion of Russia, 1812: Prince Michael Barclay de Tolly (1761-1818)[1]

The Barclay family came originally from Normandy (Berchelai or Berchelei meaning birch trees), and there is a village of that name near Frome in Somerset where in 1086 the Norman tenant-lord, under Robert Arundel, was a certain Robert de Berchelai. It may be this line which first appeared in Scottish records near the end of the reign (1153-65) of Malcolm IV in the persons of Robert and Walter de Berkeley; but nothing is known of how they got there.

Towie, or Towey, lies in the parish of Turiff in Aberdeenshire; the name is Gaelic in origin, later gallicised to Tolli or Tolly. Towie Castle was built by the Barclays in the sixteenth century and finished in 1593 in the time of Patrick Barclay.

Colonel David Barclay (1610-1686) served under Gustavus Adolphus and was converted to Quakerism in 1666. His son Robert was born at Gordonstoun near Elgin in 1648 and was educated at the Scots College in Paris, of which his father was rector. Here he withstood every temptation to embrace Catholicism and, returning to Scotland in 1664, later joined the Society of Friends, married a Quakeress in 1670, and devoted the rest of his life to the promotion of the Society.

Another Barclay, John, was born in 1582 at Pont-à-Mousson in Lorraine where his father William, a Scot born in Aberdeen in 1546, was Professor of Law. He went with his father to England about 1603, where he published his *Euphormionis Satyricon,* a politico-satirical romance chiefly directed against the Jesuits. Supplements of this work were the second part (1607), his *Apologia* (1611) and *Icon Animorum* (1614). In 1616 he went to Rome where he died, a good Catholic, in 1621. In the same year appeared his Latin political allegory *Argenis,* according to Cowper, "the best romance that was ever written";

according to others, a dreary and ponderous allegory about the Guises and the King of Spain.[2]

Yet another Barclay, William, wrote a tract in reply to James VI's famous *Counterblast against Tobacco*. His was called *Nepenthes, or Virtues of Tobacco*. In it he said: "It (tobacco) has a certain mellifluous delicacy which deliteth the senses and spirits of man into a mindful oblivion, in so much that it maketh and induceth the forgetting of all sorrows and miseries. There is such hostilitie between it and melancholie, that it is the only medicament in the world ordained by nature to entertain good companie."[3]

In 1621 two Protestant brothers, Peter and John Barclay, merchants, settled in Rostock, then already suffering from the decline of the Hanseatic League. Peter and three sons stayed on; John went to Norway and founded there a branch of the family which died out in 1907. Peter's eldest son Johann Stephan Barclay settled in 1664 in Riga in Livonia and became the ancestor of Michael Andreas Barclay de Tolly.

At that time Esthonia was a narrow strip along the southern shore of the Gulf of Finland, and Lithuania a vaguely defined area which comprised the southern part of present-day Lithuania, Courland, and other areas which were Polish. Livonia was the space in between, comprising the southern part of present-day Esthonia, all of present Latvia, and part of northern Lithuania. All these Baltic States had long been under the domination of German language and culture, the Livonian Order of the Knights of the Sword having ruled the region for three hundred years. The inhabitants were originally pagan until the advent of the German knights, who converted them to Catholicism and, after the Reformation, to Lutheranism.

Despite succeeding waves of conquest by Lutheran Swedes and Catholic Poles, and even incorporation into the Russian Empire in 1721 by Peter the Great, the only influence conspicuous by its absence was Russian; at no time up to the present day has the Russian Orthodox Church ever established itself in, or influenced, the Baltic States. The ruling class remained German in culture and language. This is of significance in explaining later the mistrust and unpopularity which surrounded the great son of Livonia who became a Russian general, Field-Marshal, Minister of War, and finally a Prince of the Russian Empire.

Johann Stephan Barclay, Michael's great-grandfather, was admitted to the bar at Riga in 1664 and became Public Prosecutor. He had three sons of whom the eldest, William, became a municipal employee of

Riga and rose to be an alderman and quarter-master. William's son, Gotthard, born at Riga in 1726, had a brief career in the Russian army, leaving it at 24 with the rank of lieutenant. He had ambitions to become landed gentry, but, falling into debt, he had to sell his estate and settle as a tenant on a small farm at Pamushis where Michael Andreas was born in 1761. Michael had an elder brother, Erich, three years his senior, who outlived him by one year. A younger brother, Heinrich, became an artillery major in the Russian army and died at 39; and nine years after Michael came his sister Christine. Their mother died a year after Christine's birth, and their father — generous and feckless as ever and now reduced to being a tenant farmer on an even smaller farm, Laiksaar — was unable to afford the upkeep of his family; so Michael, and later Christine, were adopted by their maternal aunt and her husband, the Vermeulens. Far from being "cast off," this adoption enlarged the family unit, as the Barclays, the von Smittens (his mother's family) and the Vermeulens were all inter-related. Such an arrangement had much to commend it: As the Josselsons put it, "The institution of fosterage was far from uncommon among the nobility and landed gentry of the time. It supplied parents for orphans, children for childless families, educational and marital opportunities inaccessible at home. It helped level out family size and the costs of rearing each new generation, and it greatly strengthened the bonds of Livonian interrelatedness."[4]

Michael was happy in the family of his Aunt Auguste, for whom he had always retained the deepest respect and affection, and in the company of his younger sister there was brought out in him an affectionate protectiveness which later he was to extend to the troops under his command. The household was strictly Lutheran, God-fearing but not bigoted, of moderate means and by no means uncultured. The Germanic family ideal of "Kinder, Küche, Kirche" prevailed, in marked contrast to the socially equivalent Russian family, where children were treated with either brutality or neglect. This background of duty, thrift, formality and discipline, added to the solitariness of a small boy with only a nine years younger sister as companion, was formative of the man, who became self-disciplined, self-contained, sympathetic and considerate, but no boon companion to any man. This again marked him as "peculiar": the main off-duty occupations of Russian officers being drinking and gambling, for which Barclay had no taste at all. He never lost his Baltic-German accent, and was always considered a foreigner by his brother officers.

His virtues were so outstanding as to be somewhat offensive in the milieu of military life. He was sober, industrious, studious (especially of military treatises), modest and of an unassailable honesty; qualities which, if not leavened with an imperturbable temper, a kind and tolerant attitude towards those subordinate to him, a sympathetic ear and an unpretentious lack of ambition, might have made him an insufferable prig. But even the most hostile of his contemporaries recognised his sterling qualities, though they might be chilled by his aloofness and his inability to conform to the lowest common denominator of mess life.

He was a man of imposing appearance. Well over six feet in height, with a high-domed forehead accentuated by the early onset of baldness, his portrait by George Dawe which inspired Pushkin's poem, "The Commander," shows a placid, level gaze, a straight, well-shaped nose and a generous, quizzical rather than humorous, mouth; a man who would command attention in any walk of life: self-assured, self-controlled and self-willed. The words "noble," "independent," "steadfast," immediately come to mind.

In 1791, at the age of 30, Michael married his cousin, Helene Auguste von Smitten, nine years younger than himself. The only portrait we have of her, in her forties, shows her a heavy, matronly woman, bedecked with the Order of St Catherine; under a ribboned bonnet her small, porcine eyes gaze out shrewdly and calculatingly. However, the marriage, for all the interruptions caused by Michael's absences on military duty, appears to have been successful, and his letters to her, and her sole extant letter to him, are couched in affectionate terms. Shortly after his marriage, Barclay was appointed battalion commander of the St Petersburg Grenadier Regiment, and took part in the Polish campaigns of 1792 and 1794; the latter following the Polish revolt under Tadeusz Kosciusko. This was the last and most serious attempt by the Poles to regain their independence. They succeeded in taking Warsaw and Grodno, slaughtering the Russian garrisons in both cities. After the capture of Kosciusko, Polish resistance collapsed, and the third partition of Poland reduced that unhappy country to a vestige of its former area. Barclay was promoted to lieutenant-colonel and transferred to command of the first battalion of the Estonian Jaeger Corps; he was also awarded the white cross of the Order of St George, Fourth Class.

This was the last campaign of Catherine's reign; she died in November 1796 and was succeeded by her son Paul, under whom

Barclay received rapid promotion to full colonel and then major-general in 1799. He was now aged 37 and had had a very varied experience. Paul was murdered in 1801 by a group of disgruntled officers who resented the tightening of discipline that Paul's "Prussianization" of the Russian army implied. He was succeeded by his son Alexander I, who saw himself as the saviour of Europe from the increasing domination of the continent by Napoleon. Unfortunately the young Czar had more military enthusiasm than experience, and an ill-founded respect for Austrian generals; he was surrounded by sycophants who risked disgrace if they ever had the nerve to express any criticism of the Czar's military plans.

Austerlitz (Nov. 20/Dec. 2, 1805)* was a complete victory for the French and a resounding rout for the Russians. Kutuzov, the Russian Commander-in-Chief, was dismissed to become Governor-General of Kiev, being used as a scapegoat by the Czar for the latter's own rashness and impetuosity. Alexander never forgave Kutuzov for being a witness of his own incompetence. Barclay took no part in this campaign, but distinguished himself at the subsequent and equally devastating defeat at Eylau (26-27 January/7-8 February, 1807), where he was severely wounded.

It was at Memel, during a lull between battles during which Barclay lay wounded in his quarters, that the Czar paid a call on him. No record of this lengthy conversation exists, but it was to prove the turning point in Barclay's career. The young Czar was deeply impressed with Barclay's straightforward common sense, plain speaking and evident command of his subject. He was equally impressed with the loyalty and fidelity he sensed in him. Shortly after (April 1807) Barclay was given command of the 6th Division, but he was still convalescent from his wounds when the battle of Friedland (2/14 June, 1807) was fought, and had ample time to think about problems of the future. It was here and at this time that he evolved his scorched earth policy for the defence of Russia, though it would be five years before it was required to be carried out.

After Friedland a mood of despair and defeatism set in among the Russian generals. Bennigsen and others formed a Peace Party centred on the person of the Czar's brother, Grand Duke Constantine, whose activities eventually led to the historic meeting between Napoleon and

---

*Note: See Preface for a note on dates in this chapter.

Alexander I on a raft in the river Niemen at Tilsit. From the beginning the "Peace of Tilsit" (25 June/7 July, 1807) was recognised for what it was — breathing space between hostilities. It was very unpopular in Russia, where hatred of the French was beginning to generate that patriotism which was to become such a potent force in 1812.

In order to distract the Russian people's attention from the ignominies of Eylau and Friedland, as well as to keep up the morale of the armed forces by not allowing them time to brood on past defeats, Alexander decided it was time to turn the Swedes out of Finland, which he regarded as a simple exercise. In the event it took the whole of 1808 to effect, but by December the Swedes had been routed and Finland was declared a grand Duchy of the Russian Empire, which it remained until 1917.

Barclay was active during the early phases of this war as commander of the Sixth Division, but was ill for a long period during the second half of the year, and was forced to retire to his home in St Petersburg. Whilst there he frequently attended the Czar's councils of war, where to be listened to and to take part in policy-making hastened his convalescence considerably. The invasion of Sweden was the main item on the agenda. The idea of invading across the ice in winter appears to have originated with Arakcheev, the Minister of War, but it was left to Barclay to work out the details in a memorandum which he submitted to the Czar and which was adopted.

The crossing of the Gulf of Bothnia, in temperatures from 16 to 26 degrees of frost, presented enormous and unprecedented hazards. Three columns were set up: one, under the command of General Count Shuvalov, was to make a land crossing north of the Gulf of Bothnia; a second, under Barclay, to take the middle route from Vasa in Finland to Umea in Sweden via the Kvarken Straits, a distance of about one hundred kilometres; and a third, under Prince Bagration, to cross farther south via the Åland Islands. The cold was intense, and two hundred soldiers lost one or more limbs from frost bite. The few islands that acted as stepping-stones provided neither shelter from the biting wind nor wood for fires. Moving heavy guns and ammunition over the creaking, groaning ice which threatened to break up under their weight, was only one of the problems undertaken and solved. The Swedish commander of Umea, grossly over-estimating the size of the forces under Barclay's command, hastened to capitulate; and the exhausted and frozen Russian troops were only too glad to avail themselves of the comforts afforded by the town of Umea, where they seized a vast quantity of guns and matériel. However, peace being declared a few days later, all supplies were handed back to the Swedes, and all their personal possessions were left untouched — an act of generosity which amazed the Swedes and which reaped a harvest of goodwill in the future.

The Czar made a tour of the main cities of Finland to persuade the Finns of their exalted status in the Russian Empire and to sever the ties which had held Finland to Sweden for generations. Promotions were handed out all round (and a few dismissals) and Barclay was surprised to find himself a full general, Commander-in-Chief and Governor-General of Finland.

So well and humanely was Finland treated under its enlightened and generous Governor-General that, three years later when all Russia's military resources were needed to face Napoleon's invasion of Russia, Finland undertook the defence of the Baltic shore entirely with its own troops: a dividend of incalculable value.

The Swedish war being terminated, Barclay could give his whole time to the administration of Finland, and to the establishment of a governing council over which he presided. By his personal example he quietly demonstrated to the Finns that economic progress and peace could be combined with loyalty to the Russian Crown, whilst a large degree of autonomy in Finland's internal affairs was maintained. In fact, the Finns never had it so good; and many were the expressions of thanks and regret when, in January 1810, Barclay was recalled to St Petersburg and appointed Minister of War on the resignation of Count Arakcheev. As Minister of War Barclay inherited a fairly good artillery, which was Arakcheev's chief interest, but little else. The western defences of Russia were almost non-existent. Barclay had a plan for a chain of fortresses from Dvinsk on the River Dvina to Bobruisk on the Berezina; but time was against him and the fortresses were never built. One of Barclay's first actions as Minister of War was to appoint a commission to draw up a new set of army regulations, the first since 1716. These new regulations, cumbrously titled "Regulations for the Functioning of a Large Army in the Field," but known for short, from the colour of the binding, as the "Yellow Book," were thorough, precise and concise, and they remained in force with few alterations until the 1870s.

In the meanwhile a low-key, chronic war with the Turks was draining Russia of essential war material, manpower and food. Barclay was well aware of this and made repeated efforts to get the Czar to make peace with the Turks. It was not until the Napoleonic invasion was imminent that, on May 28th, 1812 (N.S.) peace was made with Turkey at the Treaty of Bucharest.

In spite of three massive levies made between 1810 and 1812 Russia's military manpower needs were still unsatisfied. When the invasion[5] started Russia had approximately 200,000 men in arms, and the generals were still talking about pre-emptive strikes, which would have been fatal. The Russian generals' estimates of French strength ranged from 150,000 to 250,000; they would have been even more alarmed had they realised the invasion force numbered 500,000, with another 226,000 in reserve. Napoleon, on the other hand, was well aware of his numerical superiority. In a conversation with Count Balashov, Minister of Police, whom Alexander sent as an envoy, Napoleon said: "I know that a war between France and Russia is no trifling matter for either France or Russia. I have made extensive preparations, and my forces are three times as large as yours. I know as well as you do, perhaps better than you, the size of your army. You have 120,000 infantry, and 60 to 70 thousand cavalry. In a word, under 200,000 men all told. I have three times as many."[6]

It is difficult to ascertain exactly when and by whom the policy of retreat into the heart of Russia originated. It was not popular in Russia, and such was the developing spirit of patriotism amongst all classes of the people, that even talk of retreat was tantamount to treachery and *lèse majesté*. In the army opinions were sharply divided; but in general Barclay's plan, which had the support of Alexander, and which counselled defensive measures until such time as the enemy became weakened by disease (typhus had already taken its toll of Napoleon's forces) and his supply lines became attenuated to the point of non-effectiveness, was grudgingly accepted. After that, the Russian winter could take over. But none at this stage envisioned the abandonment and destruction of Moscow: even to have considered such a possibility would have been too damaging to morale.

That such a policy was being adopted was equally apparent to a number of Napoleon's entourage, but not to Napoleon himself. He was accustomed to dictating the time, venue, terrain and hence the probable outcome of his battles, and he was not prepared to listen to alternatives. Count Mathieu Dumas, Intendant Général of the Grande Armée, in a conversation with Barthold Georg Niebuhr as early as March 1812, summed up the latter's fears of the effectiveness of this policy. Niebuhr told him: "The Russian general Barclay de Tolly hoped to lure this formidable French army into the heart of Russia, even beyond Moscow, exhausting it, removing it far from its operational line, making it use up its resources and matériel, whilst husbanding Russia's reserves until, aided by the rigours of the climate, he could take the offensive and deal Napoleon a second Poltava on the banks of the Volga."[7] Dumas hastened to inform Marshal Berthier of this conversation, who no doubt transmitted it to Napoleon, but there is no record of the latter's reaction to this information.

On the night of June 24th, 1812, Napoleon crossed the Niemen. The Czar appointed Barclay commander of the First Western Army and Bagration of the Second Western Army. No commander-in-chief was appointed, the Czar presumably considering himself as such. Moreover the armies were about two hundred miles apart. Barclay's forces numbered only 92,000 men and Bagration's about 35,000; even had they been able to join and fight as one unit, the result would have been disastrous, and most historians agree that no other policy than retreat was possible. Napoleon was exasperated at the disappearance of the Russian forces and taunted Barclay with cowardice.

Napoleon's strategy was concentrated on preventing the First and Second Armies from joining together. Bagration was particularly hard pressed, being pursued by Marshal Davout with 70,000 men, Poniatowski with 35,000, Jerome Bonaparte with 16,000, Grouchy with 7,000 and Latour-Maubourg with 8,000. Bagration fought magnificently and managed to escape before the French pincers closed on him.

Meanwhile Barclay had fallen back on Vitebsk, and Bagration, avoiding Moghilev where the French expected him to make a stand, was defending the road to Dorogobuzh; neither could help the other. By this time relations between Barclay and Bagration had degenerated into open warfare on the part of the latter, who was daily irritated by and exasperated by what he considered pusillanimity, cowardice and even treason on Barclay's part. Vitebsk had been evacuated without any resistance and now Smolensk loomed on the horizon as the only place where a stand could be made before Moscow. On August 27th Bagration sent a note to Barclay: ". . . I humbly entreat Your Excellency not to retire from Smolensk, to try with all your strength to maintain your position . . . Your retirement from Smolensk would harm us greatly and could not be pleasing to the Tsar and the fatherland."[8]

The battle for Smolensk began at 6 a.m. on 5/17 August and continued throughout that day and the next. In the middle of the

Plan of Napoleon's Advance into and Retreat from Moscow

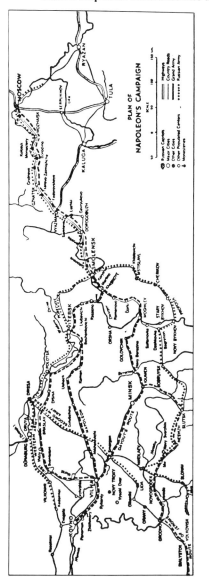

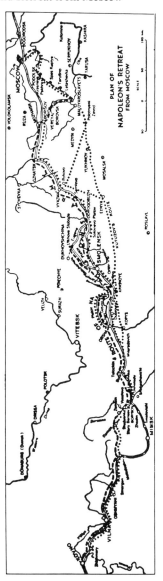

second night the Russian guns suddenly ceased firing and explosions of tremendous force began to shake the city. Barclay had ordered the destruction of the powder magazines and the evacuation of the city.

The retreating Russians, however, seized every opportunity to harass and counter-attack the advancing French. A Russian rearguard stopped Marshal Ney at Valutino and inflicted 7,000 casualties for the loss of 6,000. But the retreat continued: more and more were the people, the nobility especially, dismayed by the lack of success, as they saw it, of the Russian armies. Daily the bitter feud between Barclay and Bagration was aired, until Bagration finally asked to be relieved of his post and to fight as a common soldier anywhere so long as it was not under Barclay. On 16/28 August the Czar, yielding to pressure, appointed the retired Prince Kutuzov as commander-in-chief, who promptly endorsed Barclay and Bagration in their respective commands.

Kutuzov was 67 years old at the time and had only nine months to live. The Czar detested him and held him responsible for the ignominy of Austerlitz, though it was the Czar who had been in command on that fateful day. Years later someone tried to justify Kutuzov to him, saying the latter had tried to "restrain" the Czar from engaging in battle at Austerlitz. The Czar replied cuttingly: "He didn't restrain me enough."

Kutuzov was, however, popular with the army and with the generals who counted. Moreover he was "a real Russian," and not a "German" from Livonia. Even his sloth, his self-indulgence and reputation as a ladies' man were forgiven him because of his reputation for shrewdness, military strategy and his clout at headquarters with almost everyone except the Czar. He was considered the heir of the fabled Suvorov, even if he was too old and corpulent to mount a horse, and was habitually carried into battle in a carriage.

In fact nothing much altered; the retreat continued, but Kutuzov was shrewd enough to realise that he could not surrender Moscow without at least one battle. The battle of Borodino was, by any standards, one of the most sanguinary fought in modern times. Napoleon himself, many years later, recognised Borodino as the most terrible of all his battles: "The French showed themselves worthy of victory, and the Russians worthy of being invincible." The Russians lost 58,000 of their 112,000 men, and over 50,000 French, including 47 generals, were killed. Prince Bagration was severely wounded and died of his wounds three weeks later at the age of forty-six. He had taken part in twenty campaigns and wars, and more than 150 skirmishes and battles. Twenty-seven years later his body was brought back to Borodino and buried there. His command of the Second Army passed to Dokhturov who, at 56, was one of the oldest generals in the field. Barclay fought the whole day in a mood of suicidal despair. He appeared in full general's uniform, with plumed hat and resplendent with orders, and took no pains to conceal himself from the French.

After Borodino the retreat continued. Bennigsen believed he had found a good defensive position between the villages of Fili and Vorobevo, on the western outskirts of Moscow; but Barclay, Ermolov, Toll and others who had inspected the site roundly condemned it as untenable.

The decision whether to stand and fight or to abandon Moscow was taken at a meeting at Fili which was attended by Kutuzov, Konovnitsyn, Raevsky, Ostermann-Tolstoy, Bennigsen, Barclay de Tolly, Uvarov, Toll, Dokhturov and Ermolov. Bennigsen, who arrived late from inspecting the proposed battle site, opened the proceedings, without waiting for Kutuzov, by demanding bluntly "whether it is better to give battle before the walls of Moscow or to abandon the town to the enemy?" Kutuzov, echoing the observations of Barclay, Ermolov and Toll, summed up the position: "As long as the army remained in existence and as long as it was in condition to oppose the enemy, hope remained to finish off the enemy in the end; but once the army was destroyed, not only Moscow but all of Russia could be lost . . ." He then put the question: "Should one wait to be attacked in a disadvantaged position, or cede Moscow to the enemy?" He then turned to Barclay who restated the theme he had been so stubbornly defending ever since the invasion started; it was not any particular city but the whole fatherland that must be saved, hence the army must be preserved for this purpose. In his opinion the position was disastrous and the army risked being destroyed. In case of defeat, all not lost to the enemy in battle would be destroyed subsequently during retreat through Moscow. However painful the abandonment of Moscow might be, the seizure of the capital by the enemy could bring about the latter's downfall.

Bennigsen, who had been dismissed by Barclay after Smolensk, argued for an immediate attack on the French. His arguments were based more on emotional than practical considerations; the shame of abandonment of the capital, the loss of credibility and morale in the army, and the effect on public and foreign opinion. He also pointed out that the Russian army had received three regiments of reinforcements, whereas the French had none, and that, although the Russian army was disorganised and weakened since Borodino, the French army was in a similar or worse condition.

Barclay ignored the emotional appeal and replied only to Bennigsen's tactical proposals. It was now late night and too late for redeployment, and it was impossible to identify and disentangle units before morning, by which time the French would be upon them. "Although Kutuzov's opening statement leaves no doubt that he favoured abandoning Moscow, he had cannily left the question open for discussion, and it was Barclay who had come out with a clear proposition. According to Ermolov, 'Kutuzov was enchanted because he was not the first to propose the abandonment of Moscow and he could now put the blame on someone else.'"[9]

The discussion continued long into the night until Kutuzov brought it to an end. After a brooding pause he stated solemnly: "I am aware of the responsibility I am assuming, but I sacrifice myself for the good of our country. I hereby order the retreat."[10]

It is quite clear that, although Barclay, with his usual incisive commonsense and command of the tactical situation, had been the protagonist of the policy of retreat, it was the joint decision of the council of which Kutuzov, as commander-in-chief, had the final say. Bennigsen was playing a deep game, hoping that his stand would impress the Czar and maybe lead to his taking Kutuzov's place. Barclay, whose views were shared by Kutuzov, Ostermann-Tolstoy, Raevsky and Toll, had, at that time, no inkling that he would be held solely responsible for the decision.

The retreat continued. It was now mid-September and the weather still unbearably hot. Barclay, shivering with fever, remained in the saddle for eighteen hours, shepherding his troops through the streets of Moscow. His Cossack escort was active in preventing the thirsty troops from plundering liquor stores; and, according to Loewenstern, "It was due to such rigorous measures that General Barclay saved the army from disaster."[11] But even he could not be everywhere, and he had insufficient aides to carry out his orders, so that some six thousand troops "went AWOL" in the byways of Moscow, most of whom fell into the hands of the French.

The firing of Moscow has no place in an account of General Barclay de Tolly; but it is significant that Count Rostopchin, Governor of Moscow, had removed all fire-fighting equipment before the fire broke out, and he had left incendiary material in the hands of thousands of criminals let out of goal for this purpose.

It was not to be expected that the Czar would tamely accept the abandonment and destruction of Moscow. Reports were sent for, and Kutuzov shamelessly put the blame on Barclay, as did Bennigsen in his report to Arakcheev. Alexander, however, was experienced in reading between the lines and held Kutuzov fully responsible. He wrote later to Kutuzov. "Remember that you still owe an explanation to the offended fatherland for the loss of Moscow . . ."

After Moscow a strange lethargy settled on the Russian army. Although it was about to achieve numerical superiority over the French, and Kutuzov's main army now outnumbered the Grande Armée by some ten or fifteen thousand men, no serious operation was undertaken. The army retreated to Tarutino, some forty-six miles south of Moscow. Barclay remained in very poor health. Continuous bouts of fever racked and wasted his frame, while the sniping of his chief and colleagues behind his back further lowered his morale. Barclay applied for, and was surprisingly granted, sick leave. He took a dignified farewell of his adjutants. To Loewenstern he said: "The present is against me and I must yield to it. I foresee calmer times, times when consideration of what has happened will do justice to me . . . But I see clearly that my remaining here will stir up discord and discussion in the army. Therefore I must leave . . ."[12]

Barclay set off on a six months' leave by touring the country for two months. At a stop at Kaluga he sent off a detailed report to the Czar, vindicating his own actions by a detailed indictment of Kutuzov's and Bennigsen's mismanagement of the army. He also wrote gloomily to his wife, instructing her to sell everything that was superfluous but not his library, map collection and "certain papers in my desk," meaning especially letters from the Czar. He was accompanied by his doctor, Dr Batalin, and two aides, Major Reitz and Colonel Zakrevsky. From Kaluga to Tula, then east and north towards Vladimir province where Zakrevsky had his country house, they proceeded. It was here that an ugly incident occurred in which Barclay's disgrace reached its nadir. The people of Vladimir hated the French and all "foreigners." The day was a holiday and the people idle and drunk. A mob gathered shouting and clamouring for "that traitor" and threatening to lynch him. Zakrevsky, sword in hand, cleared the way and ordered his coachman to use his whip.

Barclay was unaware that Kutuzov's unscrupulous condemnation of him had been published in the Government Gazette. His fever continued unabated, to which deep depression was added, as he was nursed by Dr Batalin at Zakrevsky's house. The country needed a scapegoat for the disasters which had come upon it. Kutuzov's accusations went unchallenged and the Czar remained silent. The Czar had a valid excuse as he was trying to prod Kutuzov into some activity against the French; now was not the time to have a showdown with his commander-in-chief. Barclay's wounded feelings must take second place to the exigencies of the war.

On 6/18 October Kutuzov suddenly fell upon an unwary Murat near Tarutino and inflicted a severe defeat on him. On 7/19 October Napoleon started to retreat from Moscow; a bloody battle took place at Maloyaroslavets on 12/24 October and the thoroughly dispirited and disorganised Grande Armée began its miserable retreat through Mozhaisk, Borodino and Vyazma. The oft-repeated story that Napoleon was defeated by "General Winter" alone is a misrepresentation of the facts. The summer of 1812 was exceptionally hot and lingered on into a balmy autumn. Long before the first snows of winter descended on the stricken battlefields surrounding the approaches to a burned-out Moscow, the demoralised, sick and utterly dispirited Grande Armée had been, to all purposes, defeated. The severe winter which followed only finished the destruction which had started with the policy of retreat and preservation of the army so clearly pursued by Barclay.

The fine weather gradually got colder until the crossing of the Berezina River (13/25 to 16/28 November), when Napoleon once more demonstrated his genius by eluding capture and removing a large part of his forces across the river. But after November 28th heavy frosts set in and the second part of the retreat — from the Berezina to Vilna, reached on December 9th — was a calamity of unexampled severity, with temperatures dropping to nearly 40 degrees below zero.

On 24 November/6 December Napoleon took leave of his army in the little town of Smorgonia, handing over command of its remnants to Murat. He travelled in a sled with Caulaincourt, a Polish officer named Wonsonwicz, and a servant. He was completely calm. To him the whole Russian venture was but a lost gamble. "I left Paris intending not to carry the war beyond the Polish frontier. I was carried away by events. Perhaps I made a mistake in going to Moscow, perhaps I should not have stayed there so long; but there is only a step from the sublime to the ridiculous; it is up to posterity to judge."[13] Less than 30,000 men remained alive of the 420 thousand who had crossed the Niemen on June 24th, plus the 150,000 who had joined them later. The Russian losses were on a similar scale. Yet within a few months Napoleon could remark to Metternich: "A man such as I am is not much concerned over the lives of a million men."[14]

When he was well enough to resume his travels Barclay decided to return home to Beckhof via Novgorod. In Novgorod he completed a thirty-page confidential narrative of all the operations of the First Army since the beginning of Napoleon's invasion. He worked at this with enormous care, constantly referring to the mass of documents he had collected, with Zakrevsky checking the accuracy of details. This narrative was sent to Czar Alexander by the hand of Zakrevsky and acknowledged by the Czar who, carefully avoiding all reference to Kutuzov's published criticisms of Barclay, assured Barclay of his imperial master's continued interest in his career. He then turned to consider the severe strictures upon Barclay's conduct of military tactics, and ended with a promise to publish "an explicative justification of your conduct drawn from the materials you have sent me." But as the Czar was trying to get Kutuzov to pursue the French into Germany and had no wish to discourage his efforts, this promise was never kept. Instead an attempt was made to placate Barclay's injured *amour propre* by appointing him to the command of the Third Western Army which, having long felt itself neglected and unloved, welcomed the appointment of such a distinguished general with acclaim. The Third Western Army was really no more than a corps, consisting as it did of a mere 17,000 men, almost a third of whom had been detached by Kutuzov for other purposes. Moreover it lacked ammunition, boots and shirts, and, most seriously, heavy artillery. When he eventually obtained sufficient of the latter, Barclay laid siege to the fortress of Thorn which capitulated five days later — a modest enough success, but one which resulted in the capture of 57 cannon, plenty of ammunition and a liberal supply of foodstuffs at minimal cost in Russian lives or wounded. Kutuzov, always a realist, and accepting the upward rise of Barclay's popularity, publicly saluted him by ordering all the armies to celebrate a solemn thanksgiving for the capture of Thorn, while the Czar sent Barclay the diamond insignia of the Order of St Alexander Nevski and 50,000 roubles.

Meanwhile Napoleon, with the resilience which never failed to amaze his contemporaries, had rebuilt the Grande Armée to a strength of 225,000, partly with raw recruits, partly with seasoned campaigners recalled from Spain, and he soon appeared at Erfurt ready for the fray. The Russian armies, now commanded by Wittgenstein, had been too incautious in their rapid advance into Germany and were scattered too thinly over too wide a front. The Czar re-entered the field, interfering with Wittgenstein's command until the latter was content to sit under a tree and leave him to it. But when it was obvious that nothing short of full-scale withdrawal would save the Russian armies, the Czar ducked the responsibility of commanding Wittgenstein to order the retreat.

On 14/26 May, 1813, the Czar ordered Barclay to hand over command of his army to Blücher* and report to him personally; and on 19/31 May Barclay was appointed Commander-in-Chief of all the armies; at long last rewarded for his many years of unswerving loyalty and devotion to his sovereign.

The appointment was unexpectedly popular and indeed it had far-reaching consequences. The Czar refused the peace offers of Napoleon; thus encouraged, Austria decided to join the coalition against Napoleon.

But both sides were in a serious state of exhaustion. At Bautzen (8/20 May, 1813) the Russian forces were down to a mere 55,000 men, tired, out of ammunition and supplies; Napoleon was equally convinced that he needed a breathing space to build up his reserves, especially cavalry, in view of the threat of Austrian intervention.

During the truce which lasted from 21 May/2 June to 29 July/10 August the coalition against Napoleon was totally reorganised. Four armies came into being: the armies of Bohemia, of the North, of Silesia, and of Poland. The strongest was the Army of Bohemia, consisting of Austrian and Barclay's Russian and Prussian forces. It was agreed that the commander of this army should be supreme commander of all allied forces. Alexander was strongly tempted to appoint himself to the post, but regretfully turned it down; at the same time he was loath to relinquish the post to one of his own commanders (Barclay being the logical choice). In the end Prince Schwarzenberg of Austria was appointed, to the relief of Barclay, who would not have declined the post had it been offered to him, but who had already

---

*Commander of the Prussian Army

had the experience of being nominally commander-in-chief whilst his monarch interfered in the background. On this occasion the prospect of three monarchs (of Russia, Prussia and Austria) interfering was too much to contemplate with equanimity.

Throughout the German campaigns of 1813 Barclay was on his best behaviour. He had instructions from the Czar to obey Schwarzenberg implicitly, and his relations with the supreme commander remained stiff but correct. As the campaign proceeded, with much marching and countermarching over sodden roads, instead of Barclay it was Schwarzenberg who had cause to complain of the Czar's constant interference, until he was goaded into imploring the Emperor Francis to request the Czar to leave the field and take Barclay with him.

The muddle continued. In truth the armies were too large, too unwieldly and scattered over too large an area to make unified command easy or even possible. Barclay appreciated this and proceeded to carry out his own plan. The Russians under Count Ostermann-Tolstoy caught Vandamme left on the Bohemian side of the Erz Gebirge, and inflicted a severe defeat on the French First Corps at the battle of Kulm. "All through 17/29 August the battle raged around the villages of Priesten, Kulm and Nollendorf . . . Next morning Kleist, who had been following (with a 1721 map) the route Barclay had assigned to him, unexpectedly emerged from the mountains, his Prussian artillery shelling Vandamme's rear. The fate of the outnumbered French 1st Corps was sealed."[15] Vandamme, his chief of staff, many officers and ten thousand men were taken prisoner, and much booty and eighty-four cannons captured.

Although Count Ostermann-Tolstoy, who commanded the forces directly opposed to Vandamme, was the real hero of the day (he had his left arm torn off by a cannon-ball and had to leave the field), it was Barclay's strategy which led to the first large defeat of the enemy since the retreat from Moscow. This battle was justly claimed by Barclay as "the greatest victory over the French ever achieved." Barclay received from the Czar the highest of all military decorations, the Order of St George First Class, and from the Austrian Emperor the Commander's Cross of the Knighthood of Maria Theresa.

The victory was a great boost to the morale of the allies; henceforward the same contenders remained together to the end, with the addition of one further defector from Napoleon's ranks — Bavaria.

By October 1813 the allied forces, numbering 300,000 men and 1500 cannon, were advancing on Leipzig where Napoleon had encamped with 200,000 men and 916 guns. The Battle of Leipzig, also known as the Battle of the Nations, lasted from 4/16 to 7/19 October and resulted in a total defeat of the French. The Russian losses were enormous: 800 officers and about 20,000 men, three times those of the Austrians and far exceeding those of the Prussians. The French lost 38,000 killed and wounded, and another 15,000 taken prisoner, including 36 generals. Barclay was made a Count on the field of battle by the Czar.

But once again Napoleon slipped away and, despite prodigious losses, he could still command armies of over 100,000 men scattered throughout Europe. Alexander of Russia and the Emperor Francis of Austria had a race to get to Frankfurt first, which Alexander won by twenty-four hours. In December 1813 and January 1814 the allied forces crossed the Rhine in three places, Barclay being across early in January.

Barclay expected a quick end to the war; but Napoleon, although greatly weakened, was still a potent force to contend with. Reduced to the command of only 85,000 troops, mostly raw recruits, lacking horses and muskets, Napoleon inflicted a serious defeat on Blücher at Brienne on 17/29 January; but the Allies took their revenge three days later at La Rothière, two miles south of Brienne. Napoleon, however, had plenty of fight left. Blücher had imprudently divided his forces into four columns which Napoleon, enormously outnumbered in total troops, fell upon piecemeal. During February and March the Allies seemed rooted in immobility and unable to decide what to do: whether to advance on Paris, only forty miles distant from the leading units, or to try to defeat Napoleon in the field.

However, in the end Napoleon was not defeated in the field. The defections of Murat, the innkeeper's son whom he had made King of Naples, of his step-son Eugène Beauharnais, and of Marshal Augereau, although bitter pills to swallow, did not deter Napoleon from his determination to rid French soil of her enemies. The last straw was the pusillanimity of the people of Paris, who put the safety of their persons, furniture and jewellery before the needs of *la patrie*, and capitulated without even a token resistance. Napoleon was still thrashing around in western Europe like a wounded stag at bay when his brother, Joseph, who as Lieutenant-General of France was responsible for the defence of Paris along with Napoleon's old enemy, Talleyrand, made a truce with Czar Alexander and handed over the keys of Paris. With the fall of Paris Barclay was made Field-Marshal.

Then came Napoleon's abdication, exile to Elba, escape from Elba,Waterloo, and final banishment to St Helena.

It was after the first fall of Paris that Barclay paid a visit to England. He was ill at ease with the adulation of the crowds, but fortunately Blücher and the giant Cossack, General Platov, were the recipients of most of the attention. It was during this visit that he met his kinsman Robert Barclay, who told him that Towie Castle was for sale. It is clear from the conversation as recorded by Hubert Barclay, the family recorder, that Barclay de Tolly was aware of his descent from the Barclays of Towie. As to acquiring Towie Castle (which he could by now well afford), he passed up the opportunity; his destiny had been, and always would be, inseparably bound to that of Russia's, and he had no desire for any overseas possessions. Also his health was deteriorating, and he longed for nothing more than peace and rest. Back in Russia he applied for leave, which was granted, but before he could avail himself of the respite, Napoleon had escaped from Elba and Barclay found himself once more in the field, leading a Russian army of 200,000 men towards France. He had just reached the Rhine when he received the news of Napoleon's decisive defeat at Waterloo. Barclay's fighting days were over.

He was already one of the most decorated men in Europe. In addition to a number of orders from his sovereign, and those of Austria, Prussia and other allies, he now received the Grand Cordon of the Legion of Honour; on August 18th, 1815, the Duke of Wellington, on behalf of the Prince Regent, invested him with the Order of the Garter.

On September 10th, in brilliant late summer sunshine, a grand review of Russian troops was held before the Emperor Francis of Austria, King Frederick William of Prussia, and an international array of princes, field-marshals, generals and diplomats. Never before had there been such a parade, in which over 150,000 men and officers, including 87 generals, took part. The parade stretched out as far as the eye could see and much farther than the voice could carry, so that commands were given by cannon and musket salvoes. Men who had been in the field only two or three days before presented themselves immaculately turned out; the drill was precise and perfectly executed, no matter which unit was performing. The Duke of Wellington was heard to remark that he had "never imagined that an army could reach such absolute perfection," while Admiral Sir Stanley Smith said the review "was a lesson given by Russia's Emperor to other nations."

It was the zenith of Barclay's glory; more decorations were heaped upon him, and the City of London presented him with a sword studded with precious stones. At the end of the ceremony promotions and citations were read out by the Czar, who singled out Barclay for special mention and named him "kniaz," usually translated as prince.

On his return to St Petersburg just before Christmas 1815, Barclay was given a surprise reception by his grateful monarch, who presented him with a fully equipped house, including a *maître d'hôtel*, kitchen staff, and carriages, before which was drawn up a guard of honour from the Czar's favourite Semenovsky Lifeguards. Barclay was embraced by the Czar and kissed on both cheeks by the Dowager Empress. Three days of celebrations followed — receptions, dinners and a great regimental banquet at which the Czar, remembering it was Barclay's birthday (his fifty-fourth), proposed a toast to his health.

After these heady events, the next few years were rather an anti-climax for Field-Marshal Prince Michael Barclay de Tolly. In 1818, at 57 a prematurely aged man, he was thoroughly jaded and spent. He applied for leave to enable him to seek spa treatment in Bavaria. The Czar granted him two years' leave and generously threw in 100,000 roubles towards his expenses. On 28 April/10 May, Barclay and his party set off from Beckhof in four carriages. With Barclay and Auguste were their sons Magnus (Max), now aged 20, their adopted daughter Christel (daughter of Barclay's sister Christine), a lively and precocious girl of 15, a nephew and niece of Auguste, a doctor, an adjutant and servants.

But the journey did nothing to restore Barclay's health; and two weeks later, near the East Prussian town of Insterburg, he could no longer continue. On 13/25 May, 1818, he was taken to a nearby house and that evening, sitting in an armchair, he died.

A gentle tug-of-war ensued between the Czar and Auguste for his body. The Czar desired a grand state burial in St Petersburg's Kazan Cathedral which was dedicated to the war of 1812, and where Kutuzov and other heroes were buried, but Auguste wanted him buried at Beckhof. Auguste won and now sleeps beside him there.

Max died childless and the title passed to the eldest grandson of Barclay's sister Christine, the son of his niece and foster-daughter Christel, Alexander Magnus von Weymarn, who took the title of Prince

Barclay de Tolly-Weymarn; his last descendant died in Sweden in 1964.

It was Tolstoy whose adulation of Kutuzov and suppression of all mention of Barclay de Tolly in *War and Peace* rendered history so lamentable a disservice. Today Soviet historians are slowly coming to a more favourable revaluation of Barclay — a process which started with the publication, in 1836, of Pushkin's poem, *The Commander.*

Although *War and Peace* is a work of fiction, and although many of the characters are fictitious, the military commanders are all given their proper names (e.g. Miloradovich, Bagration, Konovnitsyn, Vasilievich, Davydov, Tuchkov, Platov, etc.), with the sole exception of Colonel Denis, who appears as Colonel Vasili Dmitrich Denisov. Could Tolstoy have confused Colonel Davidov's forename and patronymic and transferred them as forename and surname to this character?

Barclay de Tolly stands out in bold relief as the only commander of senior rank who is conspicuously absent from *War and Peace;* this cannot but be deliberate. The translator of the standard English edition, Aylmer Maude, is merely repeating the (then) current denigration of Barclay when, in the introduction,[16] he wrote: "It is an understanding of their heroism, sympathy with it, and belief in it, that constitutes the greatness of Bagration and Kutuzov; as lack of understanding of it, disregard of it, and even contempt of it, constitutes the misfortune and pettiness of Barclay de Tolly and Speransky."

Josselson on the penultimate page of his book[17] referred to Tolstoy's misleading masterpiece" thus:

"Pushkin was killed in a duel while the controversy was still seething. If he had lived it is tempting to think he might have written an epic poem where Barclay figured — a poetic counterpart of *War and Peace:* Pushkin did conceive of Barclay as 'a highly poetical figure.' But by itself "The Commander" cannot offset the effect of Tolstoy's misleading masterpiece. Waves of xenophobia again and again have washed out the chances of a true rehabilitation of Barclay among the Russian people. Between waves, however, scholars both Tsarist and Soviet have tried to render him his due, and among these there is hardly one who has not referred to 'The Commander'."

The one person who was never in doubt of his loyalty, devotion, and utter commitment to the cause of his sovereign and his country, was Czar Alexander I, even if at times, from consideration of overall strategy and public relations, he could not afford to come out fullheartedly in approbation of his devoted servant. The honours heaped upon him by the Czar, but above all the personal affection shown by him, were sufficient reward; history's reassessment could not be anticipated and the plaudits of the crowd were never desired by the "foreigner" whose entire life and energies were spent in personal service to his sovereign in the cause to which both were committed.

CHAPTER 8 — BIBLIOGRAPHY

1. Barclay de Tolly, like Charles Cameron *(vide infra)*, had to wait more than a century and a half before he was honoured with a full-length biography. This has finally appeared as *The Commander — a Life of Barclay de Tolly*, by Michael Josselson and Diana Josselson (Oxford University Press) in 1980. This is a work of great scholarship and painstaking research, without which it is impossible for any author to write an adequate account of Barclay de Tolly. The present author's indebtedness to this biography is obvious and total.

2. *Chambers' Biographical Dictionary*, p. 67.

3. Burton, J. Hill, *The Scot Abroad*, Vol. ii, pp. 118-9.

4. Josselson, M. and D., *The Commander*, p. 7.

5. There is, of course, a vast bibliography of Napoleon's invasion of Russia; the works listed here are only the main sources used by the present author:

   Tarlé, Eugène, *Napoleon's Invasion of Russia, 1812*, George Allen & Unwin, London, 1942.

   Brett-James, Antony, *1812: Eyewitness Accounts of Napoleon's Defeat in Russia*, Book Club Associates, London, 1973.

   Cronin, Vincent, *Napoleon*, History Book Club, London, 1971.

   Butterfield, H., *Napoleon*, Collier Books, U.S.A., 1962.

   Jenkins, Michael, *Arakcheev*, Faber & Faber, London, 1969.

6. Tarlé, E., *Napoleon's Invasion of Russia, 1812*, p. 48.

7. Josselson, *op. cit.*, p. 89.

8. Tarlé, E., *op. cit.*, p. 102.

9. Josselson, *op. cit.*, p. 150.

10. Josselson, *op. cit.*, p. 151.

11. Josselson, *op. cit.*, p. 152.

13 Tarlé, E., *op. cit.*, p. 282.

14. Brett-James, Antony, *op. cit.,* p. 265.

15. Josselson, *op. cit.,* p. 180.

16. Tolstoy, Leo, *War and Peace,* transl. by Louise and Aylmer Maude, World Classics Edition, Oxford University Press, 1922. In 3 Vols.: Vol. i. Introduction (by Aylmer Maude), p. xiv.

17. Josselson, op. cit., pp. 216-7.

CHAPTER 9

Scots Romantics in Russia

CHARLES CAMERON (1743-1812)

It is difficult to explain the extraordinary neglect of this very gifted architect, whose memory was in almost total eclipse for over a century after his death.* Three landmarks in his resurrection should be noted: In the first two decades of this century memory of him was stirred by a group of mostly Russian enthusiasts, notably Georges Loukomski, who published, in 1943, an illustrated monograph of Cameron's life and work in Russia;[1] secondly, by the promotional energies of Professor D. Talbot Rice and his wife, Tamara, who, together with A. A. Tait, organised an exhibition of his work in 1967-68;[2] and thirdly, by the publication of a biography of Cameron by Isobel Rae[3] in 1971. This last, a monument to painstaking and accurate research, brought to light many previously unknown facts about his life, especially of his early days, and corrected many erroneous assumptions.

Before Miss Rae's book, Cameron's origins were obscure and allegedly romantic; it was thought he was related to Cameron of Lochiel; was a nephew of Miss Jenny Cameron, an ardent Jacobite; was possibly one of the three unaccounted for sons of Dr Archibald Cameron, a Jacobite physician who was "out" with the '45 and was executed in 1753; was at the Court of the "Chevalier de St George" (the old Pretender) in Paris; and suchlike romantic fables. But Miss Rae has proved conclusively that he was the son of one Walter Cameron, a carpenter and builder of London, who gave the name of *his* father as "Archibald Cameron, late of Edinburgh, gentleman and deceased." None of these men appear in the family records of the Camerons of Lochiel.

He was born in London, probably in Bolton Street, where his father

---

* He is not mentioned in the DNB, the *Biographical Dictionary of Eminent Scotsmen,* in A. F. Steuart's *Scottish Influences in Russian History,* or in any 19th century reference book that I have consulted.

lived from 1740 to 1747. Earlier records give his date of birth as 1741 or 1742, but Miss Rae suggests as more likely 1743, as he was apprenticed to his father in 1760 and it was customary in the Carpenters' Company to end a seven-years' apprenticeship at the age of 24. However ardently he might proclaim his Jacobite partisanship, the household he was brought up in was absolutely loyal to George I: no trouble during the '45, no exile and no residence at the Court of the Pretender for Walter's son, who, in fact, lived under his father's roof in White Horse Street (whither Walter moved in 1747) until he was over 30. There is no record of his education, but in his book, *The Baths of the Romans,* he shows a good knowledge of the classics and of the French language. He also studied under Isaac Ware, master of the Carpenters' Company from 1763 to 1766, whose book, *The Complete Body of Architecture* (1756), would be known to him. At this time there was no clear distinction between the functions of carpenter, builder and architect, and his training under Ware was probably thorough in all these disciplines.

At a time when everyone — builders and architects — was a Palladian, it was necessary for Cameron to go to Rome. He was definitely there in 1768, professing Jacobite sympathies as it was then fashionable to do *outside Britain,* but too late ever to have met the Old Pretender, James Francis Edward Stuart, who died in 1766, aged 78 years. He probably did meet the French architect Clérisseau, who fought with everyone except Robert Adam, who was his pupil. He must have returned to Britain as he exhibited drawings in London in 1767 and 1772.

In 1772 he produced his book, *The Baths of the Romans,* the first edition[4] of which was only fifty copies, dedicated to Lord Bute, who probably subscribed to its publication. In addition to his own drawings, he drew heavily on engravings of Palladio's unfinished sketches which, so he said, Ware "had left imperfect at his death."[5] It was this book, probably brought to her attention by Reiffenstein, Director of the Russian Academy, which caused the Empress Catherine to invite Cameron to Russia. On August 23rd, 1779, she wrote to Baron Grimm: "A présent je me suis emparée de Mister Cameron, écossais de nation, Jacobite de profession, grand dessinateur, nourri d'antiquités, connu par un livre sur les bains romains."

Cameron arrived in Russia in the summer of 1779. At first he lived in Chernyshov's house in St Petersburg, but shortly after moved to

Tsarskoye Selo, where he was given a studio in Joseph Busch's apartments above the orangery. Busch* was an English gardener of the school of Lancelot Brown, who was imported to design gardens for Catherine. In 1784 Cameron married Catherine, one of Busch's four daughters.

The Empress had an itch to build. She wrote to Grimm in 1779: "Vous saurez que la fureur de bâtir est plus forte que jamais et guère tremblement de terre n'a plus renversé de bâtiments que nous n'en élevons;" and "La fureur de bâtir est chose diabolique, cela dévore de l'argent et plus on bâtit, plus on veut bâtir; c'est une maladie comme l'ivrognerie." But as in the period 1765 to 1770, by strict economies and by opening up trade with China (Treaty of Kyakhta, 1768), Catherine had turned a deficit of seven million roubles into a surplus of five-and-a-half millions, perhaps she felt entitled to spend some of it on her own projects.

Catherine recognised the limitations of Russian architects, so she established the Institute of Laureats of the Academy of Fine Arts, in order to arrange for young architects to study in Rome and Paris. It was thus that Neelov and his son, who were attached to Tsarskoye Selo Palace, Starov, Bazhenov and others, were sent abroad. Charles Louis Clérisseau (1721-1820) designed on a vast scale some fantastic projects, but nothing he designed in Russia was ever executed, though Catherine's later architects, Cameron and Quarenghi, derived much inspiration from his drawings.[6]

Cameron's first work was to alter, add to and internally decorate Tsarskoye Selo Palace, which had been built for the Empress Elizabeth by Rastrelli, and whose facade was twelve hundred feet long. Having tested him by getting him to build a little pavilion in the park, Catherine gave him his head. Indeed, throughout his long association with her he had her entire confidence and a remarkable lack of disagreement, though protocol dictated that he should consult her only through a third person. So from 1780 to 1785 he was hard at work altering and lightening Tsarskoye Selo, adding the Agate Pavilion and the Cameron Gallery (the only building in the world, it is believed, to be named for its architect), and decorating its interior in the Pompeiian style which Clérisseau and Robert Adam had popularised. Later, when Catherine

---

* Busch introduced "Russian" comfrey into England.

was too old and heavy to walk up the steps to the "Kameronova Gallereya," he added an inclined ramp (Pente douce) to assist her.

Cameron found Russian workmen thieving, lazy and incompetent, and more used to working with wood than stone; so he imported labour from Scotland. As a result of an advertisement in the Edinburgh *Evening Courant* of January 21st, 1784, about sixty or seventy workmen with their families sailed for Russia. Later another seventy or so were asked for, which caused the British Ambassador at St Petersburg to write to the Marquis of Carmarthen expostulating against the loss to British industry of so many skilled workmen. He also brought out the only two other Scottish architects known to have worked under Catherine: Adam Menelaws and William Hastie. Pavlovsk however is the first building Cameron designed *in toto* and is his masterpiece. Built for Catherine's son Paul, it was a thank-offering on the birth, in 1777, of her grandson, Alexander, which secured the dynasty. Here, however, Cameron's harmonious relations with his employer ran out. He had to put up with constant interference, arguments and acrimonious correspondence with Paul's wife, the Grand Duchess Marie Fedorovna, who detested her mother-in-law. It was sufficient for Catherine to approve to earn the disapproval of the Grand Duchess. Her tastes were not Catherine's or Cameron's. Fortunately Paul and his wife were away visiting Paris during much of the planning stage. "It may be that Catherine and Cameron, during those fourteen months when they worked together over the plans for the new palace during the absence of its future owners, were thinking too much in terms of their own taste and not making sufficient allowance for the modern outlook of the younger generation."[7]

Cameron was accused of not obeying instructions, extravagance and dilatoriness; but he would not give way. A reasonable enough man in other ways, he was adamant when his professional skill and taste were called into question. Pavlovsk was built as *he* wanted it.

In anticipation of Catherine's progress to the Crimea in 1786-87, Cameron was given the job of restoring the Khan's palace at Bakhtchisarai, "a compound of Moorish, Arabian, Chinese and Turkish architecture, with fountains, little gardens, paintings, gilt ornaments and inscriptions in every corner."[8] He was given one year to complete the task, which he did.

On his return from the Crimea in 1787, Cameron found he had been superseded at Pavlosk by his assistant, Brenna, by order of the Director of Building Operations, a German, Kuechelbecker, with whom he had had many arguments. So he employed his time on the unfinished Church of St Sophia.

Catherine died suddenly in 1796, two days after suffering a stroke. Cameron was dismissed as architect at Tsarskoye Selo and had his "grace and favour" house taken from him. Throughout the short reign of Czar Paul he was largely unemployed and was driven by necessity to sell his books in 1798. He submitted designs in a competition for the Cathedral of Our Lady of Kazan in St Petersburg, but those of Voronykhin were preferred on the recommendation of Count Stroganov, on whose estates, it is said, the Russian architect had been born as a serf. Voronykhin was also appointed to work with Brenna at Pavlovsk.

The only work Cameron is known definitely to have done during Paul's reign, probably at the request of the Empress, was the last of his garden pavilions: the beautiful little Pavilion of the Three Graces (1800). Paul was murdered in 1801 by a court camarilla led by Count Pahlen, and his son Alexander came to the throne. In 1802 Alexander I appointed Cameron Architect-in-Chief to the Admiralty. Cameron, by now somewhat soured, haggled, demanded and received a salary of 1500 roubles and the "restoration in full of all his privileges to which twenty-three years' service entitled him." Further, remembering the trouble he had had with Kuechelbecker, he stipulated that he would make his reports only to the Emperor. Thereafter he worked on hospitals and barracks at Kronstadt, and Admiralty buildings in St Petersburg; but in 1803 he returned to Pavlovsk which had been severely damaged by fire. During his absence his work at Kronstadt was taken over by Zakharov who, although twenty years younger than Cameron, predeceased him.

Cameron died in the spring of 1812. With the country's attention distracted by Napoleon's sabre-rattling in Europe, no one seems to have noticed his death. The Czar was informed on April 16th, and in June a laconic obituary notice in the *Gentleman's Magazine* stated: "At St Petersburg, Charles Cameron, Esq., formerly architect to the Court of Russia;" but no date was given. His books and other effects were sold by an auctioneer with the ominous name of Jean Grabit. He left a wife and no children. His wife received a pension of 1500 roubles from Czar Alexander and died in 1817.

This is no place for a critical appraisal of his work. He will live by his work at Tsarskoye Selo and Pavlovsk, and other buildings he designed for Catherine the Great. Though he would have been the first to admit his debt to Palladio and Robert Adam, his work improved as he developed away from his Italian roots, under the beneficent encouragement of his royal and sympathic patron.

In Russia he found an exciting new range of materials: polychromic marble, jasper, malachite, lapis-lazuli and porphyry; and, anticipating Lalique by a century, a milky glass. Wedgwood plaques, bronze and gilt, were all used to great effect. His earlier work could occasionally be over-elaborate, as in the Salle des Arabesques at Tsarskoye Selo. Perhaps the combination of youth, opportunity and a wealthy patron were too intoxicating to a young man who, although he proudly signed his book "Charles Cameron, Architect," had not, at that time, a single building to his credit. His subsequent work illustrates his development from Baroque to Neo-Classical, founded firmly on the classic art of Greece and Rome. "The influence of Palladio and of the other great Italian masters upon Inigo Jones and Sir William Chambers, that special phase of classicism which may be seen in London, was transmitted to Russia by Cameron, and that is his special distinction."[9]

In fact, it may be said that Cameron cured Russia of its obsession with the Baroque. It is possible that his fame as a decorator overshadowed, or detracted from, his importance as an architect; but that does not explain why he was allowed to sink into oblivion until rescued by a group of amateur and predominantly Russian artists more than a century after his death. Through the good offices of those noted at the start of this chapter he has been rescued, and not by British architects by whom, in 1791, he was blackballed when his name was put forward for honorary membership of the recently formed Architect's Club, which "particularly wished we might have only men of moral character and high reputation." How Cameron's "moral character" fell short of the rigid code of the Architects' Club is not easy to see at this distance of time; his reputation as an architect, however, thanks to his resurrectionists, stands higher today than ever in his lifetime or for a century and a half after his death.

MIKHAIL YURIEVICH LERMONTOV (1814-1841)

This tragic young man, one of Russia's leading lyric poets, some say second only to Pushkin, was of Scottish descent. His father, Captain Yurie Lermontov, claimed descent from a Captain George Learmont, a Scottish adventurer who entered Russian service in the early seventeenth century; and who was said to be descended from Thomas of Erceldoune, also known as Thomas the Rymer, whom Hector Boece was the first to name as Thomas Learmont of Earlstoun. (Earlstoun is a village in Berwickshire, about thirty miles from Berwick.) Robert Learmont, the last of the line claiming descent from Thomas the Rhymer, died unmarried about 1840.

That Lermontov was not only aware of his Scottish descent, but also felt some innate empathy for the land of his forefathers, is expressed in two of his poems: *The Coffin of Ossian* (1830) and *A Wish* (1831). In the former he wrote:

> Under a curtain of fog,
> Under the stormy skies, amid the plains,
> There stands the tomb of Ossian
> In the mountains of my Scotland.
> Towards it my flagging spirit flies
> To breathe again its native air,
> To seek again a second life
> From that neglected grave! . . .

Nostalgia for his ancestral origins is the very essence of *A Wish*. The author is indebted to the late Victor Ramzes, of the USSR Writers' Union, Moscow, for the following translation:

> Why am I not a bird, or a raven of the steppe.
> That has just flown over me?
> Why can't I soar in the skies
> And love freedom only?
>
> > I would rush to the West, to the West,
> > Where a field of my forefathers blooms,
> > Where their ashes rest
> > In an empty castle on the foggy slopes.
>
> There is a family coat of arms on an ancient wall
> And their rusted sword.
> I would hover over it
> And brush the dust away.
>
> > I would pluck a string of a Scottish harp
> > And the sound would rise to the dome.
> > I would listen to it alone
> > Until the last note died out.

> But dreams are in vain and prayers powerless
> Against the stern laws of destiny.
> Between me and the hills of my fatherland
> Stretch the long rollers of the seas.

> The last offspring of valiant warriors
> Is fading amid alien snows.
> I was born here, but my soul belongs elsewhere . . .
> Oh, I wish I were a raven of the steppes!

His father was an army officer and a small squire. His mother was an Arseniev and her mother, née Stolypin, was a wealthy landowner and a considerable figure in Moscow society who looked down on Captain Lermontov as a poor relation with whom her grandaughter had made a *mésalliance.* The future poet's mother died when he was only three years old, and his grandmother Mme Arsenieva took the boy off to her country estate.

He remained in his grandmother's care until he was twelve: spoiled, indulged, and lacking any company of his own age. He read omnivorously, chiefly of the late eighteenth century romantics and, like so many of his generation, fell totally under the spell of Byron. He started writing poetry at the age of thirteen. He was a shy, self-conscious and sensitive child who developed, in a society of numerous, chiefly female, cousins and acquaintances, an arrogance and a vanity as a carapace to cover the raw places of his morbid sensitivity. He began to model himself on Childe Harold, magnifying his adolescent puppy-loves into *grands amours,* and wallowing in self-pity over his circumstances (such as his mother's early death and separation from his father).

He entered Moscow University in 1830, stuck it for two years only and left in order to enter St Petersburg University, but, for some reason which does not appear, changed his mind and entered the School of Ensigns of the Guard of Cavalry Cadets, which was a depository for gilded youths in receipt of handsome allowances from indulgent relatives. He did not like St Petersburg or the School, but adapted himself, suppressing his self-consciousness under a veneer of smart cynicism. Romantic love, the dominant sentiment of his Moscow days, was concealed under a callous and calculated libertinism. The only poems he wrote during this period were too coarse to be printed, but earned him a cheap popularity among his fellow cadets. In 1834 he was given a commission in the Hussars of the Guard.

His first major poem was on the tragic and unnecessary death of Pushkin, who was killed in a duel in 1837. In this poem, which was said to have been on the streets within twenty-four hours of his receiving the news of Pushkin's death, words tumbled out of him in a cascade of despair at the death of what he considered Russia's greatest glory, rage at the "alien murderer" (Pushkin's assailant was a Frenchman, Baron Georges d'Anthès), scorn and hatred of the base and unworthy courtiers who had allowed a foreigner to strike down the poet. The poem, of course, could not be printed but nevertheless achieved a wide circulation, and its authorship was immediately recognised. Lermontov was arrested, court-martialled, dismissed from the Guard and transferred to a regiment of the line in the Caucasus. His sentence however was light and within a year he was back in St Petersburg, but this time as a well-known poet and literary lion. His stay in the Caucasus produced a long tale in verse, *Hadji Abrek,* and several other poems. He then started on his main work, a novel, *A Hero of Our Times,* which brought him instant recognition.

In 1840 he fought a duel, over some trivial matter, with M. de Barante, son of the French Ambassador. No blood was spilt, but Lermontov was arrested and sent to the Caucasus again. This time he took part in several campaigns and proved a brilliant and brave officer. He was mentioned in despatches and recommended twice for awards but, not being popular in official circles, he received nothing.

In the summer of 1841 he went to Pyatigorsk, a watering place in the Caucasus, and there met several friends including a Major Martynov. Martynov and Lermontov courted the same young lady. Lermontov made Martynov's life most unpleasant with his sneering and teasing in the presence of the lady. Martynov bore it for a while but eventually challenged him. The duel with pistols took place on July 15th, 1841; Martynov fired first and the last of Russia's lyric poets fell dead on the spot.

It is impossible for anyone not conversant with the Russian language to pass judgement on Lermontov's work as a poet. Most Russian authorities agree that there are no good translations of Russian poetry into any other language. Comparisons of Lermontov's and Pushkin's work are inevitable. Pushkin is still one of the most widely read authors in Russia today, in prose as well as in verse; and Lermontov, after suffering various ups and downs of popularity, has recently made a strong come-back. Whilst both owe much of their inspiration to

Byron, both moved away from this base; probably it is to Shelley that Lermontov bears the closest resemblance.

Pushkin was better educated, especially in the classics and in French. His language was more precise, controlled and less extravagant, his line shorter and more terse. Lermontov's reputation rests on the output of his last four years or so. As one critic sums them up: "Lermontov's mellifluousness is more purely musical than Pushkin's. It is not tempered by the precise classical training of the older poet."[10]

However, there are other striking parallels in their lives. There are some people who seem to be born for a rendezvous with violent death. In the works of both poets the probability of early and violent death is foreshadowed. In Pushkin's *Evgeny Onegin,* Onegin kills his best friend, Lensky, in a duel. In Lermontov's *A Hero of Our Times,* Pechorin, the Lermontov-like hero, kills the fop Grushnitsky in a duel — a reversal of what might be expected, however. Both poets lost their lives over a woman; in both cases a woman who did not really mean very much to either of them. (Baron d'Anthès was suspected of paying too much attention to Pushkin's wife, but she was a frivolous, empty-headed girl from whom the poet had largely drifted away.)

Turgenev saw Lermontov at a ball in 1839. "There was something fatal and tragic about Lermontov. His tanned face and dark eyes evinced a grim and evil force, passion, pensiveness and disdain. His fixed and oppressive gaze was in discord with the tender, almost childish shape of his full mouth. His stocky torso, his cavalry legs and big head set on sloping shoulders did not create a pleasant impression. But it was impossible not to feel the force, even the might, of this man."[11]

One of Lermontov's poems, *Laugh Not at My Prophetic Grief,* contains these lines: "I shall not find fame, glory or happiness. The fatal hour will strike: I shall fall covered with blood, and envious enmity will blast my genius in its bud; and I shall perish, leaving never a trace of my hopes and torments."[14]

Prophetic, but not accurate. He would probably never find happiness. His hopes and torments live in his works. Fame and glory continued to accrue to him after his death. Who knows what he might not subsequently have achieved? He was 27 when he died.

SIR ROBERT KER PORTER (1777-1842)

The Porters were a remarkably talented family who originally came from Durham. Their mother, left a widow in 1779 with five children, returned to her native Edinburgh, where Walter Scott was a frequent visitor to the house, and subsequently removed to London (before 1803), where the family lived in a house once tenanted by Sir Joshua Reynolds. There, through Robert, they met the artists Benjamin West, Flaxman and Northcote, and writers Hannah More and Mrs Barbauld.

Robert had two elder brothers, Dr William Ogilvie Porter and Colonel John Porter. He, the fourth child, was sandwiched between two sisters, Jane (1776-1850) and Anna Maria (1780-1832), the latter being born after her father's death.

It is alleged that Jane Porter, in her childhood, met Flora Macdonald and was inspired by her to write historical novels. Her first romance, *Thaddeus of Warsaw,* appeared in four volumes in 1803; and by 1810 it had reached its ninth edition, being translated into German, and had fallen into the hands of Kosciusko, the Polish patriot, who wrote Jane his expressions of admiration and approval. A tenth edition was dedicated to Kosciusko, and subsequent editions appeared in 1831, 1840, 1860 and 1868.

Her second work, *The Scottish Chieftains,* in five volumes, appeared in 1810. Founded on the life of William Wallace, it had an immense success in Scotland, was translated into German and Russian, and was reprinted nine times between 1816 and 1882. It is one of the few historical novels written before *Waverley* that have lived. There is no truth, however, in the legend that she inspired Sir Walter Scott to write historical novels; or vice versa. She wrote several other works and a few unsuccessful plays.

Anna Maria Porter also wrote novels: *The Hungarian Brothers,* in three volumes, was published in 1807; *Don Sebastian, or the House of Braganza,* in four volumes, in 1809; and *The Knight of St John,* in three volumes,1817, which had the distinction of being the book which Prince Leopold read to Princess Charlotte before her death in childbed at Claremont in 1817.

Robert started painting at a very early age, and in 1790 Benjamin West, impressed by his precocity, secured him admission to Somerset House as an academy student.. At one time he was employed as a scene painter at the Lyceum Theatre, London, but his main interest was in historical pictures and altar-pieces. In 1798 he painted an altar-piece on the subject of "St John Preaching in the Wilderness" for St John's College, Cambridge, in which he portrayed his sisters, Jane as

Faith and Anna Maria as Hope. The DNB is in error in stating that the picture is still there.*

In 1800 he pioneered a new style of panorama painting with his *Grand Historical Picture of the Storming of Seringapatam, on May 4th, 1799.* This enormous canvas, 120 feet long and consisting of 2550 square feet of canvas, containing several hundred figures and "designed from the most authentic and correct Information relative to the Scenery of the Place, Costume of the Soldiery, and the various Circumstances of the Attack," was said to have been painted in six weeks. After successful exhibition in London, the panorama, which was fan-shaped and apparently shown as an early example of a "moving picture," being suspended on two giant rollers, was taken on tour and exhibited "in a New Temporary Building, erected for that purpose, in Ingram Street, Glasgow," at an admission fee of one shilling. The descriptive pamphlet concludes with these words: "The Place is rendered agreeably warm by Stoves, in which Fires are constantly kept;" and this proved the nemesis of the giant picture which was destroyed when fire broke out in the temporary building shortly after the pictured was exhibited.

This new form of panorama picture became very popular, especially in France. Other successful works included the *Battle of Lodi* (1803), also exhibited at the Lyceum Theatre; *Defeat of the French at the Devil's Bridge, Mont St Gothard, by Suwarrow in 1804; Agincourt; Battle of Alexandria,* etc., etc. In all he painted thirty-eight pictures between 1792 and 1832, the majority of them historical or landscape.

In 1804 he was appointed historical painter to Czar Paul and immediately started on a series of vast paintings with which he

---

* In 1799 a member of St John's College, Cambridge, presented as an altar piece a painting of St John Preaching in the Wilderness, by Sir Robert Ker Porter. At some time much later Miss Porter, presumably Jane, visited the College to view her brother's painting. By this time the picture had become blurred and indistinct and she induced her brother to paint another one to take its place. It is supposed that the earlier one went back to the Porter family.

This second picture was a "marvellous picture of the Angel of Revelations surrounded by a Rainbow." There is no mention of the College retaining the earlier picture, and its poor condition makes it likely that it went back to the family.

In 1841 a picture of the Descent from the Cross by Anthony Raphael Mangs (1726-1779) was given to the College. This picture was evidently preferred by the College, as it displaced the second Porter picture, which was removed to the library. However, Miss Porter returned to the College and was highly indignant at the removal of her brother's picture from its original place in the Chapel; she could be pacified only by being allowed to take the picture away; from that time the College has no trace of its former property.

decorated the Admiralty Hall in St Petersburg, recently completed by Charles Cameron. During his stay there he fell in love with Mary, daughter of Prince Theodore von Sherbatov. His feelings were reciprocated by the lady but not by her family, who no doubt had higher ambitions for her than marriage to a penniless and untitled painter. Shortly after Robert left Russia and travelled in Finland and Sweden, where he was knighted by the eccentric Gustavus IV in 1806. He then visited several German courts and in 1807 was created Knight of the Order of St Joachim of Württemberg.

He subsequently accompanied Sir John Moore (whom he had met and captivated whilst in Sweden) to Spain, and was present at Corunna and at Moore's death.*

In the meanwhile he published, in 1809, *Travelling Sketches in Russia and Sweden 1805-1808*, in two volumes,[13] which however show neither any great literary faculty nor any special powers of observation.

In 1811 he revisited Russia, and on February 7th, 1812, triumphantly married his Russian princess. He was subsequently well received in Russian military and diplomatic circles, and was well acquainted with the Russian version of the 1812 campaign against Napoleon, of which he gave a graphic account in his *Narrative of the Campaign in Russia during 1812*.[14]

He returned to England prior to publication of this book and was knighted by the Prince Regent. From 1817 to 1820 he was occupied in travelling in Persia and the Caucasus, which resulted in his *Travels in Georgia, Persia, Armenia, ancient Babylonia, etc., during the years 1817-1820*, in two volumes, London, 1821-22.[15] This book was a great advance on his previous efforts and was widely acclaimed. Whilst in Teheran he painted the portrait of the Persian monarch, Futteh Ali Shah, from whose hand he received, in 1819, the insignia of the Order of the Lion and the Sun.

His wife died of typhus in St Petersburg in 1826, leaving one daughter. It was probably this which caused him to take up an appointment as British Consul in Caracas, Venezuela, where he resided for fifteen years, carrying out his consular duties, painting, and building up a reputation for hospitality. During this period he painted a portrait

---

* Sir John Moore (1761-1809) and Sir Ralph Abercrombie (1734-1801), both Scots, were largely responsible for building up the discipline and training of the British Infantry, which was finally to be the decisive factor in defeating Napoleon.

of Simon Bolívar, the liberator of Bolivia and Columbia; and several large altar pieces, including the one in St George's Church, Esher, Surrey.[16]

In 1832 he was created Knight Commander of the Order of Hanover in recognition of benefits he conferred on the Protestant community of Caracas.

In 1841 he relinquished his post in Venezuela and returned to England. A year later he went to Russia, for the last time, to visit his daughter, Mme Kikine.

Anna Maria Porter had died in 1832 and Jane, now aged sixty-six, set off in 1842 to visit her brother in Russia, prior to his intended retirement to England — a journey formidable enough for younger folk to contemplate in those days. A few weeks after her arrival, her brother suddenly died of apoplexy as he was returning in his drozhky from a farewell visit to Czar Nicholas I. Jane, now utterly alone in the world, was left to face the journey home and the long days ahead until she died in 1850.

It is a pleasant task to end this book with a portrait of such a charming and well-rounded character. There have been in Russian history, as we have seen, Scots of fame and infame — warriors, doctors, saints and sinners — many of whom left an imprint, at least temporarily, on the Russia of their day. But in Sir Robert Ker Porter we encounter a man of universal popularity and of varied attainments; distinguished alike in the arts, in diplomacy, in war and in literature; a man warmly and hospitably at home with himself and a large circle of friends; a man possessed of the art of ingratiating himself with kings, diplomats, soldiers, and people from every walk of life. He was a splendid horseman and excelled in field sports. He was a generous host and an entertaining guest. He was the idol of his own domestic circle; and his sister Jane adored him. Can the gods offer more than this?

CHAPTER 9 — BIBLIOGRAPHY

1. Loukomski, Georges, *Charles Cameron, 1740-1812. An Illustrated Monograph of his Life and Work in Russia, particularly at Tsarskoye Selo and Pavlovsk,* Nicholson & Watson, The Commodore Press, London, 1943.

2. Talbot Rice, Tamara and A. A. Tait, *Charles Cameron,* Catalogue, Arts Council Exhibition, 1967.

3. Rae, Isobel, *Charles Cameron, Architect to the Court of Russia,* Elek Books, London, 1971.

4. Cameron, Charles, Architect, *The Baths of the Romans, explained and illustrated with the restorations of Palladio corrected and improved,* etc., George Scott, London, 1772. The copy in the National Library of Scotland is the first edition of 1772.

5. It was probably this "borrowing" of Palladio's sketches and Ware's engravings of them that caused Catherine to describe Cameron, in a letter to Baron Grimm, as the "editor" of the work. See Carmichael, Joel, *A Cultural History of Russia,* Weidenfeld & Nicholson, 1968, pp. 102-3

6. Catherine to Grimm, 1780: "This sparkling mind is a great admirer of Clérisseau, whose sketches help Cameron in decorating my new apartments."

7. Rae, Isobel, op. cit., p. 59.

8. *Memoirs of the Life of Prince Potemkin,* London, 1812, quoted by I. Rae, op. cit., p. 63.

9. Loukomski, G., *Charles Cameron,* op. cit., p. 61. For a complete list of Loukomski's articles in *Apollo, Connoisseur, Country Life, Architectural Review,* etc., see the *Illustrated Monograph* quoted above.

10. Mirsky, D. S., *A History of Russian Literature,* Routledge & Kegan Paul, London, 1949, p. 135.

11. Quoted by Marc Slonim in *The Epic of Russian Literature,* Oxford University Press, 1950, p. 115.

12. Slonim, op. cit., p. 114.

13. *Travelling Sketches in Russia and Sweden, 1805-1808,* published in two Vol., London, 1809.

14. *Narrative of the Campaign in Russia during 1812.*

15. *Travels in Georgia, Persia, Armenia, ancient Babylonia, etc., etc., during the years 1817-20*, 2 Vols., London, 1821-22.

16. Anderson, Ian G., *History of Esher,* Wolsey Press, Esher, 1948, p. 91.

To the Memory of Dr Arcadios Alexandrevich Lempert

So, Arcasha Alexandr'ich, I have at last completed the task which originated in a conversation we had in D D's Restaurant, Avenue Joffre, Shanghai, in 1938. This book, dedicated to your memory, must have about the longest gestation period in the history of book-making!

On that occasion I remember we discussed the affinity of Scots and Russians; how both got on better with each other than with the English; how compatible was Celtic mysticism with the soul of Mother Russia; and how, despite multiple dilutions of alien blood, the nordic origins of Scots and Russians persist to this day.

Even in such small matters as the ability of both to put their tongues (or rather, palates) to the aspirated h (X, kha, as in *loch*), a feat which separates the Nordic languages from the Latin; for, as a medieval writer put it (I have forgotten who), "the letter H, though said to be *no Letter,* was enough to choak the conquering Normans, as a grape-stone served Anacreon, the Laureat of Bacchus."

I remember once asking how you came by such an un-Russian name. Your father was Commissioner of Public Health for Siberia under Czar Nicholas II, and your family had been in Russia for centuries; you thought your family originated in Belgium (as it is today, though more properly the Netherlands when your family sojourned there). I suggest that your family name was originally LAMBERT, and that you came from one of those Scots families who traded with, or took part in the military adventures of, the Dutch in the seventeenth century.[1]

Many Scots names got transmogrified when the families settled in Russia: the Kerrs (or Carrs) founded a noble house of Kar; there was a Brusovski Street[2] in Moscow, named for the many Bruces who settled there; and who would recognise that Goloday Island (now the Island of the Decembrists, separated from Vasili Island by the River Smolenka) owed its name to the Scots Doctor Halliday?

Not that the Scots were very consistent in the spelling of their own names: Argyle or Argyll, Kerr or Carr or Ker, Dalzell or Dalyell or Dalziel.[3]

So, wherever you may be wandering or your shade be at rest, please accept this belated tribute to a valued friendship of treasured memory.

ENVOI — BIBLIOGRAPHY

1. The Cathedral at Liège is dedicated to St Lambert.

2. Renamed Nezhdanova Street, after a famous ballerina, in 1962.

3. The name Dalzell or Dalyell was actually spelt no less than 220 different ways, of which about 20 variations are in current use. *Sc. Hist. Society.* Vol. vii (1910), p. 69.

Czars of Russia:

THE HOUSE OF RURIK

Ivan IV (1533-85). Known as "The Terrible," but better translated as "The Awe-Inspiring." The House of Rurik had lasted from 862, and its members called themselves Grand Dukes of Muscovy, being descendants of Ivan I (Ivan Kalita), who reigned from 1328-40. Ivan IV was the first to call himself Czar. "Kalita" is a nick-name meaning "Moneybags."

Fedor I (1585-98). Fedor, son of Ivan IV, a scholarly and ascetic recluse, was the last of the House of Rurik. During his reign the functions of monarchy were largely usurped by Boris Godunov.

Boris Godunov (1598-1602). Boris was elected Czar by the Zemsky Sobor. His sister Irina had been married to Fedor.

THE TIME OF TROUBLES

(1602-13). This was the Time of Troubles with the False Dimitris as pretenders to the throne. Prince Vasili Shuisky (1606-10).

THE ROMANOVS

Michael (1613-45). The first of the House of Romanov was elected by the Zemsky Sobor at the age of 14 to end the Time of Troubles. He reigned mostly under the control of the Boyars.

Alexis (1645-76). Alexis was the son of Michael.

Fedor II (1676-82). Fedor II was the son of Alexis by his first wife Maria.

Ivan V (1682-89). Brother of Fedor II, he was deposed in 1689.

Sophia and Ivan VI and Peter I (1689). Sophia, the eldest child, Ivan her imbecile brother, and Peter, her youngest brother, were equal heirs to the throne. Sophia ruled nominally under the actual rule of Prince Golitsyn. Ivan was ignored. Peter succeeded Sophia after the palace revolt of 1689.

Peter I (1689-1725). Known as "The Great," son of Alexis by his second wife Natalia. He married a Lithuanian peasant's daughter, originally named Martha Skavrouska, who had been previously married to a Swedish dragoon and who later became the mistress of Prince Menshikov. On Peter's death she succeeded to the throne as Catherine I.

Catherine I (1725-27).

Peter II (1727-30). Grandson of Peter I and Catherine I.

Anna (1730-40). Niece of Peter I and Catherine I, and daughter of Ivan V.

Ivan VI (1740-41). Great-nephew of Anna.

Elizabeth (1741-62). Daughter of Peter I and Catherine I.

Peter III (1762). Grandson of Peter I, he was an imbecile and was deposed by his wife Catherine and subsequently murdered.

Catherine II (1762-96). Known as "The Great"; widow of Peter III, she was succeeded by her son Paul.

Paul (1796-1801). Son of Catherine II, father disputable. He was murdered in 1801.

Alexander I (1801-25). Son of Paul.

Nicholas I (1825-55). Brother of Alexander I.

Alexander II (1855-81). Known as "The Emancipator," son of Nicholas I. He was murdered in 1881.

Alexander III (1881-94). Son of Alexander II.

Nicholas II (1894-1917). Son of Alexander III. Murdered by the Bolsheviks along with all his family and near relatives of the House of Romanov.

INDEX

Adolphus, Gustavus: see Gustavus Adolphus.

Adrianople, Peace of, 1829: 87

Agriculture, backwardness in Scotland, 4; short tenures, 6, 6n, 8; fishing 7; rural housing 6; wool trade 7, 8

Alberoni, Cardinal Giulio, 1664-1752, Prime Minister of Spain, 92

Aleksei Mikhailovich, Czar of Russia, r. 1645-1676: 46

Alexander I, Czar of Russia, r. 1801-1825, 120, 121, 124ff, 137ff

Alexander III, King of Scotland, 1249-1286, 14

Alexander, Sir William, *An Encouragement to Colonise*, 1624, i

Alison, Sir Archibald, British delegate to peace talks, Paris, 1815, 124.

Andrew of Wyntoun, c. 1350-c.1425, 3, 14

Apraksin, General-Admiral Count Fedor Matveevich, 72-5

Aptekarskii Prikaz ('Medicine Chancery'), 103, 105, 105n, 114

Arakcheev, Count Aleksei Andreevich, Russian War Minister, 138, 139

Archangel (Arkhangelsk), founded by Russia Company 1583, 33, 34; visited by Peter I 1693, 71; attacked by Swedes, 72

'Arcticus': see Guthrie, Dr Matthew.

Armada, the Spanish, 1588: 19

Auchleuchries, 29, 30, 56, 65

Augustus II, Elector of Saxony, 1670-1735, 56, 88; death of, 93

'Auld Alliance,' 37

Austerlitz, battle of, 1805, 122, 137, 143

Azov, sieges of, 66-7, 72

Bagration, General Piotr Ivanovich, Prince, 138, 141-4

Bakhtchiserai, palace, 160

Balashov, Count, Minister of Police, 140

Balfour, Gilbert, of Westray, 38

Baltic trade, v-vi

Bannockburn, battle of, 1314, 14

Barclay, Colonel David, 1610-1686, promoter of Society of Friends, 133

Barclay, Hubert, family historian, 152

Barclay, Johann Stefan, fl. 1664, grandfather of Prince Michael Barclay de Tolly, 134

Barclay, John, 1582-1621, author of *Argenis*, etc., 133

Barclay, John, merchant of Rostock, fl. 1661, 134

Barclay, Peter, merchant of Rostock, fl. 1661, 134

Barclay, Robert, 133, 152

Barclay, William, author of *Nepenthes*, 134

Barclay de Tolly, Helene Auguste, wife of Prince Michael, 136, 146, 153

Barclay de Tolly, Field-marshal Prince Mikhail Bogdanovich, 1761-1818, subject of chapter 8: origins and family connections, 133; at battle of Eylau, 1807, 138; at battle of Friedland, 1807, 138; invasion of Sweden across ice, 138; Governor-general of Finland, 139; Minister of War, 139; 'Yellow Book,' 139; invasion of Russia by Napoleon, 139ff; Council at Fili, 144; crossing of Beresina River, 147; honours and decorations, 148, 150, 152; death, 153. Abbreviation: BdeT.

Barclay de Tolly-Weymarn, Prince Alexander Magnus, 153-4

Batalin, Dr, BdeT's doctor, 146-7
Baths of the Romans, The, Charles Cameron's book, 158
Bautzen, battle of, 1815, 149
Beaton, Cardinal David, 1494-1546, assassinated 38
Beckhof, BdeT's home, 148, 153
Beggars' Summonds, 16
Belau (or Balau), Dr Johann, Holsteiner doctor at Russian Court, 103
Bell, Dr John, of Antermony, doctor to Peter I, 1714, 108
Belsky, Bogdan, Russian boyar, 103
Berezina river, crossing of, 147
Bezborodko, Count, 119
Blücher, Marshal Gebhard von, 151, 152
Boece, Hector, c.1465-1536, Scottish historian, 3, 5, 163
Bomel, Dr, German doctor to Ivan IV, 102
Bonaparte, Jerome, 141
Bonaparte, Joseph, military governor of Paris, 151
Bonaparte, Napoleon: see Napoleon Bonaparte.
Borodino, battle of, 1812, 143-4
Bothwell, James Hepburn, Earl of, 1536-1578, 19
Briansk, shipbuilding yard, 72
Brienne, battle of, 1813, 151
British Factory: see Companies.
Brodie, Sir Alexander, of Brodie, 23n
Brogat (brogwort, bragwort or bragget), 3n
Brown, Richard, English shipbuilder, 73n
Bruce, Alexander Romanovich, son of Robert (q.v.), 1705-1751, major-general 1739,
    retired 1751, 49
Bruce, Count, Senator, General-in-Chief, Governor of Novgorod and Tver, married
    Praskovia Alexandrovna Rumiantsova (q.v.), 99
Bruce, Count James Aleksandrovich, 1742-1790, Governor of Moscow 1781-86, 49-50
Bruce, James Daniel (Yakov Vilemovich), 1669-1735; negotiations with Sweden 1721;
    Senator 1718; Count 1721, 48-9
Bruce, John, grandfather of Peter Henry Bruce, 49
Bruce, Robert (Roman Vilemovich), 1668-1720: accompanied Peter I on his travels
    1697-98; commandant of St Petersburg 1704-20, 48-9
Bruce, Colonel William, of Airth, arrived in Russia 1650; died 1680, 48
Bruges, wool staple at, 8, 32
Brusovsky, House of, Russianised name of Bruce family, 51, 173
Buchanan, George, Scottish humanist, reformer and historian 1506-1582, 17
Bucharest, Treaty of, 1812, 140
Bulloch, James, father of Jean Stobo (q.v.), 25
Bulloch, Maria, mother of President Theodore Roosevelt (q.v.), 25
Busch, Joseph, English garden designer, 159
Butler, James. See Ormonde, Duke of.

Calderwood, Dr Lewis, 108
Cameron, Archibald, grandfather of Charles Cameron, 157

Cameron, Dr Archibald, leading Jacobite, 157

Cameron, Charles, architect, 1743-1812, subject of chapter 9; origins 157; *The Baths of the Romans* 159; arrival in Russia 158; work at Tsarskoye Selo and Pavlovsk 159-160; work under Czar Paul 161; death 161

Cameron, Miss Jenny, ardent Jacobite, 157

Cameron, Walter, father of Charles Cameron, 157

Campvere (Veere), wool staple at, 8

Carmichael, General, governor of Pskov, 38

Carmichael, Sir John, of Hyndford, uncle of General Carmichael, 40

Carne (or Garne), Colonel Thomas, 46, 55

Carr, Captain Robert, 41; House of Kar 41, 174

Carron Company: see Gascoigne, Charles, and Companies, trading.

Catherine II ('the Great'), Empress of Russia 1762-1796, founded civil hospitals and medical college 110-1; relations with Samuel Greig 77-84; relations with Charles Cameron 158-61

Caulaincourt, General Armand-Augustin-Louis de, Duke of Vicenza, 147

Chancellor, Richard, 32-4

Charles I, King of England, 1600-1649; visit to Scotland 1641, 20; Russian reaction to his execution, 35, 46

Charles II, King of England, restoration of, 55n, 60

Charles VI, Holy Roman Emperor 1711-1740, father of Maria Theresa, 95

Charles XII, King of Sweden, 55, 106

Chernikov, General, 124

Chesme, battle of, 1770, 80-83

Chistovich, Yakov, Russian historian, 110

Christian II, King of Denmark 1481-1559, massacre of Stockholm, 38

Christian IV, King of Denmark 1577-1648, 30, 38, 42, 46

Christina, Queen of Sweden, r.1644-1654, 43

Clérisseau, Charles Louis, French architect, 158, 159, 171 note 6

Collins, Dr Samuel, physician to Czar Alexis, 101

Colson, John: see Schools.

Commander, The, poem by Pushkin, 154

Companies, trading: Russia, or Muscovy, C., later known as British Factory, 31-36; 'regulated' and joint-stock CC. 35; East India C. 35; Africa C. 35; Hudson's Bay C. 35; C. of Scotland (see also Darien Scheme) 23-5; Eastland or Baltic C. 35; Merchants Adventurers C. 32; Carron C. 84

Concordat of Leith, 1572, 20

Conservator of Scottish Privileges, vi, 8

Cook, Dr John, entered Russian service 1735, 108-9

Covenant, National, 1638, 20

Cranston, Lord, vi

Crawfurd, Colonel Daniel, son-in-law of General Patrick Gordon, 59, 65-6

Crécy, battle of, 1346, 14

Crichton, Sir Alexander, physician to Czar Alexander I, 121

Crichton, Sir Alexander William, nephew of above, 121

Dalgetty, Dugald, character in *The Legend of Montrose,* 44

Dalrymple, John, second Earl of Stair, 2n

Dalyell (Dalzell, etc.), Thomas, the 'Muscovy general,' 1599-1685, 53-4, 174

Danzig, Scottish consulate at, v-vi. See also Gordon, Patrick, of Bracho.
Darien Scheme, 23-5
Dashkova, Princess, director of Russian Academy, 109, 119
Daun, General, Austrian general, 96-7
Davout, Marshal Louis-Nicolas, Duc d'Auerstadt, Prince of Echmühl, 141
Davydov, Colonel Denis Vasilievich, 154
Dawe, George, English painter, 136
Dee, Dr Arthur ('Artemy'), English physician at Russian Court, 97
Dee, Dr John, father of above, 103
Denmark, typhus in, 11
Dimsdale, Dr Thomas, later Baron, 111
Dokhturov, General Dmitri Sergeevich, 132-3
Dolgoruki family: Princess Anastasia Mikhailovna and Princess Yekaterina Aleksievna, 47
Douglas, Count Gustav Otto, 1687-1763, Governor of Finland 1717; seizes bones of St Henry 1719; governor of Reval 1737-41; retired 1751; still living 1763, aged 76, 45-6
Douglas, General Patrick: Brothers William, Archibald and Richard all served in Russia, 54
Dugdale, Lieut. Robert, at battle of Chesme, 76, 78
Dumas, Count Mathieu, Intendant-General of the Grande Armée, 130-1
Dunbar, William, c.1460-c.1522, Scottish poet, 5

Edict of Restitution (1685), which reversed the Edict of Nantes (1598), q.v., 42
Elizabeth I, Queen of England, 4; executed Mary Queen of Scots, 19
Elizabeth, Empress of Russia 1741-1762, interest in Navy, 76-7
Elphinston, Rear-admiral John: commissioned in Royal Navy 78; delayed at Copenhagen 78; attacks Turkish fleet at Nauplia 79; in command at battle of Chesme 79-81; grounded the Sviatoslav 83; rusticated to Leghorn 83; and death 83
Engine to empty dry-dock at Kronstadt, 84
Ermolov, General Aleksei Petrovich, 144
Erskine, Dr Robert, first Scots doctor in Russian service, 101, 104-5
Eylau, battle of, 1805, 138

Farquarson, Henry, Liddel Mathematical Tutor, 74
Ferdinand II, Holy Roman Emperor 1619-37, 31, 41-3, 55
Ferdinand III, Holy Roman Emperor 1637-57: made peace with France and Sweden at Peace of Westphalia 1648, 43
Fili, council at, 1812, 144
Fitzherbert's *Book of Husbandry*, 4
Fletcher, Andrew, of Saltoun, 9, 22
Flodden, battle of, 1513, 14, 15
Food, in Scotland: grain crops 2; swedes, potatoes and turnips 2; Scotsmen's fare in 1590, 2-3; liquor 3
Forbes, Captain James, 46
Foula, island of, 4n
Frederick I, Duke of Holstein, 38

Frederick of Hohenzollern, 41
Frederick ('The Great'), King of Prussia 1712-1786, 77, 95ff
Friedland, battle of, 1807,138
Froissart, Jean, c.1337-c.1410, traveller and historian; visited Scotland 1364, 3, 14-15

Gangut (or Hangö Head), battle of, 1714, 72-3, 81
Garbett, Samuel, of Carron company, father-in-law of Charles Gascoigne (q.v.), 85
Garde Ecossaise, 35
Garne, Colonel Thomas; see Carne.
Garvine, Dr Thomas, expedition to Pekin 1715-1718, 106-8
Gascoigne, Charles, Scots engineer, inventor of carronade (gasconade), 84-5
Gegn, Steven, navigation tutor, 74
'General Winter,' 1812, 147
Gilbert, Captain David, 40-1
Godunov, Boris, 1552-1605, Czar from 1598, 73, 103
Golitsyn, General Prince Vasili Vasilievich, favourite of Princess Sophia, sister of Peter I, 62-3
Golovin, Admiral, 76
Gordon, Colonel Alexander, of Auchintoul, author of *A History of Peter the Great*, 63; arrived in Russia 1634, 54; opinion of General Patrick Gordon's character, 63; account of second siege of Azov, 67; opinion of Russians sent abroad for training, 73
Gordon, John, killer of Wallenstein, 43, 59
Gordon, Patrick, 'of the Steel Hand,' captain, later general, 59
Gordon, General Patrick, 1635-1699, 29-30; subject of chapter 4: birth and siblings 56; leaves for Russia 57; in Polish service 57; captured by Swedes 58; enters Swedish service 59; marries Katherine von Bockhoven 60; at siege of Chigirin 1678, 61; promoted Lieut.-general 61; promoted full general 62; association with Peter the Great 62ff; death of wife and remarriage 65; second siege of Azov 1695, 66ff; death and funeral 68
   Children of: John, eldest son, 65; George Stephen, second son, 61, 65; Katherine Elizabeth, eldest daughter, married Colonel Strasburg (q.v), 68; Mary, younger daughter, married Colonel Daniel Crawfurd (q.v.), 65, and subsequently Colonel Alexander Gordon of Auchintoul (q.v.), 66
Gordon, Admiral Thomas, 1662-1741; entered Russian Navy 1719, 83; active at Peace of Nystadt 1721, 83ff; letter to Mr Willians 113n; death 84
Gordon, William, seaman, 54
Gordon, Captain William, fl.1631, 54
Gordon, William, 7th Earl of Menteith 1591-1661, denounces Scottish mercenaries, 39
Görtz, Count, chief minister to Charles XII of Sweden and Swedish Ambassador at the Hague, 1716, 106
Graham, James, of Claverhouse, later Viscount Dundee, 54
Gramann, Dr Hartmann, German doctor at Russian Court, 103
Greig, Captain, commander of artillery 1611, 39
Greig, Admiral Aleksei Samuilovich, 1775-1845, son of Sir S. Greig (vide infra), 87
Greig, Admiral Sir Samuel, 1735-1788: subject of chapter 5; entered Russian Navy 77; battle of Chesme 80-3; reorganises Russian Navy 83; battle of Hogland, 1788, 86; death and funeral 86

Greig, Vorontsov Alekseivich, son of Aleksei Samuilovich (vide supra), 88
Grice, Richard, navigation tutor, 74
Grieve, Dr James, physician to Empresses Anna and Elizabeth, 113
Grieve, Dr John, physician to Empress Catherine II, 113
Grimm, Baron, correspondent of Catherine II, 84
Gustavus Adolphus, King of Sweden 1594-1632, 38, 39, 42-4
Gustavus Vasa, King of Sweden 1496-1560, 38
Guthrie, Dr Matthew, 1743-1807, physician to Catherine II, 115-118; pen-name 'Arcticus'
    117; married Countess Marie de Romont 116; literary works 117
Gyllenborg, Count, Swedish Minister in London 1716, 106

Halliday, Dr Matthew, physician to Catherine II, 111-3, 174
Halliday, Dr William, son of above, 113
Hamilton family, the 'Swedish Hamiltons,' 40, 109
Hamilton, Lady Mary Danielovna, executed by Peter I, 109
Hanseatic League, 31
Hastie, William, Scots architect, 160
Hastings, Lady Mary, lady-in-waiting to Queen Elizabeth, 102
Henryson, Robert, c.1425-c.1500, Scottish poet, 5
Hepburn, James. See Bothwell.
Hepburn, Sir John, commandant of a brigade under Gustavus Adolphus, later the Lothian
    Regiment, later the Royal Scots, 144-5; died a Marshal of France 31
Hepburn, Samuel ('Samuel Khebron'), commanded a regiment of Scots in Sweden
    1612, 39, 44
Heron, Robert, author of *History of Scotland*, 1799, iv
Heresbach's *Four Books of Husbandry*, 5
Hertford, Earl of, 'rough wooing' of, 14
Hildburghausen, Prince, Austrian commander, 96
Hill, Thomas, author of *The Profitable Art of Gardening* and *The Perfect Ordering of
    Bees*, 5
Hochkirch, battle of, 1757, 97
Hogland, battle of, 1788, 86
Horsey, Sir Jerome, director of Russia Company, 36, 37, 38, 40, 102
Howard, John, prison reformer, 1726-1790, 110
Hume, Captain Tobias, 45-6
Hundred Years' War, 1337-1453, 14

'Ill Years' (or 'Dear Years'), 9, 23
Illyn, Lieut. Dmitri, Russian sailor at battle of Chesme, 82, 83
Islay, island of, v
Ivan IV ('The Terrible'), 1533-1585, first Czar of Russia, vi, 33-4, 36, 101-2
Ivangorod, Peace of, 1704, 55

Jacob, Dr Robert, English physician to Russia Company, 102
James I, King of Scotland 1394-1437, scholar, 5
James I, King of England (James VI of Scotland), 1603-1625, 39, 42

James II, King of England, 1685-1688, deposition and abdication 63; attempted restoration 64

Jessop, Dr Joseph, appointed to Ivan IV but died, 102

Jones, John Paul, Rear-admiral, 1747-1792, 88-9

'Kalita' ('Moneybags'), nickname of Ivan I, 1328-41, first Grand Duke of Muscovy, 34

Kang-hsi, Emperor of China, 1662-1723, 106-8

Keichen, Baron von, hospital builder, 111

Keith, Sir Andrew, of Forssa, 38

Keith, Field-marshal James Francis Edward, 1696-1758, subject of chapter 6; in Spanish service 92; entered Russian service 92; entered service of Frederick the Great 95; battle of Leipzig 96; attended by Dr J. Mounsey 113; operation in Paris 114; death and eulogies 97-9

Keith, George, brother of above, Governor of Neuchâtel, 95

Keith, Robert Murray, British ambassador in Vienna, 97

Khmetensky, Captain, Russian naval officer, 83

Killiecrankie, battle of, 1689, 54

Kitai Gorod ('China City'), suburb of Moscow, 40

Klokachev, Captain, Russian naval officer, 83

Knowles, Admiral Sir Charles, adviser to Russian Navy, 84, 127

Knox, John, 16, 18, 19

Konovnitsyn, General Piotr Petrovich, 144, 154

Korsakov, Count, lover of Catherine II, 51

Kosciuzko, Tadeusz, Polish patriot, 1746-1817, 136, 167

Koslyaninov, Admiral Tymothey, 86

Kriegspiel (war exercises or manoeuvres), 95

Kronstadt, Russian naval base, fire engine at, 84

Kutusov, Field-marshal Mikhail Illarionovich, Prince Golenishchev-, Russian military commander, 137ff, 154

Kvarken Straits, crossing of, 1809, 138

Lacy, General Peter de, later Russian Count and Field-marshal, 1678-1751, 93

Lange, Lorenz, Swedish diplomat, fl. 1715-38, 107

Laud, Archbishop, his Liturgy, 21

Learmont, Thomas, of Earlstoun, ancestor of Lermontov, 163

Learmont, Lieutenant, 39

Lee, Dr Robert, 1793-1877, 126

Lefort, François Jacob, 1653-1699, General; entered Russian service 1675; contemporary and rival of General Patrick Gordon (q.v.), 51, 51n, 63, 66

Leighton, Dr, physician to Russian Navy, 122

Leipzig, battle for, 1757, 96

Leipzig, battle of, 1813, 'the Battle of the Nations,' 151

Leslie, Alexander, of Kininvie, 46n

Leslie, Alexander, later Earl of Leven, 46n

Leslie, Sir Alexander, of Auchintoul, Governor of Smolensk, died 1661, 46n

Leslie, George, Capuchin monk, 46n

Leslie, John, Bishop of Ross, 1527-96, author of a *History of Scotland,* 2, 5

National Covenant, 1638, 19
Nemetskaya Sloboda ('dumb suburb'), suburb of Moscow, 40
Nepea, Osip, 34
Nerchinsk, Treaty of, 1689, 71
Nicholas I, Czar of Russia, r. 1825-55, 120, 125
Niebuhr, Barthold Georg, diarist of Napoleon's invasion of Russia, 140
Nördlingen, battle of, 1654, 43
Nystadt, Peace of, 1721, 46; 'Articles du Paix,' 88

Ochakov, battle of, 1737, 94, 113
Ogilvy, Field-marshal George, 1648-1710, 55-6
Ogilvy, Baron George, father of F-m. Ogilvy, governor of Spielberg, 55
Ogilvy, Lord James, of Airlie, father of Patrick Ogilvy, 55
Ogilvy, Mary, mother of General Patrick Gordon, 29, 56
Ogilvy, Patrick, of Muirtoun, father of Baron George, 55
Orkney, Earl of, 37
Orkneys and Shetlands, acquired from Denmark 1468, v, 30
Orlov, Admiral Count Aleksei, at battles of Navarino and Chesme 1770, 79ff, 83
Orlov, Admiral Grigori, brother of Aleksei, 81
Ormonde, James Butler, second Duke of, 1665-1746, 92
Ostermann-Tolstoy, General Aleksandr Ivanovich, Count, 144, 150
Oxenstiern, Count Axel, 1583-1634, Swedish chancellor, 43

Pahlen, General Peter, Count von, military governor of St Petersburg, 122
Paris, Treaty of, 1763, 77
Paterson, William, founder of Banks of England and Scotland, and originator of Darien
    scheme (q.v.), 24ff; relationship to Dr J. Mounsey, 113
Paul, Czar, r. 1796-1801, 120, 122, 126, 136, 160
Pavlovsk, palace of, 160
Peter I ('The Great'), Czar of Russia, 1689-1725, 47ff; relations with General Gordon,
    62-8; founder of Russian Navy, 71ff
Philaret, Patriarch of Russia, father of Czar Mikhail Romanov, 44
Pinkie, battle of, 1547, 15
Pitt, William, Prime Minister of England 1784-1801, 85
Plague in Scotland, 10-12, 23
Platov, Hetman Count Matvei Ivanovich, 1757-1818, 124, 152
Poltava (battleship), 72
Population of Scotland 9-11; of Islay, v; no census before 1790, 9; Alexander Webster's
    unofficial census 1755, 9; William Seton's estimate 1700, 9; Sir John Sinclair's
    1707, 9
Porter, Anna Maria, 1780-1850, authoress, 167, 170
Porter, Jane, 1776-1850, authoress, 167, 168n, 170
Porter, Sir Robert Ker, 1777-1842, Scots painter, traveller and diplomat, 160ff; scene
    painter at Lyceum Theatre, 167; fate of giant panorama, 168; appointed court
    painter to Czar Paul, 168; appointed British Consul at Caracas, Venezuela, 169;
    death in Russia, 170
Postnikov, P.B., first Russian medical graduate, 103

Potemkin, Field-marshal Grigori Aleksandrovich, Prince, 89
Primogeniture, 29
Pushkin, Aleksandr Sergeevich, 1799-1837, Russian poet, author of *The Commander*, 136, 162-6; comparison with Lermontov, 165

Raevsky, General Nikolai Nikolaievich, 144, 145
Ramsay, Colonel Alexander, 37
Ramsay, Colonel Andrew, brother of above, 39
Raey, Lord: see Mackay, Sir Donald.
Reiffenstein, Baron, Director of Russian Academy, 158
Reitz, Major, Barclay de Tolly's aide-de-camp, 146
Renaissance and Reformation in Scotland, 15ff
Reynolds, Dr, English physician to Ivan IV, 102
Rheum palmatum (rhubarb), 115, 115n
Richard, John, traveller in Russia 1775, 109
Richelieu, Cardinal Armand Jean Duplessis, Duc de, 1585-1642, 42
Ridley, Dr Mark, English physician to Boris Godunov, 102
Rizzio, David, murder of, 18
Robison, Dr John, 1739-1805, Scots savant, 127-8; in Russia, 84
Rogerson, Dr John, 1741-1823, physician to Catherine II, 118ff; Rogerson family, 120n
Roonaer, Elizabeth Barnoe, General Patrick Gordon's second wife, 65
Roosevelt, President Theodore, 25
Rostislav, Admiral Greig's flagship, 86
Rostopchin, General Nikolai Nikolaievich, Governor of Moscow, 146
Royal Scots Regiment: see Hepburn, Sir John.
Rumiantsev, General, 51
Rumiantseva, Praskovia Aleksandrovna, married Count Bruce (q.v.), 51
Russia, or Muscovy, Company, 31ff, 101
Rutherford, Baron Robert, financial advisor to Catherine II, 85
Rutherford, General, 39
Ruthven, Sir Archibald, of Forteviot, v, 39
Ruthven, Lord, Lord Treasurer, 38
Ruthven, Sir Patrick ('Rotwein'), later Earl of Forth and Brentford, 39
Ryswick, Peace of, 1697, 104

St Petersburg, building of, 49, 72; naval academy of, 75
Schools: Royal Mathematical S. at Christ's Hospital, 74; John Colson's S. at Wapping, 74; Moscow S. of Mathematics and Navigation, 74; Admiralty College, St Petersburg, 74; St Petersburg Naval Academy, 74; Louis XIV's Naval SS. at Toulin, Brest and Rochefort, 74; Dalmation naval SS., 74
Schwarzenberg, Field-marshal Karl Philipp, Prince, Austrian commander, 149
Scotland: agriculture in 16th century, 4; diet in 16th century, 2-3; housing of tenants, 6; tenure of leases, 6, 6n; plague and pestilence in, 10-12, 23; population of, 9-10; wool trade, 7
Scots Greys (regiment), originally Tom Dalyell's Dragoons, 54; see Dalyell, Sir Thomas.
Scott, Reginald, author of *A Perfect Platform for a Hop Garden*, 5

Scott, Sir Walter, 1771-1832, author of *The Legend of Montrose*, 44; *Tales of a Grandfather*, 54; *Minstrelsy of the Scottish Border, 109n; Waverley* 167; relationship with the Porter family (q.v.), 167
Scottish levies, v, vi
Scottish Privileges, Conservator of, vi
Ségur, Louis-Philippe, Comte de, 87, 120
Seton, William, of Pitmidden, his population estimate, 9, 23
Seven Years' War, 1756-1763, 77, 95
Shuisky, Vasili, pseudo-Czar, r. 1606-10, 41
Sievers, Admiral, 76
Simpson, Dr Robert, surgeon on the *Rostislav*, 86
Sinclair, Captain George, 39
Sinclair, Sir John, author of *Analysis of the Statistical Account of Scotland*, 1826, 9
Skene, Sir John, his *Law Dictionary*, vn
Skornyakov-Pisarev, Grigori Grigorievich, 75
Smith, Adam, and son, Alexander, engineers, 84
Smolensk, battle of, 1812, 141ff
Solway Moss, battle of, 1542, 14
Sophia, Princess, sister of Peter I: bid for power, 62; banishment, 63
Soubise, Prince de, French general, 96
Soymonov, Fedor Ivanovich, Vice-admiral, Senator and Governor of Siberia, 75
Spaar, Baron, Swedish Minister in Paris, 1716, 106
Spanish Succession, War of the, 1701-1713, 26
Spens, Sir James, of Wormiston, 39
Speransky, General Mikhail Mikhailovich, 154
Spiridov, Rear-admiral, 78-83, 82n
Standish, Dr Ralph, English physician to Ivan IV, 101
Stanhope, Lord, British Secretary of State 1716, 106
Stewart, Colonel William, of Egilshay, 38
Stobo, Archibald, Darien survivor, 25
Stobo, Jean, daughter of above, married James Bulloch (q.v.), 25
Streltsys, 62, 66, 68
Stuart, Prince Charles Edward ('The Young Pretender'), 108
Stuart, James Francis Edward ('The Old Pretender'), 157, 158
Sutherland, Baron Richard, 1739-91, investment advisor to Catherine II, 85
Sybelist, Dr Wendelin, Holsteiner doctor at Russian court, 103

Talleyrand, Charles-Maurice, Comte de Périgord, 1754-1838, 122, 124, 151
Talbot Rice, Professor D., and wife Tamara, 157
Thirty years' War, 1618-1648, 30, 31, 41, 58
Tilly, General Jan Tserklaes, Count, 1559-1632, 42-3
Tilsit, 'Peace' of, 1807, 138
Toll, Colonel Karl Friedrich, Baron von, 144
Tolstoy, Count Lev Nikolaievich, 1828-1910, author of *War and Peace*, 154
Towie Castle, 133
Trevenen, James, naval historian, 82
Trubetskoi, Prince Ivan, 48